I0082926

THE MAN
IN
THE SPIDER WEB
COAT

THE MAN
IN
THE SPIDER WEB
COAT

BY

PHILIP R. ACKMAN

www.penmorepress.com

THE MAN IN THE SPIDER WEB COAT by Philip R. Ackman

Copyright © 2016 Philip R. Ackman

All rights reserved. No part of this book may be used or reproduced by any means without the written permission of the publisher except in the case of brief quotation embodied in critical articles and reviews.

ISBN-13: 978-1-942756-48-4(Paperback)
ISBN   :-978-1-942756-49-1(e-book)

BISAC Subject Headings:
FIC037000FICTION/Political
FIC052000FICTION/Satire
FIC014000FICTION / Historical

Editing: Chris Wozney
Cover Illustration by Christine Horner

Address all correspondence to:

Penmore Press LLC
920 N Javelina Pl
Tucson AZ 85748

"There is no such thing as government," said the Professor. "Just the armed gang running the place at the time."

DISCLAIMER

This is a work of fiction. A number of historic figures, institutions and locations from the time have been incorporated into the story to create a sense of realism. But the Splendid Islands do not exist and therefore—by definition—nothing related to the Splendids is true, including the fictional conversations between historic figures, or between historic figures and characters created by the author. The author does not suggest any of the figures from history acted other than in the highest loyalties to their nations or institutions. It is one of the puzzles of international relations; everyone acts with honor, but the outcomes are sometimes not to quite so high a standard.

PREFACE

The journey that would produce *The Man in the Spider Web Coat* began more than thirty years ago on the front seat of an Australian Holden Belmont station wagon bumping along a dirt road about three hundred and fifty miles north of Perth, which is to say, in the middle of nowhere.

Beside me, hunched over the wheel, puffing a Winfield cigarette, sat Leonard Casley, a crowbar thin, homespun revolutionary, amongst whose feats was to have formally declared war on Australia a few years earlier.

Leonard—Prince Leonard of Hutt River Province—as he prefers, is the self-styled monarch of a twenty thousand acre wheat farm, and has been battling the West Australian State Government and Australia's Federal Government since the 1960s.

Most military strategists would warn against a war on two fronts, but for Prince Leonard, forty thousand bushels of wheat he was not allowed to sell, and his right to join the international community as a fully-fledged state, made for battles on many fronts, and against countless government agencies, including the Post Office, the Treasury, Tax, Western Australia's Primary Industry Ministry and, of course, Australia's Federal Department of Defence.

The world was a simpler place back then, and documents were more likely to be taken at face value, but I remember thumbing through several Hutt River Province passports in astonishment. They were filled with entry and exit stamps from numerous countries. Superbly contrived fakes, perhaps, but I could think of no good reason why anyone would bother. In accordance with the principle of Occam's Razor, the simplest answer was the passports had been used as nature intended.

I also mailed postcards bearing Hutt River Province stamps from the official Hutt River Post Office, to my home, thousands of miles away, in Melbourne on Australia's east coast. The postcards arrived.

And a few days before his retirement, I spoke to a senior tax official in Western Australia, who confirmed Prince Leonard's outrageous claim that Hutt River paid no tax on income earned inside the province.

Too damned hard and too little to bother about, were the words, as I roughly recollect them.

This surprising response confounded me in light of the long established behavior of tax authorities across the globe: no sum of money too trifling to chase. It is only in pursuit of huge sums that the taxman backs off. The little man feels the full force of his wrath.

Hutt River Province's remarkable journey to 'statehood'—it exists to this day—was navigated by its self-appointed monarch with a natural instinct for getting to the bottom of every piece of legislation, no matter how arcane. I can picture it still; a skinny future prince, a desolate farmhouse, a bare dining room table lit by a flickering kerosene lamp, and a battered copy of the Encyclopedia Britannica turned to the section on international law.

The journey culminated in a declaration of war against Australia. When, after three days, no troops, fighter aircraft, or tanks had appeared on the horizon, the no doubt relieved Prince fired off a second telegram to Australia's Governor General declaring the war to be over—but as a state undefeated by war, Hutt River, he now claimed, was a real country under the rubbery principles of international justice.

I ran the painstaking details of Prince Leonard's machinations past that rarest of all beasts, a constitutional lawyer. There was much ah-hemming, but again as I recall, the lawyer agreed with each of the steps, then choked on what I saw as the inescapable conclusion: Prince Leonard had pulled it off. Hutt River Province was legit. The joke was on us.

Ten years earlier, as a young reporter, I found myself witnessing a more conventional battle. Like so many others, I had discovered I could extend my European working vacation by holing up on a kibbutz in Israel. The deal was simple enough. Free food and board in exchange for labor; in my case, throwing eighty pound bunches of bananas onto the back of a tractor trailer as it chugged majestically through a sweltering plantation on the banks of the Sea of Galilee, just a short ride from the Golan Heights and the peace-loving peoples of Lebanon and Syria.

I was at lunch at midday on October 6, 1973 when I heard the roar of jets overhead. I rushed outside and climbed the water tower to witness a surreal dog fight between Israeli and Syrian pilots. I watched in awe as a Syrian MiG spiraled out of the sky and crashed into the distant hills. A blotch of charcoal smoke marked its fatal descent. Thus began what came to be known as the Yom Kippur War.

Fast forward a few days when I found myself on a bus with some of the world's most distinguished reporters—American network correspondents in fake battle drill and coiffed hair, Fleet Street veterans whose careers charted the war, but for some reason never the peace, less exalted correspondents from less prestigious publications, and finally, at the bottom of the heap, your terrified author. Chaperoned by Israeli military media handlers, we headed north into the Golan Heights, paused briefly at the abandoned border, and then entered Syria unopposed.

Borders, every backpacker had long ago learned, were dangerous places: the natural center of the spider's web for the nastiest agencies any government ever dreamed up. Form a line. No talking. Return air ticket in hand. Passport. Cash. Answer the questions and, with luck, an official nod in the form of a search for an empty visa page and a new stamp.

I remember lying in a ditch on a rocky desert plain as the Syrians launched what seemed like a perfunctory artillery barrage from an Arab town shimmering in the distance. For whatever reason, they were rotten shots, unable even to hit the side of our bus, which had broadsided to a halt while the cream of the world press and I took cover. Maybe the Syrians figured they had to shell us for reasons of national duty, while also deciding that blowing a bus full of journalists to smithereens might not play well in the court of international opinion.

What struck me more than anything else, however, was how easily a border could be abandoned; how effortlessly raw power could erase lines on a map.

Fast forward again to 2010, and I am sitting by a tropical lagoon in Rarotonga, capital of the Cook Islands, with Sir Geoffrey Henry, the Cook's two-time former Prime Minister and about-to-be-appointed Speaker of the House in the new Parliament, whose election, by chance, is a few days away. The Cooks lie in the middle of the Pacific Ocean, four hours by jet, north-east of Auckland, New Zealand, and most definitely far from the beaten track.

What took me to Rarotonga was pursuit of the question which is central to The Man In The Spider Web Coat: How does one take control of a nation? Since there is no less natural condition than a power vacuum, how are kings, presidents and prime ministers dislodged?

As famous American slave and abolitionist, Frederick Douglass, noted more than a century ago: "Power concedes nothing without a demand. It never did and it never will."

Possibly in a few cases, world leaders do spontaneously surrender power to 'spend more time with their families', but the job, even from the outside, looks like so much fun, I doubt it. As an example, consider the financial clout of even the most modest leader.

The smallest economy in the world is generally reckoned to be Tokelau, a tiny island in the south Pacific. At a million and a half dollars a year, as Head of Government of Tokelau you would still have your hands on a flow of cash far greater than most households in the United States.

Next biggest is Niue, also in the south Pacific, whose population of less than fourteen hundred nevertheless manages to secure a gross economy of more than ten million dollars a year.

Nauru, essentially a pile of bird poo, again in the south Pacific, has an economy of approximately sixty million dollars a year.

The Falklands, desolate and wind-swept in the South Atlantic, has an economy worth around one hundred million dollars a year. No wonder the British went to war with Argentina in 1982 to retain possession.

By the time you get to American Samoa, yet another impoverished south Pacific paradise, you have joined the billion dollar economy club. Not too bad, considering there are still around a hundred and ninety-five countries to go.

Impoverished, of course, refers only to the masses, not to the elite, of whom the country's leader is usually top dog. The Philippines is a dirt poor nation of one hundred million people, but the notorious President Marcos and his shoe-loving wife ripped off billions during their twenty-one year reign. Amongst their plunder is said to have been a three-foot high statue of Buddha that weighed two thousand pounds of twenty-two carat solid gold. Since Marcos' official salary for his entire reign amounted to three hundred thousand dollars, it seems clear he fully participated in the riches of office. Imelda reportedly spent more than that in a few hours—three hundred and eighty four thousand dollars to be precise—in a shopping trip to New York during a slow day at the United Nations in late 1977.

In 2011, when Egyptian strongman, Hosni Mubarak, left office after eighteen days of national protests, western intelligence agencies reported he had salted away as much as seventy five billion dollars—making him possibly the world's richest man, almost half again as rich as Bill Gates.

With so much at stake, it is no wonder the number of countries in the world has quadrupled since Cuba led the charge to independence in the late 1890s. At the time, there were only fifty-five countries. Depending on how you define the term, there are about two hundred countries today, as we motor through the second decade of the Twenty-First Century, and the number looks certain to rise as old power structures crumble and new ones arise. Better to lead a small country than be an army lieutenant, senator, or business mogul in a large one.

And so I sat with Sir Geoffrey Henry, hoping for some insight into how power was seized, much as Sir Geoffrey's controversial cousin and the founding Prime Minister of the Cooks, Albert Henry, had done in the mid 1960s.

I selected the Cooks because I knew Sir Geoffrey from a much earlier assignment, tracking cancer surgeon Milan Brych, who had set up in New Zealand, Australia, and then the Cooks, before being jailed in California for medical quackery.

In such a tiny place, I reasoned, the rules for seizing power, while no doubt universal, might nevertheless be easier to uncover.

Or was I completely in error? Does gaining power, like catching cold, or winning the lottery, turn mostly on chance?

Politicians—successful ones at any rate—would surely know the answer. But madness seemed to lie down the path of trying to unlock these rules, which determine the two hundred figures who lead the other seven billion of us who weren't quite quick enough to get the job.

Nothing is less helpful, I discovered, than political autobiographies, filled as they are with righteous self-justification, saccharine accounts, if any at all, of what must have been eviscerating battles with rivals, and rewrites of history designed to locate the writer alongside Mother Teresa.

And then I came across the work of Gene Sharp, the eighty-seven year old founder of the Albert Einstein Institute, a non-profit dedicated to the study of non-violent activism. A four time nominee for the Nobel Peace Prize, Professor Sharp's work might just possibly illuminate the path to power.

So there you have it. A self-appointed monarch, who benevolently overseers the second largest country in Australia, the two time Prime Minister of one of the world's smallest nations, the work of a little known American academic who might—but probably won't—win the Nobel Peace Prize, and my own contemplation of power as I sheltered in a ditch during the Yom Kippur War.

The Man in the Spider Web Coat is the outcome. I hope you enjoy it.

MAP OF THE PACIFIC

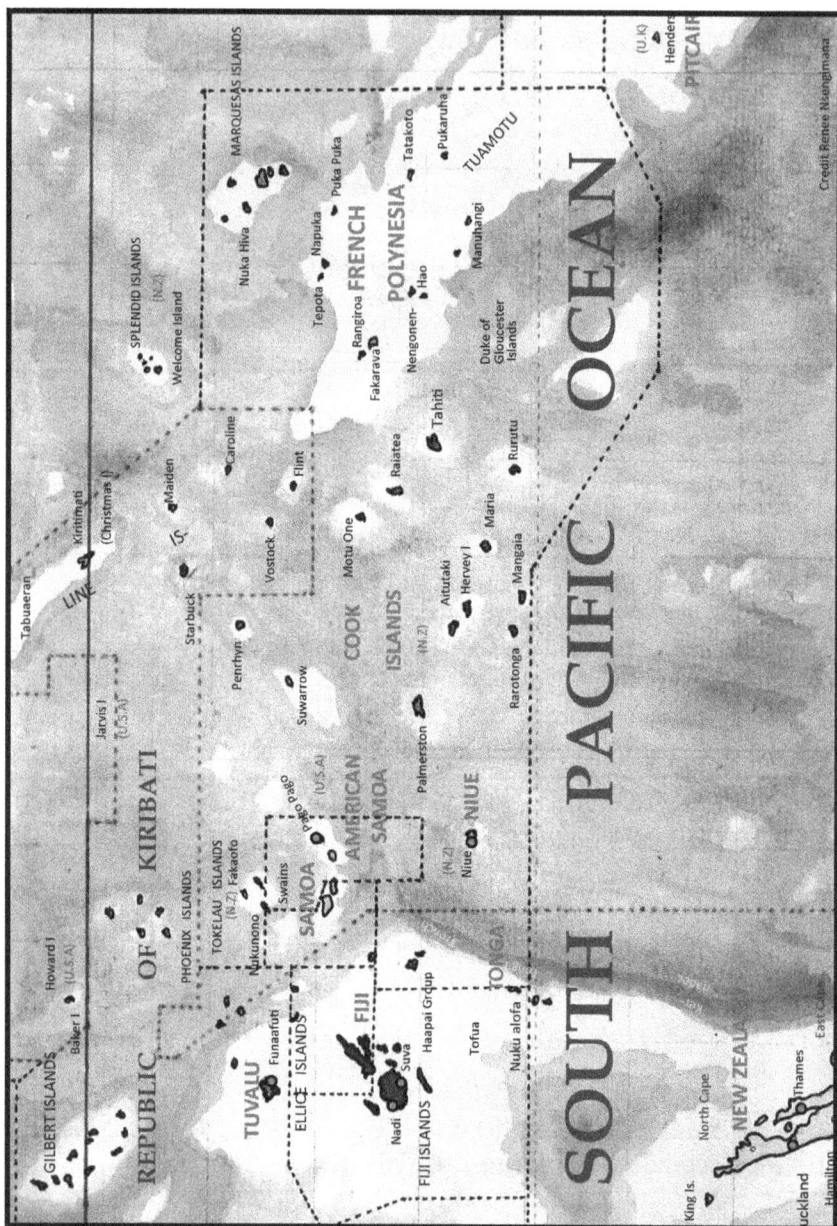

Map showing imagined location of the Splendid Islands.

PART 1

CHILDREN'S WAVES

CHAPTER 1
THE WINDS OF CHANGE

December, 1960 began with the launch and fiery failed re-entry of the five ton Russian Sputnik 6 and the deportation from Hamburg, West Germany of a couple of musicians who nailed a condom to the wall of their cheap apartment in the early hours of the morning and then set it alight. The musicians, guitarist George Harrison and drummer, Pete Best, returned to Liverpool, England. Best failed to make the cut, but Harrison, along with John Lennon, Paul McCartney and Best's replacement, Ringo Starr, went on to become the most famous rock group of all time. Such is the fickle finger of fate.

In other momentous developments, John F. Kennedy was declared America's thirty-fifth President after the count in Texas put him narrowly over the line, and French President Charles De Gaulle's visit to Algeria sparked riots, leaving one hundred and twenty-seven dead.

In what came to be known as the New York Air Disaster, United Airlines flight 826, inbound to Idlewild Airport from Chicago, and Trans World Airlines flight 266, inbound to La Guardia from Dayton, Ohio, also selected December, 1960 to collide mid-air, killing all one hundred and twenty-eight passengers onboard the two flights as well as six people on the ground. Flight 826 crashed into the Park Slope section of Brooklyn, setting fire to ten apartment buildings, a church, a funeral home and a Chinese laundry. Soldiers, searching for bodies which plummeted from the doomed aircraft, invented the term "bathtubs" to describe the blood-rimmed craters the bodies made when they hit the ground at around one hundred and twenty miles per hour—terminal velocity for a free-falling human being.

Just a few days earlier, a US Navy pilot and his navigator had provided reassuring confirmation that flight to great altitudes was safe when they climbed their carrier based supersonic A-5 Vigilante bomber to an altitude of ninety-one thousand, four hundred and fifty feet and nine inches.

December 14 in midtown Manhattan began with the third day of a snow storm which dumped eleven inches of ice and sludge along the east coast from the Carolinas to Connecticut. The General Assembly was in session and a long line of skidding limousines and fish-tailing taxis deposited their distinguished passengers into the slush outside the United Nations headquarters on 1st Avenue.

During the course of the day, a seventy-five page report from the Committee on Information from Non-Self-Governing Territories thudded onto the table for the attention of the UN's illustrious member states. In mournful bureaucratese the report boiled down to an 'expression of confidence', whatever that might mean, that countries responsible for the administration of these 'territories', as they were politely described, would bring the report to the attention of the appropriate authorities, which was presumably themselves.

Later in the day, acting on the report, and by a vote of eighty-nine to nothing, the General Assembly proclaimed Resolution 1514, which enshrined the principle that all people should have the right to self-determination. By the genteel standards of UN diplomacy the proclamation was a bombshell whose fuse was now lit. The world body had finally proclaimed an end to colonialism, though like most things, it was a little more complicated than that.

*****

Five thousand, five hundred and sixty miles southwest of New York, on a tiny speck of land quite near the equator, two small boys scrambled onto the back of an eight-foot wave as it crashed through a break in the reef not far from Welcome Harbour, capital of the Splendid Islands. The wave crested and dumped the boys into a sea of white foam. They shrieked with excitement and then swam back to catch the next comber as it neared the end of its long journey across the Pacific. The boys were surfing the sting in the tail of cyclone 1960–01, a Category 1 tropical cyclone producing winds of eighty miles per hour and a storm surge in excess of four feet. Cyclones didn't have names back then, but 1960–01 was a first-of-the-season cyclonic toddler compared to the freight-train Category 3, 4, and the feared Category 5 cyclones that created winds sometimes in excess of a hundred and sixty miles an hour and storm surges of seventeen feet or more.

The waves crashing ashore that day were called children's waves, and by tradition, children were believed to be fully safe in such dangerous seas unless a misguided adult intervened. It is why none of the onlookers on the ramshackle pier looked anxious or worried. Most were probably reminded of their own lazy childhood as they watched the boys mount the next wave and slide down its salty face. Plump clouds scudded across the morning sky. There was a faint smell of cooking in the sweet air.

Across the road from the pier, a whitewashed church squatted in the cool shadow of a flowering flame tree. Next to the church and connected to it by a short path sat the rectory, windows open, curtains flapping briskly in the wind. A small, trim figure emerged from the front door and ran across the road to the pier, a slow missile in an apron aimed at a short, pot-bellied man in suit pants and a half-unbuttoned white shirt.

"Reverend," she called, as soon as she judged he was within range. "Telephone. From America. They will call back in two minutes."

Not much happened in Welcome Harbour, so children's waves and a phone call from America on the same day were the island equivalent of high drama. The pot-bellied man hurried across the road in the excited wake of his housekeeper. There had been rumors about the two of them for years, but Reverend and housekeeper was as much as anyone could ever prove. As he entered the rectory the phone, one of only nine telephones on the whole of Welcome Island, rang again.

There was a brief delay before the operator came on the line. "Is this Reverend Geoffrey Brown?"

"Yes, of course. Is there an emergency?"

The operator ignored the question. "I have a person to person call from Boston. Mr. Oxide Brown. Are you willing to pay the charges? If so, please hold for your caller."

There was a hollow sound, as if the call came from the bottom of the ocean—which, thanks to the undersea cable, it actually did—and then Reverend Brown heard the voice of his son.

"Father! When I come home for Christmas, I would like to bring someone with me."

"This is why you called me from the other side of the

world? What is her name?"

"It is a man, father. The most fascinating man I ever met."

There was a long pause before Reverend Brown replied. "Very well. You must bring to your home whoever you want."

*****

Oxide Brown and his companion left New York in another snowstorm. Six days later they arrived at the bravely named Briggs International Airport in the Splendid Isles. It was the night before Christmas. The two men had caught a Pan Am 707 to London and then a British BOAC 707, which had stopped to refuel in Zurich, Beirut, Delhi, Bangkok, Singapore, Perth, Sydney and finally Auckland, New Zealand. They'd transferred to a TEAL Lockheed L188 Electra for the remainder of the trip—the 'Coral Route' as it was described in the brochure. The Electra shuffled slowly into the summer sky, like an old man climbing a staircase, and set course almost halfway back to the United States. The four propellers dragged them across the Pacific via Nadi, Pago Pago in American Samoa and then Tahiti. When they resumed their seats for the final thousand-mile leg to Briggs Field, they were the only passengers on the plane.

Reverend Brown was mid sermon in the first of two packed Christmas Eve services, so his housekeeper, Piata Hana, was dispatched to the airport to retrieve Oxide and his mysterious companion. She waited patiently outside the terminal, a barn-sized shed with open sides that served for arrivals, departures and freight handling. The immigration post was vacant, so the two men walked straight out onto the street. Mrs. Hana hit the horn of the idling Austin A40, a gunmetal gray, four-door saloon, built in 1948 and purchased by the Splendid Isles Christian Church shortly thereafter.

After brief greetings, the car pulled into the light traffic and accelerated with considerable complaint to twenty miles per hour. Eventually Mrs. Hana found top gear and the Austin surged forward to almost twenty-five miles per hour. Oxide and his companion slumped exhausted in opposite corners of the cramped back seat.

Oxide had grown a little taller, thought Mrs. Hana. And the food must be good in America because he looked heavier than she remembered. The other man was an odd fish. As old as the Reverend himself, she decided.

He appraised her, however, in a most irreverent way. He swept his eyes across her breasts as he clambered into the car, before reluctantly meeting her steady gaze with a naughty schoolboy grin which put paid to the unspoken question that had hung in the air since the phone call a few days earlier. He was almost bald with a wispy comb-over, which suggested a certain vanity, but tufts of white hair sprouted from his ears, which suggested no vanity at all. She couldn't see much more through the rearview mirror. Before she had traveled more than a mile she heard gentle snoring and realized he was asleep.

Given the many duties of Reverend Brown on Christmas morning, and the complete exhaustion of Oxide's companion from their flight three quarters of the way around the world, the three men did not see each other until the roast turkey was laid on the table at precisely noon on Christmas Day. Also on the table were green drinking coconuts, fresh shrimp in coconut sauce, baked breadfruit, yams and other island delicacies. When Mrs. Hana and her daughter, Tanisha, came in from the kitchen, Reverend Brown steepled his fingers and offered a short thanksgiving prayer.

"Father," said Oxide, as Reverend Brown helped himself

to a large serving of shrimp and breadfruit, "I want you to meet Professor Titus Buchanan, who has come all the way from America to see you."

The Reverend surveyed the guest with mild interest. "I hope you won't be disappointed," he said at last. "How do you know my son?"

"Professor Buchanan runs a think tank at Williams College."

"I don't believe I have heard of it," said the Reverend.

"It's the most prestigious liberal arts institution in America," said Oxide. "Even more respected, by those in the know, than Harvard, which is only a hundred miles away."

"Associate professor," corrected Buchanan. "I am an associate professor. Even though I'm quite old." He smiled apologetically. "Not in a fashionable field, you see."

"And what field is that?" asked the Reverend.

"The Professor is an expert on the United Nations."

Reverend Brown turned to his son. "Oxide, I'm sure Professor Buchanan can speak for himself. But we should take this up later over cigars and a little sherry, while Mrs. Hana and Tanisha are washing up."

With that, everyone resumed their Christmas dinner. The turkey and the seafood were accompanied by fruit mixed with poke—raw fish—and rukau, which is the leaves of the taro plant simmered in coconut cream. The resultant sweet, fishy paste is a delicacy in the Splendid Isles and highly valued. Mrs. Hana had a reputation as a particularly accomplished cook, so by the standards of Welcome Harbour, Christmas dinner was a fine feast indeed.

After the meal, Mrs. Hana and Tanisha cleared the table while the men adjourned to the Reverend's study.

"Oxide's all grown up," said Tanisha to her mother, once they were safely back in the kitchen. "Do you think he will return to Welcome Harbour when he has finished his studies?"

"I expect so." Mrs. Hana looked carefully at her daughter. "But who can know?"

The Reverend, Professor Buchanan and Oxide Brown puffed on stale cigars and sipped the Reverend's sherry. A grandfather clock ticked in a corner of the room. There was the occasional tinkle of dishes from the washing up, but the rectory had otherwise settled into a lazy afternoon.

"Perhaps I should tell you why I've come," said Professor Buchanan. "Are you familiar with Resolution 1514, adopted by the General Assembly of the United Nations in New York, eleven days ago?"

"There isn't much coverage of anything outside Welcome Harbour in the local paper," said Reverend Brown, "so I'm afraid not."

The Professor looked up at the ceiling, as if his memory had fled and was hiding in the rafters. "I need to summarize," he said. "It's rather long. Well now. The General Assembly, recognizing the passionate yearning for freedom in all peoples, solemnly proclaims the necessity of bringing a speedy and unconditional end to colonialism in all its forms and manifestations."

The Reverend drew on his cigar and raised an eyebrow. "There is some point here, but I am not sure what it is?"

"Thirty-eight countries have gained independence since 1945," said the Professor.

"And you think this is the moment for the Splendid Isles to cast off colonial rule from New Zealand? Become number thirty-nine? Is that your point?"

"Father," said Oxide Brown, "I'm not sure you understand this might be a moment in history."

But both Professor Buchanan and Reverend Brown

ignored Oxide's interjection.

"Have you heard of Sir Leslie Knox Munro?" the Professor asked.

"No," said the Reverend.

"New Zealand diplomat. Fine fellow. He was President of the 12ᵗʰ session of the General Assembly in '57," said the Professor. "Knows what's going on behind the scenes. Have you heard of Alex Quaison-Sackey?"

The Reverend shook his head.

"African chap. Chairman of the Committee on Information from Non-Self-Governing Territories. Heard of it?"

"No," said Reverend Brown again.

"Their report was tabled on December 14, the same day the General Assembly adopted Resolution 1514."

"Coincidence?"

"My dear fellow, Quaison-Sackey's report helped shape Resolution 1514."

"Are you American?" asked the Reverend.

"English," said Professor Buchanan. "Quaison-Sackey was the main architect of Ghana's independence in March '57. He's a rising power at the UN. Played cleverly, the Splendid Isles could ride his coat tails to independence."

"New Zealand might have something to say about that."

"On the other hand," countered the Professor, "they may not figure it out until you're well down the track."

"Why not?"

"Their new Prime Minister down there—Holyoake—hates Sir Leslie Knox Munro. Old enemies. Won't listen to a word he says. Might not appreciate the significance behind 1514."

"Still doesn't get us to independence," said the Reverend.

"You have to be sure that's what you want."

"Wanting is the easy part. I want a cathedral. Doesn't mean I'm going to get one."

With that, Tanisha entered the sitting room. She had been listening for some time. "I have come to take Oxide for a walk," she announced.

CHAPTER 2
A CALCULATION AND A HUNCH

Three thousand, four hundred and thirty-two miles southwest of Welcome Harbour, at 41 Pipitea Street, Wellington, sat Keith Holyoake, the newly elected Prime Minister of New Zealand. It was early in the morning in the national capital, and Holyoake was in shirt sleeves, a fine china cup of steaming tea on the desk in front of him. The prime ministerial residence, brick but unprepossessing, occupied a block of land with an oil company on one side and a brewery a few yards down the road. A nearby construction site threw up a mist of powdered concrete, and a jackhammer was already at work. If there was any security for the newly minted Prime Minister of this South Pacific nation of two and a half million, it was not apparent. His desk was a simple table, pressed into service from an earlier life. The room was bare of books or decoration of any kind. A packing crate lay unopened on the floor. In a corner, a bucket collected drips from the ceiling, although there had been no rain for some time.

It was the day after Christmas—Boxing Day, a public holiday—but Prime Minister Holyoake, elected just a few days earlier, was hard at work. An aide knocked on the door to the PM's study and entered. "The Attorney-General and the Finance Minister have arrived. Shall I send them in?"

Neither of the men who entered the study a few moments later could have been described as imposing. Harry Lake wore horn-rimmed glasses and looked exactly what he was, a rural accountant. He was now the second most powerful man in Cabinet, officially at least, but still he could not hide his nervousness. Lake's elevation to Minister of Finance had come as a surprise to better qualified men, but his loyalty to Holyoake was unquestioned. His cabinet colleague, Attorney-General Ralph Hanan, was a former lawyer, junior infantry officer and small-town mayor. Hanan was also the Minister for the Splendid Islands, although he would eventually assume responsibility for all of New Zealand's colonies, or protectorates, as they were more politely known.

"Very well," said Holyoake. "What does Her Majesty's Government of New Zealand think of UN Resolution 1514?"

"We voted in favor, as instructed, but we see it as a guideline only," said Attorney-General Hanan. "Perhaps a long-term goal. Nothing we feel the slightest need to act on."

"And this is the view of—?" The Prime Minister's voice trailed away.

"My department, naturally," said Hanan.

"Not Leslie Knox Munro?" asked Holyoake, who looked as though he were about to say something unpleasant, since his feud with New Zealand's Special Representative to the United Nations was well known.

"Good gracious no," said Hanan.

"Because I don't care to hear that fellow's opinion," said the PM, who, like most men, could be petulant when it suited him.

"We have also studied the Committee Report on Non-Self-Governing Territories, which led to the resolution," Hanan continued. "It notes our position that many of the problems discussed in the report are not pertinent to the New Zealand-administered territories of the Cooks, Niue, Tokelau and the Splendid Islands, since they have no natural resources, or minerals and generally poor soils." The four territories were a collection of tiny islands spread over a huge swathe of South Pacific Ocean. They stretched well out to the east of New Zealand and more than halfway to Hawaii. The Splendids were the most distant of all; they straddled the equator and lay northwest of the Marquesas Islands, about a thousand miles northeast of Tahiti.

"Is that right?" said Holyoake. "Because, if so, perhaps there's no good reason for us to hang on to them."

"If I might come in?" said Finance Minister Lake. "The Splendids, in particular, have some value for us. We export almost two million pounds a year of goods to them and import considerably less than a million pounds of coconuts and whatever in return. The balance of trade, though small, is strongly in our favor. We also collect taxes on their behalf and, naturally, some of these revenues are retained by us as a fee to defray the cost of administration. Finally, we own the only shipping line that services the Splendids, so we get the freight revenue, which is very profitable."

"Small beer though," said Holyoake.

"Not so very small," said the Attorney-General. "The five islands of the Splendids make up only a hundred and fifty square miles of landmass, but—" he paused for effect, "they cover thousands of square miles of the Pacific Ocean. With a three-mile territorial limit the area is significant."

"So what?" said Holyoake, who had allocated fifteen minutes for a meeting on such a minor matter.

"Two years ago, Iceland got into a shooting war with Britain over extending their territorial limit to twelve miles. And they won."

"Doesn't sound like a great deal to go to war over," said Holyoake, who'd left school at the age of twelve to work on the family farm.

"On the contrary," said the Attorney-General. "Is the Prime Minister aware of what has happened with Peru, Argentina, Chile and Ecuador?"

"Refresh my memory," said Holyoake. Which meant no.

"Each of these countries has achieved international recognition for a two-hundred-mile limit. If the Splendids were to achieve such a result—surely possible, since there is no nearby country to contest it—we would control three quarters of a million square miles of Pacific Ocean. The fishing rights alone could be worth a fortune."

"How much?" said Holyoake, who had a habit of cutting to the bone.

"If I might come in again?" said Finance Minister Lake. "Ralph and I discussed this. I asked my Department for an estimate."

"And?" prodded Holyoake.

"Making all sorts of assumptions about the price of fish, population densities, competition between various national fishing fleets for access to the grounds, recovery costs and so on—"

"Yes, yes," said the Prime Minister impatiently.

"One million pounds a year," replied the Finance Minister.

"And for this we would have to do precisely what?"

"Assuming a two-hundred-mile limit and a fishing agreement in place?"

"Yes," said Holyoake.

"Why, nothing at all, Prime Minister."

*****

THE MAN IN THE SPIDER WEB COAT

At Welcome Harbour, on the other side of the International Date Line, it was still Christmas Day. Young couples held hands and strolled the beach in the slowly fading afternoon sun. Oxide Brown and Tanisha Hana did not stroll or hold hands. They had known each other all their lives—since Oxide was a toddler and Tanisha a babe in arms. Oxide hurried along, as if on his way to an important meeting. Tanisha struggled to keep up. He was annoyed, she decided, annoyed because she had extracted him from the meeting with his father and the mysterious English professor who lived in America and taught at a famous college nobody had heard of. Eventually, Oxide's anger subsided and he slowed to a more conversational pace.

"The Professor seems like a nice man," Tanisha ventured, though this was far from her real view. She did not like the Professor at all. When it was clear Oxide had nothing to say, she went on "It seems a long way to come to meet your father."

Again, Oxide Brown did not respond.

"Is he important?" she asked.

"He could be very important," said Oxide.

"Could be?" said Tanisha. Her eyes flashed. "If he was going to be important, surely it would have happened by now."

"I meant important to us."

Tanisha considered this for a moment. "He wants your father to do something, doesn't he? It's why he's come all this way. I don't like him," she announced more candidly. "Promise me you will say 'no' to whatever he wants."

"Why ever would you ask that?" said Oxide, surprised.

"Some people are dangerous," said Tanisha. She grabbed Oxide's hand and squeezed it briefly before letting go.

CHAPTER 3
A DANGEROUS PROPOSAL

The two men sat in silence as the old Austin skittered around corners, lurched through potholes, of which there were many, and clambered uphill to the lookout above Welcome Harbour. Reverend Brown stopped in the baking heat of the empty parking lot and got out of the car. Professor Buchanan followed, but one had the sense it was more out of politeness than interest.

"See where the waves curl on the reef?" The Reverend gestured through a gap in the trees.

"What of it? asked Professor Buchanan, squinting at a cobalt blue breaker as it smashed into foam and rippled, exhausted, across the lagoon.

"On the other side," said the Reverend, "the reef drops away. It's like plunging down the face of a mountain. So they say. A few yards offshore, the water is five thousand feet deep."

"I don't suppose you've got any more of your terrible sherry?" said the Professor, for whom underwater geology seemed of scant interest.

"Afraid so," said Reverend Brown. "I did ask Mrs. Hana to put a bottle in the trunk, and a couple of glasses."

"Excellent," replied the Professor, brightening visibly. "I

don't really consider myself an expert on the United Nations. My interests are narrower than that. Or broader. Where did you say the sherry was?"

"I'll get it," said Reverend Brown. He returned with the bottle and two chipped tumblers, which he filled generously with the rich amber fluid.

Professor Buchanan swirled the sherry in his glass before raising it in a silent toast.

"I'd be fascinated to hear where your research interests do lie," said the Reverend.

"I have made a study of the most effective way in which dictatorships can be brought down," the Professor replied.

Overhead, a seagull wheeled. A native canoe made steady progress across the lagoon, the tiny figure of a man in the stern. From somewhere below, they heard the toot of a horn. A yacht, trapped in the harbor by the cyclone season, tugged cheerfully at its mooring. There was the crunch of gravel behind them as another car pulled into the lot. "I think I would like to know why you're here," said the Reverend.

But Professor Buchanan was not to be hurried. "Five thousand feet deep," he reflected. "The edge of the reef must go almost straight down."

The churchman waited for Professor Buchanan to go on. The next one to speak loses, he thought; but the Professor must have had the same thought because there was silence for a very long time. Both men drank their sherry. Mrs. Hana had also put a packet of crackers in the boot; the Reverend fanned them onto a paper plate. But neither man was hungry. "I do need to know why you're here," the Reverend repeated at last, breaking the silence. On his own analysis this meant he had lost.

"I've developed a formula," said the Professor, after a further age had passed. "It is a mathematical formula. It looks at a host of factors. Nature of present government. Gap between rich and poor. Degree of political representation. Alignment with the people. Credible alternative leadership. Twenty-four factors in total."

"I see," said Reverend Brown, who was not sure he saw at all.

"My formula has predicted many of the thirty-eight countries that have achieved independence since World War Two."

"So you said on Christmas Day."

"Still, it is encouraging, don't you think?"

"Your formula?" mused the Reverend. "Perhaps it is encouraging. Perhaps it is just good luck."

The Professor ignored the churchman's reply.

"More remarkably," he said slowly, "it predicted the Ivory Coast and the Central African Republic would both achieve independence this year—and in the correct order."

"I see," said the Reverend again.

"My dear chap, you don't see at all. The Ivory Coast achieved independence on August the seventh. The Central African Republic won freedom on August the thirteenth."

"The formula predicted they would achieve independence six days apart? When did you say your formula made these predictions?"

"In January 1957. I was in Ghana at the time."

"But you said these countries gained independence this year."

"Yes."

"You predicted when two countries would gain their freedom more than three years into the future?"

"Yes." There was no immediate response from Reverend Brown, so the Professor went on: "I have run my formula farther into the future as well."

"I sense we have arrived at the center of things now," said the Reverend.

"The Cook Islands will achieve independence from New Zealand in 1965. Niue will follow in about ten years." Both the Cooks and Niue were neighbors of the Splendid Isles. "Tokelau may never achieve independence. This is a matter I do not yet understand." The Professor was right on all counts. Fifty years later, Tokelau, a tiny nation of three islands, was still a New Zealand territory. Both the Cooks and Niue had achieved self-rule.

"Which, of course, leaves the Splendid Isles," said the Reverend, "and what I imagine is the purpose of your long journey."

"Yes," said Professor Buchanan. "It is why I am here. The Splendid Isles could become independent in less than one year."

"I doubt that," said the Reverend.

"But," said the Professor, "there is an important condition not yet in place."

"Oh yes?"

"Naturally, the formula requires an alternative to the current regime. My research does not reveal the emergence of a compelling candidate."

"Probably because there is none," said the Reverend.

Professor Buchanan ignored the comment. "There is a Farmers' Federation, yes?"

Reverend Brown nodded.

"But there is no strong leader? How can that be?"

"The shipping company is powerful. The only shipping company. Any farmer who stood out would be blackballed. His crops would die in the ground. That is the fear, anyway."

The Professor went on: "There is also a second condition which must be in place. It is the desire of the people to be free."

"I do not know how badly our freedom is desired. I have not heard it much discussed," said the Reverend.

"The desire can be created," said Professor Buchanan, "by a leader who is right for the job. As I said, thirty-eight countries have been successful. Many others have not."

"Because?"

"It is a dangerous path if freedom is to be won."

"I have a question," said Reverend Brown. "New Zealand is not a dictatorship. We are perhaps unjustly treated in the Splendid Isles, but we are not under the heel of a jackboot. How then can your dictatorship formula be relevant to us?"

"The answer has long troubled me," said Professor Buchanan. The 'dictatorship formula', as you call it, does not seem to care whether the ruling elite are despots or a more benevolent power. It is enough the people have no say in their own affairs."

"But the path to independence is, as you say, dangerous?"

"It has always been the case. Yes."

"Professor. You are English, you said. I cannot put a finger on it but your accent is not quite English at all."

"Forgive me," Professor Buchanan replied. "I was born in Germany and moved to England as a younger man. It is not so good to be German, even fifteen years after the war. But this is not the important thing in today's discussion. I have developed a thesis, you see. I have determined what must be done for a country to achieve independence with the lowest risk of bloodshed and the highest likelihood of success."

"You have studied this?"

"Extensively! I have visited every one of the thirty-eight countries that have gained their freedom since 1945. I have analyzed, most carefully, what they did right—and what they did not."

"And from this you have developed a recipe for revolution? Surely it cannot be so simple."

"Reverend Brown, I did not say it was simple."

Once again, the two men stood in silence. They watched as the afternoon sun turned the waves beyond the reef to emerald green.

"So that is your proposal?" Reverend Brown turned to face Professor Buchanan, examining the man closely for the first time. The Christmas guest did not flinch. "You would like the Splendid Isles to become a test-tube for your thesis?"

"Yes."

"Even though on your own admission it is dangerous?"

"Yes. It depends how badly freedom is desired."

"And the issue of a leader is critical, according to your theory?"

"Yes."

"And there is none you can identify?"

But to this the wily professor did not reply.

CHAPTER 4
A STRANGE GATHERING AND A FATEFUL EVENING

In a three-story row house in Sicard Street, SE Washington DC, a few hundred yards from the filthy Anacostia River, five miles or so from the Pentagon and quite near the Washington Navy Yard, the headquarters of the National Turtle Research Foundation was located, as proclaimed by a small sign in gold letters by the front door. The row house was neither smart nor part of a row any more, situated as it was in a street taken over by organs of the US Government. The Naval Criminal Investigation Service was a few doors away, as was a National Guard district facility. Traffic in the once quiet street was mostly military vehicles, delivery vans and government cars. There was little parking, but one spot was reserved out front. It was occupied by a nail polish-pink 1958 Cadillac.

On the second floor, opposite the stairs, lay the boardroom, a far grander name than the room deserved. There were two fold-up card tables, pushed together and camouflaged to look like one with a large, heavily starched cloth. Around the table, in simple metal chairs, sat five middle-aged men. Each wore slacks, an open-neck Polo shirt and a thick sweater. They looked like corporate executives who had come together on the weekend to play poker rather than swing a golf club or mow the lawn. Behind the man at the head of the table sat a sixth man—clearly some kind of observer.

If you had been in the room you would have heard Wendell Steinbeck clear his throat to bring the meeting to order. "So," he began, running his hand through a carrot-colored crewcut slowly losing the battle with gray, "Harvey has once again had some luck raising funds." He turned to a taller man on his right. "Harvey," he said, "Why don't you fill us in?"

"Thank you, Wendell," Harvey replied. "Cutting to the chase, as they say in Hollywood, we have been able to raise some money that is going to be very exciting, I think, for our friend, the *Chelonia mydas agassizii*." This was the scientific name for the endangered green sea turtle, a four hundred pound, five-and-a-half-foot long ocean-going reptile reportedly sighted over many years in both the Atlantic and the Pacific oceans. Some of these sightings had been from Turtle Foundation facilities at Paihia, on the east coast of northern New Zealand, some from the foundation's newest facility at Punta Galera, a surf-riding community in Ecuador.

"That's great, Harvey," prodded Wendell. "For the benefit of the Board, maybe you could give us a little more detail."

"I was getting to that. Where was I? Ah, yes! We've been able to raise two hundred and eighty thousand dollars." Harvey beamed. Given the pink Cadillac sold for around five thousand dollars at the time, two hundred and eighty thousand was a good deal of money indeed.

"Splendid," said one of the other men, to a chorus of general approval. "Where is the money coming from?"

"Once again we are indebted to our friends from Navy," replied Wendell. He turned to Harvey again and prompted,

"Why not tell us the whole story, Harvey?"

"With pleasure," said the younger man. He paused for a moment to assemble his thoughts. "Most importantly, the money is allocated—yes, allocated—but not yet paid."

"Why not?" asked one of the others.

"Subject to final approval by the Department of Navy, Assistant for Administration, we can draw down the funds at any time over the next year. After the Ecuador experience, Navy rather hopes for a country that is stable and meets certain other requirements." Ecuador was wildly unstable in the early 1960s and suffered from military rebellions and guerrilla warfare.

"Requirements like what?" interrupted one of the men, who looked a good deal younger than the others.

"They're not being specific about it at the current time," said Harvey, "but they would like us to build a more sophisticated facility on this occasion. That's why the amount is so generous. In addition, the Navy would provide us with an engineer to work on the design."

"Why would they do that?" someone asked.

"This is the really exciting part," said Harvey. "They're going to allow us to connect all three of our stations—New Zealand, Ecuador and the new one—to their satellite that has recently been launched into outer space." The US was well into its covert Corona/Discoverer satellite program by this time, and in the previous few weeks had launched a spy satellite and one other, whose mission was said to involve missile detection. How Harvey, and presumably Wendell, came to know of this was not discussed. "We'll be able to capture a whole lot more information about *Chelonia mydas agassizii,* our little friend," Harvey explained. "If we are able to tag the turtles with a new kind of miniature radio transmitter developed by the Office of Naval Research, then we can track them using the satellite." Inspired by the inventor of the light bulb, Thomas Edison, the Office of Naval Research was America's pre-eminent military scientific facility. It had contributed to the development of the atom bomb, US national security radar and various long range communications devices.

"Isn't that great news?" Wendell flashed a set of perfect teeth. "Is there anything else?" he prompted.

"Oh yes! How could I forget? They–" Harvey stopped mid-sentence and looked at the man who sat behind Wendell. "Wendell, I think this is something you might like to share with us."

"Sure," said Wendell. "Wilson, why don't you stand up so everyone can get a good look at you?"

The man behind the Chairman got to his feet. He was trim and of medium height but otherwise unremarkable. He had a crewcut, and a pair of dark glasses raked back off his eyes, although the sky in wintry Washington was the color of slate and snow was forecast later in the day.

"Wilson Tuttle is an engineer who understands exactly what the Navy needs. Isn't that right, Wilson?" The man smiled and sat down again. "He works for Brown and Root," Wendell went on, "the big engineering outfit in Texas that's done a lot of work for the Government."

"They're the guys close to Lyndon Johnson?" asked one of the men. Lyndon Johnson was three weeks from becoming Vice President to the newly elected JFK, and had been the senior senator from Texas for many years.

"Used to be. Not anymore," said the man they now knew as Wilson Tuttle.

"Sorry, Wilson?" said Wendell.

"I said I used to work for Brown and Root. Not anymore."

"Of course," said the Chairman.

"At the moment I freelance for Navy."

"They have suggested Wilson might help us find the right location for the new research station," said Harvey. "Both Wendell and I are impressed with him."

"Tell them the rest of it," said the Chairman.

"Wilson also has a fascination for turtles, don't you Wilson?"

"Sure," agreed the engineer personably.

"Why don't you tell us which of the seven species is your favorite?" pressed Harvey.

There was a moment's silence before Tuttle replied. "I love 'em all."

"But that's not the best part, is it Harvey?" said the Chairman.

Harvey looked puzzled for a moment and then remembered. "Of course not." He slapped the side of his head for effect. "If we work with Wilson, it won't cost us a thing."

"He's on the Navy's dime?" asked one of the men.

"Gentlemen," interrupted the Chairman, "If Mr. Tuttle would be kind enough to wait outside, I think we might be ready to vote."

*****

It was late night at the rectory, well after dinner, when Reverend Geoffrey Brown, his son Oxide and Professor Buchanan talked again. The two older men were mellowed from another bottle of the Reverend's sherry. Cigar smoke hung in the air like the remnants of a World War One artillery duel, though no one had yet fired a shot. The Professor and Oxide would leave for America the next afternoon, so this might be the last opportunity to return to the subject that had brought them together in this tiny Pacific paradise.

"I think I'm starting to like your sherry," said Professor Buchanan, staring into his glass. "Even the cigars seem better."

"In that case you'll be wanting a refill," said the Reverend, reaching for the decanter. They skirted the only topic that mattered, as men will sometimes do when there is something of importance between them. It was Oxide, fueled by the impatience of youth, who finally took aim. "Professor," he said, "have you come to a firm view whether the Splendids should try to break away from colonial rule?"

"My view has not changed since I came here, if that is your question. The formula I have developed does not require any revision."

"Since the formula is of such importance to the future of the Splendid Isles," volleyed the Reverend, "possibly you can explain a little more as to how it works." This was a brave call for a lay preacher who had left school at fifteen with an understanding of mathematics that went little beyond calculating the grocery bill. "I assume each of the twenty factors, as you call them, has a score, and these are then added together to produce the result?"

"Twenty-four," corrected Professor Buchanan, "and no, it is not as simple as that. The variables are in families, which resolve into values. It is a matter of polynomial equations, in the end."

"But you are confident the formula is right?" said the Reverend, well out of his depth.

"My dear fellow. I would not be here—"

"Twelve months you say?"

"Yes."

"Could it be more?"

"Yes."

"And the path is dangerous?"

"Yes."

"But you have developed a thesis, you say, that makes it less so?"

"Yes," said the Professor, in what was becoming his standard reply.

"How can we know the thesis is correct?"

"We cannot know, but I am certain in every fiber of my person it is correct," he said.

"Then I think it is time for the thesis to be explained fully to us."

"Reverend Brown, without a leader, any talk of the thesis is wasted time." The Professor paused. "And there is no leader."

"Oxide has told me you discussed this matter with him."

"It is an important matter," was Professor Buchanan's rejoinder.

The Reverend opened fire. "You told my son he might be the leader?"

"I did."

"Even though it is dangerous?"

"He could lead it," said Professor Buchanan. "He is young. He desires freedom. Revolutions are often led by the young." He paused and looked steadily at the churchman. "There is a better candidate, of course."

Finally, the proposal the Reverend most feared was on the table. "And who might that be?" He could not help asking.

The Professor, however, chose not to answer this question—at least not directly. "We are not children, Reverend."

"I am old," said Reverend Brown, answering the question himself.

"Old enough," agreed the Professor.

"I am a man of peace, not revolution."

"A man of peace is required."

"I do not have the energy for such a task."

"You do."

"You told me you could not find a leader in the Splendid Isles."

"I lied. It can take time for a man to accept his destiny."

Reverend Brown turned to his son. "Oxide, what do you say about this?"

"Father, I agree with Professor Buchanan."

Like a small yacht in a gale, Reverend Brown tacked to a different heading. "This United Nations resolution you spoke of. What was the vote?"

"Eighty-nine to nothing."

"So New Zealand favors independence for the Splendid Isles?"

"Yes, but in their heart they will not want to let you go. Once they realize what is happening they will try to stop it, no matter how they voted."

"But it is a start."

"A beginning, I agree. With the correct plan and a wise leader...."

And so, late on the evening of the twenty-ninth of December, in the rectory next to the flame tree, across the road from the pier, which was sometimes pounded by hurricane children's waves, two old men and a sapling of twenty-five cast the fate of a tiny nation to the wind, although there was no wind that night. It seemed as though the Splendid Isles held its breath.

*****

The following morning, Tanisha Hana arrived at the house. Oxide was packing for the long flight home, but Tanisha insisted on a walk. And when Tanisha insisted, she usually got her way.

They picked a path along the beach, watched a plump dog dozing in the shade of a tree, and skipped stones across the still waters of the lagoon.

"I would like you to tell me what has happened," said Tanisha.

It never occurred to Oxide not to comply. He needed to hear the plan out loud to see if it made sense, even to him, and Tanisha was a good listener. In any event, he told her everything. And then wished he hadn't, because after he had told his story, she became quite angry.

"He is an American, who is actually English, who is actually German," she said icily. "From a college no one has heard of."

"It's a famous college to those in the know," protested Oxide.

"A fortune-teller masquerading as a Professor," she barreled on. "With a mysterious formula no one can understand. A theory where the Splendid Isles is a laboratory rat experiment."

"Tanisha, this is not how I would put it. The Professor is a brilliant man."

"New Zealand will do nothing while we wrench ourselves from her tit?"

"The Professor believes the risk is low."

"And he wants your father, a gentle old man, to lead this —this revolution? After he asked you to lead it?"

"He believes my father will have better success."

"We are a rich country," said Tanisha. "New Zealand will send soldiers. There will be fighting. People will die. Your father! Others! You and I!"

"I do not believe it will come to that," said Oxide.

"He is a dangerous man," said Tanisha. "He will lead us to ruin."

"Are you talking of my father or Professor Buchanan?"

"Both now," said Tanisha, with a cold anger that Oxide had never before witnessed in all the years they had known each other.

In the warm lagoon, though neither saw it, swam a large green turtle. Resting from an epic journey across the vast Pacific? About to embark on a new voyage? The turtle and the Splendid Isles had something in common that day. A few yards offshore, the waters were five thousand feet deep, and almost totally unexplored.

Back at the rectory, another conversation was taking place between two dangerous old men, as Tanisha now saw them, although it was Professor Buchanan who did all the talking.

CHAPTER 5
THE MAN IN THE SPIDER WEB COAT

When the Pan Am 707, trailing inky smoke from its four jet engines, touched down at Idlewild Airport, Oxide Brown and Professor Buchanan went their separate ways. Oxide waited for one of the infrequent connecting flights to Boston's Logan Field. Professor Buchanan took a yellow cab for the twelve-mile ride to the art deco Beekman Tower Hotel at East 49th and 1st Avenue in midtown Manhattan. It was no more than a two-hundred-yard stroll from the world headquarters of the United Nations.

He checked into his room on the fifth floor and slept for eleven hours. The front desk phoned with a wake-up call at 9.30 pm. He caught an elevator to the Top of the Tower cocktail bar on level twenty-six, ordered a vodka and lime, and sat looking across the New York skyline.

There was a polite stirring in the bar with the arrival of a young African man, who wore dark slacks and a collarless smock slashed with gold, black and red.

"Mr. Chairman," said the Professor. He rose to his feet.

"Titus," acknowledged Alex Quaison-Sackey, head of the UN Committee on Information from Non-Self-Governing Territories.

"Forgive the national dress," he said in perfect Oxford

English. "I have come straight from a function at the Russian Legation. We are something of allies since Khrushchev's shoe-banging incident in the General Assembly." He mimicked the Soviet leader: 'Unless the most urgent measures are taken, colonialism is capable of causing still more suffering.' Something like that anyway. Set the scene for my committee report." Premier Khrushchev's famous outburst the previous October had made headlines around the world, but it was the tantrum shoe-banging on the lectern that lent weight to the words. "The Macallan. 1940. Double. Ice," said Quaison-Sackey to a waiter who hovered nearby. This was a rare, wartime vintage, single-grain malt whisky. Fifty years later it would sell for several thousand dollars a bottle. "So tell me, Titus, were things as you expected?"

"Exactly," said the Professor. "I believe Reverend Brown will lead the independence movement. I see no reason why he cannot achieve the necessary result in the time-frame predicted by my formula."

"That is good news," said the African, who was also Ghana's Ambassador to the United Nations, and a major figure in his country's successful battle for independence three years earlier. By the early 1960s, however, Ghana was sliding into a socialist dictatorship with anti-American sympathies. The regime was overthrown in a military coup in 1966 rumored to have been backed by the CIA. Alex Quaison-Sackey's boss was either a cold-blooded despot or a messianic man of the people; like most things in history, you could take your pick. "You do not see any other candidate," asked Quaison-Sackey, "in case your calculations are less than perfect?"

"There may be coups in Brunei and possibly Ceylon in the next few years, but I think they will be very bloody and may, in any event, fail," said the Professor. "Argentina and the Dominican Republic may also see regime change shortly, but affairs in these countries are, you might say, volatile."

"My committee does not want to be seen to be close to a revolution at this delicate time," said the African, "if it demonstrates that new leadership might be worse, or less stable, than what is already in place."

"Algeria is also a possibility," the Professor added, "but again, may be difficult. The French will fight hard to keep the Algerians in the fold."

"But not the New Zealanders? They will care little if the Splendid Isles break away?"

"They will care, and they will try to stop it," said the Professor. "I have made that clear to Reverend Brown, so he does not lose heart at the first sign of official resistance."

"But they will not try too hard? Crush the independence movement? Make the price too high?"

"My formula says no."

"Ah yes, the formula. But if we might migrate from mathematical theory to politics for a few moments?"

"Very well," said the Professor, slightly irritated. "The New Zealand regime is comparatively benign, if I can use such a term to describe any government. And the Splendid Isles is many thousands of miles away. It would be difficult and expensive to deploy other than token military power over such a distance."

"That is something," conceded the diplomat.

"Also, most New Zealanders will have never heard of these Splendid Isles, so defeating the revolution may not be a matter of national pride."

Alex Quaison-Sackey nodded slightly and took a sip of his expensive drink.

"This must be contrasted with the French and Algeria."

Quaison-Sackey continued to not speak.

"Finally," said the Professor, "the economic contribution of the Splendid Isles to the New Zealand economy is completely trivial. A few coconuts, vegetables and bananas. As your own report noted: 'The territories have limited natural resources, no mineral deposits and generally poor soil.' So, also in this aspect, there is not a lot to fight over."

"Perhaps you are right," said the African, "but I am reminded of the words of the famous American slave and abolitionist, Frederick Douglass: 'Power concedes nothing without a demand. It never did and it never will.'"

"It is why I have a secret weapon," said the Professor. "Which I hope need not be used. As I have said, the Splendids have no profile in New Zealand. But ten percent of the New Zealand population are Maori, who migrated originally from Polynesia, including, in all probability, from the Splendid Isles." In this, the Professor may or may not have been right. In the early twenty-first century, anthropologists still debated whether the Maori originated from Polynesia, Hawaii, Taiwan in Southeast Asia, or Central America.

"I think I see," said Quaison-Sackey.

"If the Maori in New Zealand learned of the plight of their brothers in the Splendid Isles...."

"Now I understand," said the African. "But why not use this weapon immediately?"

"Race relations has started to become a political issue in New Zealand. If this were added to the pot—"

"–it could be hard to control." Quaison-Sackey completed the sentence. "So it is a weapon of last resort? If things move too slowly?"

"Exactly," said the Professor.

"You have answered another question that has troubled

me. The vote on Resolution 1514 was unanimous, but there were nine abstentions—America, Australia, Great Britain, the Dominican Republic, France, Portugal, Spain, South Africa and Belgium, I think. All of the significant colonial powers. Except New Zealand."

"There was an election in New Zealand at the time of the UN vote," said Professor Buchanan. "They dared not abstain, in case it became a Maori issue."

"So the New Zealand Government is not nearly as benign as you described."

"There is no such thing as a government," said the Professor. "Just the armed gang running the place at the time."

Alex Quaison-Sackey ignored the aside. "So tell me, where did you learn all this?"

"Leslie Knox Munro."

"The New Zealand diplomat at the UN? But he's out in the cold, isn't he?"

"Very cold. Yes," said the Professor.

"Well done. I think you have found the final lever."

The men paused while the waiter brought them fresh drinks.

"I met with Dag this morning," resumed the African. Dag Hammarskjold was the Swedish diplomat who had been Secretary General of the UN since the early 1950s. In a few months he would be dead in a suspicious plane crash. "The Secretary General assured me there was a strong push for my committee to be reconstituted, with more teeth. I would possibly stay on as Chairman. He also told me something else, which would be a great honor for Ghana, and for me personally."

"What is that?"

"There is talk Ghana could join the UN Security Council

next year."

"That is exciting news," responded the Professor.

"As President, I could possibly help balance the tense relationship between the Americans and my new allies in Moscow."

"'President'? You said 'President?'"

"Yes, my friend. As early as summer next year, I could be President of the UN Security Council." In fact, Alex Quaison-Sackey went on to serve twice as President of the UN Security Council, and also became President of the UN General Assembly in 1964.

"That calls for cigars," said the Professor, signaling the waiter once again.

"So you can see why a successful, non-violent transfer from a colony to a free nation could be helpful for me. For them too, of course," he added quickly. "It would add greatly to my Committee's prestige."

"I understand," said the Professor, who judged it was time to put business aside. "The coat you are wearing is most magnificent."

"It is a kente coat," said the African, settling into the glow of a third twenty-year-old Macallan whisky. "It is made of cotton and silk. Legend holds the weave is inspired by two Ghanaian villagers who observed how spiders make their web and copied the technique." He paused. "There is one other matter. I sometimes sail with a fellow on Long Island Sound. His name is Wade Bode. Dr. Hendrik Wade Bode. He's a mathematician at Bell Laboratories and he's an expert on all sorts of things. Electronic communications is one of them. He developed some kind of weapon they used on the beach at Normandy." This was the site of the successful D-Day landing—the beginning of the end of World War Two.

"He's also quite close to the Pentagon," continued

Quaison-Sackey. "Navy, I believe. And he chaired a committee on space surveillance for NACA a couple of years ago. NASA as they are now." The diplomat leaned closer. "This is probably classified, but Wade told me there are big advantages to launching rockets near the equator. Something to do with the rotation of the Earth. Have you ever heard that?"

"Not my field, I'm afraid."

"He also has the ear of the Brookings Institute, which produced a report, the same day as mine actually, about the international use of space. And they have the ear of the new Kennedy administration."

"Is that so?" said the Professor. His face was a blank.

"Your Splendid Isles are quite near the equator, are they not?"

"Yes," said Professor Buchanan. "Yes. They are."

CHAPTER 6
GARDENING FOR BEGINNERS

In mid-January 1961, Reverend Geoffrey Brown was walking on a path far above Welcome Harbour. The night was lit by an unhelpful sliver of new moon, and he could see little of the way ahead. It did not matter. He had traveled the route so often, his feet seemed to know the way. The path rose slowly into the cooling hills behind the rectory and continued along a ridge. It passed a rocky outcrop and then rose again, until it funneled into a large pasture sheltered by a dozen trees. At the north end was a shed built from rough-hewn logs, rusting corrugated iron, slabs of old concrete and other anonymous materials that gave no hint of their origin. A small generator hummed. Above a wide door, hung on too few hinges, was a sign:

SP ENDID ISLES GARDENING CLUB
EMBERS ONLY

Inside the shed a dozen or so men were gathered around a steel refrigerator with glass doors, of the kind then becoming popular in clubs and bars. On the center shelf, bathed in fluorescent light, sat a single rose. Even to the untrained eye it was magnificent. The bloom shimmered like shot silk, one moment delicate purple, the next soft pink. Viewed from another angle, it changed color to resemble the sun itself.

The men wore shorts or overalls and work boots. Some wore gardening gloves, but most had such tough, weathered skin they had no need for gloves at all.

"Evenin', Reverend," acknowledged one of the men, glancing towards the door. Several others muttered greetings, without lifting their eyes from the fridge.

"So I imagine this is it," said Reverend Brown. He bent down to take a closer look. "Oh my! It truly is magnificent."

"I said so. Didn't I say so?" the man replied.

"You did, Tom. You did," confirmed another man, who wore a drooping moustache, pince-nez glasses and a knitted cap.

"We should call the meeting together on this historic occasion," said the Reverend, to the tune of scraping chairs being pulled into a circle. "I declare this meeting of the Gardening Club officially open. Now then. Order of business."

"Let's get straight to Tom's rose," said one of the men, to calls of "Hear! Hear!"

"Very well," agreed Reverend Brown. "Tom. Why don't you come up and join me? And Iwi!" He turned to address one of the others. "You are our official minute-taker tonight. Make sure you get everything down."

Most of the men worked their fields during the day, tending their bananas, coconuts, breadfruit, taro and other crops. The Gardening Club was mostly good company, lending each other machinery and discussing how to deal with agricultural pests. There wasn't a rose fancier among them; even Tom had learned everything he knew about the unlikely topic from a crumbling book in the Welcome

Harbour Library.

"Tell us the story again. For Iwi to write down," urged one of the men.

"I was drinking with this sailor from the *Jalisco Belle* at Trader Mike's," began Tom. "He bet me he could score a bull's-eye with his eyes closed. You know all this."

"Keep going," said someone by Tom's side.

"I won, see. He didn't have the two quid so we settled on a rosebush he got from some fellow in Wellington. It was in his cabin on the ship. Said the bush was dying from all the salt air. He was right about that. Anyhow, I took the bush and put it behind my shed in the shade. Gave it plenty of water and goat poo. It started to shoot real good. After a while it got a white bloom on it. I showed it to Mrs. Tehiri and she told me she had a rosebush and it was red." Mrs. Tehiri was the wife of Welcome Island cab driver Dan Tehiri.

"What happened then?" someone asked.

"Mrs. Tehiri said, 'Why don't we mate them together to see what we get?' But we didn't know how to do it, so I went to the library. Mrs. Tahata got me a book on roses, given to them when old Sam Rewi died. There was a section on hybridization, which I didn't understand. But there were some pictures about how to do it. So we mated the two roses together and this," he hooked a finger behind him in the direction of the fridge, "this is what came out."

"I have also spoken to Mrs. Tahata," said the Reverend, "and she told me it is tradition for the owner of a new hybrid to give it a name."

"What sort of name?" said Tom.

"Anything you like," replied the Reverend. "There are at least ten thousand roses with names. Some of them are famous."

"Give us an example," said Iwi.

"Are we all in this, the whole club, or is it just Tom?" interrupted another of the men.

"Tom?" asked the Reverend, deferring to the owner of the rose in the fridge.

"I'm not much good at names," Tom replied.

"Everyone then," said the Reverend. He retrieved a piece of paper from his pocket. "Here are some of the roses Mrs. Tahata found. Marilyn Monroe. Frank Sinatra. Gene Kelly."

"They're Hollywood movie stars," said one of the men.

"And also the names of roses like Tom's."

"Anything else?" asked another man.

"There are traditional names as well," said the Reverend, consulting his list. "Gallica. Alba. Centifolia."

"What do they mean?" called someone from the back.

"Gallica might have been around since the Crusades in the thirteenth century," explained the Reverend. "There are hundreds of famous roses of the Gallica variety."

"So we can call Tom's rose anything?" asked the man.

"What about Tom Bedall's Rose?" said another.

"It won't do," said someone else. "We should have to call it Tom Bedall's and Mrs. Tehiri's Rose, which is much too long."

"How about Jalisco Belle?" This from a man who stood by the door. "After the name of the ship?"

"Tom did all the work. Why should the ship get the credit?" said another. Which put paid to that.

This went on for a few minutes with more and more exotic suggestions. But Reverend Brown did not participate, and nothing seemed to quite find the mark.

Eventually someone noticed the club president was the only one who had not volunteered an idea. "What about you, Reverend? You haven't had a go."

"I have had an opportunity to give this some thought and I consulted with Mrs. Tahata. It is an important rose. It deserves an important name."

There was a general murmur of assent.

The Reverend fixed the men with a steady gaze. "I propose we call it the Splendid Islands Independence Rose."

There was silence for a few moments and then Tom, who had grown tired of the exercise, said: "That's good enough. I like it."

The meeting moved to weightier issues and the rose was not mentioned again.

CHAPTER 7
A JOURNEY BEGINS—AND A FLAP

It was cold by the standards of Welcome Harbour. Misty rain hugged the ground. Even the breeze had a ruffled edge. None of this was good news for Reverend Brown as he hand-cranked the old Austin. If it had ever had an electric starter, it had long ago ceased to function, which meant hand-cranking was the only option. Unfortunately, the car started reliably only if the weather was pleasant. Today, manifestly, it was not.

The Reverend held the crank in the approved manner, his fingers cupped below the handle to minimize the risk of a broken thumb. Cranks were unpredictable—they could spin without warning in either direction, depending on whether the engine chose to start properly, or backfire. Cranking a car was a little like stroking a venomous snake.

Mrs. Hana waited discreetly at the door but did not intervene. She knew the ways of the old Austin better than the Reverend, but he would not thank her if she started the engine while he stood impotently to one side. She wondered why he wore his clerical collar, since it was not a church day and he had no other engagements. And why he had asked her to find Tanisha's birth certificate, which was stored in a trunk under the stairs? Finally, he had wanted a recent photograph of his housekeeper's daughter, for reasons he did not disclose.

Eventually, on the fourth attempt, the tiny motor sputtered to life and the crank handle politely disengaged. As Mrs. Hana retreated into the house she heard the Reverend crunch the gears. He was a fast driver but a poor one. She heard the gears crunch again. He's over-revving, she thought, and sighed in sympathy for the little car.

*****

The Tasman Empire Airways office was no more than a counter at the airport. It was staffed mornings only—unless a flight was arriving later in the day—by Mrs. Tahata, who was also Welcome Harbour's part-time librarian.

"Did you find a good name for Tom Bedall's rose?" she asked.

"Satisfactory, I believe," replied the Reverend. "I have come to you over something else."

"He hasn't mated another one?"

"Good heavens, no! It is not that. My housekeeper's ex-husband lives in New Zealand, as everyone knows."

"How is Piata?" said Mrs. Tahata.

"Mrs. Hana is fine," said the Reverend patiently. Business in the Splendid Isles was conducted in the cracks between gossip. Sometimes the cracks were narrow. Occasionally, there were no cracks and business had to wait for another day. "Now, what is the cheapest way to get her daughter to her father?" tried the churchman. "Something important has happened."

There was no need for Mrs. Tahata to consult the schedule, which was in any event erratic. She knew the fares for the few flights off by heart. "One hundred and eighty-one pounds," she promptly replied. "It is a lot. Then again, it is very far." Wellington was, in fact, almost three and a half thousand miles by air, and the trip took two days.

"I hoped there might be a cheaper way," the Reverend said.

"And how is Iwi?" she asked. Mrs. Tahata was a widow and known to be sweet on the President of the Church Parish Council.

"Iwi is excellent," said Reverend Brown.

"You and he must come to dinner." The offer sounded almost—but not quite—casual.

"That would be wonderful," he replied after faint hesitation.

"And Piata too, naturally."

A foursome then, thought the Reverend. "About this airfare?" he tried again.

"Well," she replied. "How much could you afford?"

"Maybe ninety pounds. The church does not have more."

"Ah! If it is a church matter, then possibly a way could be found. The airplane has a spare seat in the cockpit. The 'jump seat,' it is called. Sometimes, as a favor, the Captain may allow a passenger to use it without a ticket."

"That would be marvelous," said the Reverend. "Could it be arranged?"

"For the church?" said Mrs. Tahata. "I see no reason why not. But it is only one-way. For the flight back to Welcome Harbour a fare will have to be paid."

Reverend Brown's next port of call was the government administration building. It was the tallest structure in the Splendid Isles, soaring two stories into the sky. He climbed the stairs to the top floor where passport applications were processed. The passports were issued by New Zealand, since the Splendid Isles was a protectorate and not a country in its own right. At least not yet, thought the Reverend, as he took his turn at the counter. The Austin idled in the street. He could not face cranking it again, and car theft in the Splendid Isles had yet to be invented as a crime.

At the pharmacy he purchased a roll of Kodachrome film for ten shillings, which was equivalent to about one American dollar. He drove back to the rectory and asked Mrs. Hana for a blanket. This he huddled under as a makeshift darkroom while he threaded the film into his Yashica Electro 35, a popular camera at the time. Then he headed up the hill to the Gardening Club. The heavy camera jiggled on its strap, but Reverend Brown was so absorbed by his thoughts he did not seem to notice.

The Independence Rose was in the refrigerator, which was turned off but still quite cold. The Reverend reached in and took the rose outside into the sun. He consumed the entire roll of film before he was satisfied. He returned the rose to its sanctuary, locked the door of the Gardening Club and retraced his steps to the rectory.

Later in the day, he drove to the office of the *Splendid Islands Telegraph* to meet with editor and occasional parishioner, Aaron Trieger, who was quite tall and crowbar thin. He had been a journalist in Fleet Street, London, rumor said, and had toured the South Pacific for a travel feature from which he never returned. That bit was definitely true, since he had been in Welcome Harbour for almost ten years.

He'd worked at the *Telegraph* as chief reporter until the owner, old Sam Rewi, died. Now he was editor, chief reporter and proprietor. The paper was quite openly pro New Zealand, and Trieger drank now and again with the country's Resident Commissioner, out-to-pasture Wellington civil servant Randolph Herd. Trieger was also an occasional guest of the Queen's Representative, Sir Jonathan O'Dowd, who lived at Government House, the island's grandest home.

He was a man of the Establishment, as editors in small places are wont to be; but had always been fair to the locals. He had, for example, reported the speech of the admittedly drunk President of the Farmers' Federation when he lamented the punishing freight costs required to ship the Splendids' produce to New Zealand. Settling into his stride, the hapless President had also complained about the low prices the shipping company paid farmers for their goods. Trieger just as scrupulously reported the furious reply from Sir Brendan Court, Chairman of Pacific Islands Shipping in Wellington, including his alarming threat the service could be withdrawn at any time. The debate died at that point and the Farmers' Federation replaced their President with a more temperate fellow, an accountant who was not on the land. A little less exuberant, was what they hoped.

Trieger uncoiled from his seat when the Reverend entered, and stuck out a bony hand.

"I have come to talk to you about a flower," said the head of the Splendid Isles Christian Church. He dropped a photograph of the 'Independence Rose' onto the editor's desk.

"Righty-oh!" said Trieger. "Shoot away."

*****

England was cold as always in midwinter. It was Wednesday the 25th of January, 1961. The evening shift of the eight hundred London staff to Queen Elizabeth the Second shivered in their various offices of the seven-hundred and-seventy-five room Buckingham Palace. The two-and-a-half-century-old royal residence may have been one of the most identifiable buildings in the world, but the heating was legendarily abominable. One of the coldest offices, despite its physical proximity to the Queen, housed the Press Secretary, Commander Richard Colville. It was 8pm. Not unreasonably, he had gone home.

Sarah Sarnow, however, a pallid twenty-four-year-old, was at her desk. She had been frankly astonished when her application to join the prestigious office had been accepted three weeks earlier, since she was not of distinguished parentage, although her father had recently retired from a mid-level job at the domestic British spy agency, MI5. Nor did she have an outstanding academic record. But she was keen. So when the teleprinter in the corner chattered to life, she immediately went to investigate. Curling out of the machine were the headlines from newspapers throughout the huge roll-call of countries for whom the thirty-four-year-old Elizabeth the Second was Monarch. Sarah scanned the headlines from Australia, Canada, India and New Zealand, before the teleprinter coughed out the headlines from the *Splendid Islands Telegraph*. One, in particular, caught her eye:

UNIQUE INDEPENDENCE ROSE BRED HERE

The Queen was reported to have recently developed an interest in the thorny shrub, so, with considerable initiative, Sarah Sarnow pounced.

A list on the wall identified the Queen's Representative to the Splendid Isles, Sir Jonathan O'Dowd, and his telex number. She pursed her lips and began to type.

*****

It was 10 am at Government House on Welcome Island. Sir Jonathan was buttering a slice of toast and about to reach for his prized English marmalade when his aide-de-camp entered the conservatory.

"Your Excellency, I have a telex from the Palace. I think

you should see it."

"The Palace?" queried the QR incredulously. In his almost three years in the post he had never once heard from Buckingham Palace. Almost all communications came from Viscount Cobham, the Governor-General of New Zealand, who was senior to the QR and his immediate boss. Once or twice he had received instructions directly from the New Zealand Government. In her enthusiasm to impress, Sarah Sarnow had breached protocol in a way that galvanized Sir Jonathan into action.

"The telex refers directly to the Queen," said the aide-de-camp, as if it were necessary to fire a second flare into the sky. Again, in her innocence, Sarah had blundered. The Queen was never mentioned in official communications unless she was directly involved.

"Give it here," said the QR, barely resisting the temptation to snatch the telex from his aide.

*****

The Chief Administrator of the Splendids, Resident Commissioner Randolph Herd, was breakfasting at Trader Mike's on that Wednesday morning. The weather was considerably better than in London, England. He was partway through his breakfast cocktail of brandy, milk, sugar syrup and nutmeg, which constituted his usual first meal of the day, when an assistant rushed in.

"There's a flap," the assistant announced. "You need to be in the office right away."

Herd was irritated by the interruption to a lazy day, but flaps always needed to be handled with care. He drained his breakfast and hurried across the road. The phone on his desk rang immediately.

"Randolph," said the QR without preamble. "I need to

know everything about some blasted rose. I have to report back to the Palace tonight."

The Resident Commissioner fumbled for a pen and a sheet of paper. Rose? Palace? Tonight? What the hell was going on? "If we could slow down a little," he said ponderously.

"The Queen has expressed interest in our Independence Rose." With that, the QR hung up, leaving the Resident Commissioner with a dead phone, a mild but growing headache and a mission that made little sense.

He turned to his hovering assistant and began to bark instructions.

*****

All police vehicles in the Splendids had sirens. Who could resist such an urgent display of power? But they did not often wail on Welcome Island, where urgent might be defined as a fish on the line, or the soup getting cold. So Mrs. Hana and Reverend Brown were open-mouthed in surprise when they saw a squad car scream up to their front door under both siren and lights. Police Chief Ned Tanner and three junior officers bounded up the steps. The air cracked with adrenaline as they entered the house.

Throughout the island the scene was repeated. Two motorcycle police found Tom Bedall oiling his tractor from a hook-nosed can. They inspected the bush from which the Independence Rose had come and sketched its exact location.

When they ran out of questions, they visited the *Telegraph*, entered the editor's office and closed the door. By 2 pm, every member of the Splendid Isles Gardening Club had been interviewed. Nor did the urgent enquiries end there. Police vehicles rushed to the airport and to the

Welcome Harbour Library in search of Mrs. Tahata, though she was treated with greater care because her son was also police. They examined old Sam Rewi's rose book and took it with them 'for further investigation', as they told the alarmed librarian.

They visited Mrs. Tehiri, who had contributed half the parentage of the adolescent rose, and asked to be shown the shrub behind her toolshed, if for no other reason than investigative thoroughness. She seemed unsurprised when the bush in question could not be found. "Maybe it died," she told police—which might have explained the absence of the rose, but surely not its remains. "My Dan might have pulled it out," she added, attempting to improve her answer. Dan was her husband, and the only taxi driver on Welcome Island.

A wheezing Ned Tanner and a party of fellow officers also accompanied Reverend Brown to the Gardening Club headquarters, far above Welcome Harbour. They inspected the increasingly famous Independence Rose, now wilted in the no longer cold fridge. But the rose was neither arrested nor detained for questioning.

*****

At another, more subterranean level, a different kind of investigation kicked into gear. The New Zealand Secret Service—the NZSS, as it was called at the time—had a representative in Welcome Harbour, who also happened to edit the paper. It was what they described as 'natural cover', because Aaron Trieger could be as nosy as he wanted and no one would wonder why. He had a license to dig out both rumor and fact. Newsmen and spies thrived on either. The four-year-old intelligence agency had a generous budget and operated, quite literally, outside the law. By happy oversight, none had been drafted to cover it.

Trieger received a call from Wellington and by lunchtime he, too, was on the job.

Late that night, the Queen's Representative signed off on the exhaustive Independence Rose Report, as it was grandly titled, and a six-thousand-word document was telexed to London. In accordance with protocol, the telex did not go to Sarah Sarnow but to her boss, Press Secretary, Commander Richard Colville. Since the Queen was directly referred to in the original request, a copy of the report was also sent to the most powerful man in the royal household, the Sovereign's Private Secretary, Lieutenant Colonel Sir Michael Adeane, who had once shot a tiger in Nepal after the Queen declined to do so. A courtesy copy went to Viscount Cobham, famed English cricket batsman and feared right-hand bowler, who also happened to be Governor-General of New Zealand and Sir Jonathan O'Dowd's occasionally fractious boss.

*****

Though no copy was sent to Prime Minister Keith Holyoake—he was outside the royal chain of command—it was not long before he too was in the loop. Shortly thereafter, Brigadier-General Herbert Gilbert was summoned to an urgent meeting. 'Gallant Bill', as he was known by all, was a conspicuously brave soldier who had served with distinction in the legendary World War Two battles at Tobruk and Cassino. He was currently Director of the NZSS and, by chance, an avid breeder of rhododendrons, whose *vireya* tropical variety happened to grow wild in a tiny corner of the Splendid Isles.

"I know something about flowers but nothing about roses," he told the PM after scanning the Palace report.

Holyoake waved a hand in dismissal. "I don't care about

roses," said the Prime Minister. "We have a man in the Splendid Isles?"

"Yes," confirmed the country's most senior spy. "We have assets in all our territories." In the secret world, an 'asset' was an on-the-ground agent under the control of a spy. At a more remote level, they might also be a human being who slept, ate, and made love, but 'asset' somehow seemed tidier. They could be discarded if the need arose. Much as accountants review, monitor and revise assets on a balance sheet, spymasters control their assets on a balance sheet of a darker kind.

"Good," Holyoake grunted.

"The brief is what exactly?" asked Gilbert.

"The Splendid Isles Independence Rose," said the PM. "I want to know where they got the name."

And so, after extensive investigations by police, newspaper reporters, intelligence operatives and top officials reaching almost to the Queen of England herself, it was the twelve-year-old-early-school-leaver turned Prime Minister of New Zealand who finally got to the heart of the thing.

CHAPTER 8
A SCENT OF SOMETHING ELSE

It was a bright afternoon and Tom Bedall rode his bucking 1912 steam tractor around the small, flinty fields on which he managed to grow vegetables and, on the higher ground, a few pawpaw that struggled out of the thin soil on this less favorable side of the island. The twelve-ton tractor pulled far better than a team of horses, which were in any event few and far between in the Splendid Isles, so despite its age, the ancient vehicle was a valuable machine. Tom had ridden the JI Case, as proclaimed in copperplate on the boiler, since his father had worked the same fields decades earlier. He loved the noisy solitude as he sat atop the ten-foot monster, and he loved its hissing power.

Tom was a simple man, though he had been described less generously as 'slow' at the Welcome Harbour primary school he'd attended briefly before his father died. He lived alone in a rough-built three-room shack without running water or electricity. A stew of vegetables and goat meat bubbled permanently on a wood fire. He had an icebox for beer, which he replenished from time to time. His first love was his tractor, which—perhaps like Tom himself—was slow and simple. Several nights a week he rode it to Trader Mike's where he sat, sometimes alone, sometimes with others. He was fond of darts and there was a competition Tuesday nights. He also attended meetings of the Gardening Club, though it was a long walk past the lookout and through the hills far above Welcome Harbour. Finally, he was a member of the Farmers' Federation, which represented the interests of growers like Tom who depended on exporting their produce to New Zealand to survive.

He had few friends and many acquaintances, but none drove a blue pickup like the one that came hurtling towards his shack at breakneck speed. The vehicle slewed to a standstill and the door opened to reveal Aaron Trieger, who also drank at Trader Mike's, but with folk far beyond Tom's humble circle. The two men exchanged greetings and adjourned inside, which was dark as a cave except for shafts of light shining through old nail holes in the roof. Tom made a pot of tea, which he poured into enamel mugs. The newsman complimented Tom on his farm, admired his vintage tractor, and approved the tea. He lauded the beauty of the location, which he described as a Turner watercolor—a subject he clearly knew little about, since Turners are famous for their delicate pastels, whereas the Splendids were bold sunsets, chocolate earth and glaring white sand. Eventually, he turned to the subject he admitted was the purpose of his visit.

"Righty-oh! I'm thinking of a follow-up story on the rose, old chap. Bit more of the color."

"Depends on the light," said Tom, relieved to have arrived at a subject requiring a useful reply. "It's pink from one angle."

"Gracious! Not that sort of color," said the newsman.

"You already put it all in the paper," said Tom in polite protest.

"Not everything," said Trieger. He sipped his tea and, old

hand that he was, waited for Tom to reply.

*****

Later that evening, the hissing tractor picked its way along the road past Welcome Harbour, its yellow Cyclops headlamp searching for the turnoff to the rectory.

Tom and the Reverend sat in the study while Mrs. Hana fussed over them, brought more tea and a plate of warm scones wrapped in cloth, as if they were some living thing too delicate for exposure to the sweet tropics air.

"Reverend," said Tom, "I need to change me story a bit. About the rose."

"Go on, Tom," said the head of the Splendid Isles Christian Church. He was used to confession, no stranger to sin.

"We had a bet, but he passed out before we could settle up."

"The sailor from the *Jalisco Belle*?"

"I carried him back to his cabin on the ship," Tom continued, "but he was still out, so I took the rose."

"Why?" asked the Reverend.

"It looked sick and I like to make things green. I also spied a pound lying on the floor," Tom hurried on. "His wallet might have fallen out of his pocket. Could be why it was there. So I grabbed it."

"The wallet or the pound?" said Reverend Brown.

"That's right," said Tom, who may have been simple, as people said, but who understood an ambiguity when one was required. "Mrs. Tehiri's rose never took. We tried a couple of times. Then it died. Said she knew where there was another one. Her Dan could get it."

"And where was this rose?" asked Reverend Brown.

"Round the other side. Near Government House."

"I never noticed any roses along the road there," the Reverend prompted.

"Could have been just near the gate," agreed Tom, taking a hasty sip of his tea.

There was silence for a moment while Reverend Brown processed Tom's new story. One parent of the Independence Rose stolen from a drunken sailor whose wallet, almost certainly, had suffered the same fate. The other parent stolen from the official residence of the Queen's Representative.

"I thought it's what he had a sniff of," continued Tom.

"Who?" said the Reverend.

"The big man from the paper. Mr. Trieger."

"And what made you think that?"

"But he didn't want to know nothing about it. Pretended he did. But he didn't."

"And what did he want to know?" the Reverend said softly.

"Why we called it the Independence Rose. What it meant. Who came up with the name. He thought it was you."

"That's what you told him?"

"He went and visited with Iwi before me," said Tom. "Iwi told him."

CHAPTER 9
THE PRICE OF FRUIT

The Farmers' Federation met in the Mechanics Hall in the middle of town. Vehicles were piled up out front, as though they had been deposited there by some great flood. Inside the hall was a trestle table laden with homemade cakes and buns. There was a coffee urn at one end, flanked by columns of plastic cups. Milk curdled in a jug covered with a weighted cloth. Spilled sugar lay on the table, like gravel from trucks departing a quarry. Chairs grated as men juggled cakes, buns and cups of steaming coffee while finding somewhere to sit before the meeting got underway.

On stage sat the new Farmers' Federation President, RW Rumsey—RW, as he liked to be called. Unlike the audience, he wore a ballooning white shirt with metal armbands. An assortment of pens protruded from a bulging pocket. The chain of a fob watch disappeared into his pants. He looked like a riverboat gambler down on his luck. In fact, he was the accountant retained by many of the growers in the hall. By his side sat Reverend Geoffrey Brown, wearing a black vest and clerical collar; and next to him, Tanisha Hana in a blue dress cinched at the waist by a plain leather belt.

RW rose to his feet. "Welcome to this meeting of the Farmers' Federation. As your new President I want to

59

welcome Reverend Brown, who I am sure is known to you all. I also want to welcome Miss Tanisha Hana, who you will know is the Reverend's housekeeper's daughter." Both the Reverend and Tanisha half rose in acknowledgment. "The Reverend has asked to speak to us later tonight, and I think we all want to hear what he has to say. In the meantime, I have prepared what I would call the pro forma accounts for a typical farm in the Splendid Isles so everyone can better understand the situation we are in."

There was a gentle murmuring in the hall.

"As you know," the President continued, "the *Jalisco Belle* will be back in a month, now the cyclone season is coming to an end. So we need to understand what must be achieved if everyone here is to get a fair return from his work." RW cleared his throat before beginning a lengthy financial presentation. "... so you can see the gross profit needs to be higher than fifty percent," he concluded, "if—I repeat, if—you are going to meet your expenses and make a decent living."

"That is all very good," said a farmer near the front of the hall, "but it does not help us understand the price we should set for our crops."

"You all know what you achieved last year," replied RW.

There was a general nodding of heads.

"And since I imagine most of you have now completed your books, you will know the profit you made." This was somewhat disingenuous of the accountant, who had personally completed the accounts for most of the farmers present.

"Profit?" said a man at the back, bitterly. "What profit was that?"

A few laughed. Most shook their heads in agreement.

Then another man spoke. "The shipping company doesn't

care about our profit. They are only interested in their own."

At this, Reverend Brown rose again and turned to catch the President's eye.

"I think this would be an excellent time to hear from our guest," said RW.

There was a further outbreak of murmuring. What could a churchman know about their problems—a man who spent his day indoors in a suit while they labored outdoors in their fields?

"A few days ago," began Reverend Brown, as though he were delivering a sermon at the cathedral he had always wanted. "A few days ago, Miss Tanisha, who is with me tonight—" He paused while the farmers looked more closely at the pretty brunette. "A few days ago," he began again, "Miss Tanisha returned from a long trip to New Zealand. She traveled there at my request." He stopped as though struck by a sudden idea and turned to Tanisha. "Why don't you stand up, my dear, and tell us what you did?"

The housekeeper's daughter coughed nervously before she began. "The Reverend asked me to visit a number of greengrocers in Wellington, and a supermarket which had just opened."

"Why don't you explain what a supermarket is, dear?" encouraged the Reverend.

"It is a huge shop selling groceries and fruit, which you select for yourself. There are aisles with shelves to the top of your head. When you are finished you line up and pay at what they call a 'checkout'. I looked on all the shelves to find the fruit and vegetables from the Splendid Isles."

"And did you find any?" coaxed the Reverend, an elderly cowboy riding herd.

"Oh yes!" said Tanisha.

"And what did you do next?" He galloped ahead.

"What you told me, Reverend. I wrote down all the prices on a pad."

"And do you have the pad with you tonight?" Steering her towards home.

"Of course," she said. "I have it right here." Tanisha fumbled in her handbag and extracted a small yellow writing pad, which she held above her head for all to see.

"Did you find any bananas on the shelves?" asked the Reverend.

"Yes," she said.

"And how much were they?"

Tanisha looked down at her notes before replying. "Eight pence."

"That was per bunch?"

"No," she said. "They were eight pence each."

"I see. Were there any coconuts?"

"Yes, of course."

"And how much were they?"

"A shilling."

"What about passion fruit?"

"Sixpence," she said.

Some of the farmers tried to calculate the numbers in their heads. Most waited for whatever would come next.

Reverend Brown turned to RW for assistance. "Mr. President," he said, "I wonder if the meeting could help me here? I believe we sell our bananas by the case. Is that right?"

A number of the men nodded vigorously.

"And there are about eighty bananas to a case?"

Once again there was a vigorous nodding of heads.

"So a case of bananas would sell in New Zealand for—eight pence per banana—multiplied by eighty bananas." He paused to do the arithmetic in his head. "Six hundred and forty pence," he said at last. Paused again. "Per case. And Mr.

President?"

"Yes?" said RW, playing for effect.

"Could the meeting advise me how much the shipping company pays the men in this room?"

The meeting erupted as several farmers competed to supply the answer.

"I believe I heard forty pence per case. Is that correct?" But he did not wait for an answer. Having lit the fuse, he hurried on. "Now I would like to turn your attention to passion fruit. Is that all right with you, my dear?"

"Perfectly," replied Tanisha, but those in the room barely heard her. Some men rose to their feet. Some cradled their head in their hands. Some were merely stunned. One man looked at the Reverend and his eyes filled with tears. He worked from sunup to sundown to sell his bananas for a little more than three shillings a crate, which were sold on to housewives in New Zealand for nearly three pounds.

The farmers of the Splendid Isles sold their oranges, mangoes, limes, grapefruit, lemons, star fruit, coconuts, passion fruit and a dozen other kinds of fruit and vegetables at prices that kept them barely above the poverty line, while Pacific Islands Shipping grew fat. By the time the *Jalisco Belle* arrived at Auckland, New Zealand's largest city, two weeks later, the same fruit and vegetables were worth up to twenty times as much.

RW tried to bring the meeting to order, but it was a hopeless task.

"Come, my dear," Reverend Brown said to Tanisha, as the pair threaded their way through the boiling crowd. "I think we have achieved everything we planned."

The Austin A40 dozed in its parking place across the road. Amazingly, its tiny engine started on the first crank.

CHAPTER 10
A ROSE BY ANY OTHER NAME

It was an odd party picking its way along the hill track far above the rectory in the fading afternoon light: one man in a clerical collar, a camera swinging heavily around his neck; a slightly younger man in suit pants and a crumpled white shirt with armbands, old-fashioned even for 1961; and a pretty girl in a willowy skirt and canvas tennis shoes. There was no breeze, so the two men sweated and the girl perspired as they arrived at the high-pasture address of the Splendid Isles Gardening Club.

Even from a distance, they could see there was something wrong. The clubhouse was a wonder of engineering, built as it was from any available material and assembled by volunteers in their spare time. But somehow it had developed a drunken lean. One of the main supports had lost its grip on the earth and tipped away from the building. The door, which had always hung on too few hinges, now hung on none at all. The sign remained, but the only part that could still be read said 'EMBERS ONLY', which seemed perfectly to describe the scene. Inside, chairs had been flung in every direction. Shards of glass covered the floor. The bar fridge lay on its side in a pool of purple soup. Its door had burst open and the most recent bloom of the Independence

Rose, wilted from the heat, looked as though it had been slashed with a machete. The stem was broken, the bloom cleaved in two. The generator still worked, but something had happened to the fuel mix, because it belched black smoke. A dozen men, fellow members, wandered the wreckage.

Reverend Brown took all this in with a sweeping gaze. He climbed onto a small table that had been left undamaged. "Find anywhere you can to sit," he said, "even if it is on the floor or the bare earth."

After a few moments, the sad meeting came to order.

"A madman did this," said Tom Bedall.

"No," said Iwi. "It is too methodical for that."

"Who, then?" demanded one of the men.

"Someone who hates the club or somebody in it," said another. Several names were mentioned, but all were quickly dismissed.

"The police," said another man. "Looking for something they couldn't find."

But there was no good reason for the police to trash the building, so this theory, too, was set aside.

Eventually, the flame blew out and the men waited for whatever might happen next.

"The question is not 'Who did this?'" said Reverend Brown. "The question is 'Why?'"

"I reckon it was kids from the school," someone replied. "It's the kind of damage kids would do."

"This is not the work of madmen," said Reverend Brown firmly. "It is not the work of children. It is not someone with a grudge."

"Who then?" asked another, who stood at the back.

"It does not matter," said the Reverend. "It is why they

did it that matters, and I think I know the answer." There was silence as they waited for the puzzle to be solved.

"Tanisha," said the churchman, "you have just returned from New Zealand, have you not?"

The men turned to look at the girl no one had noticed in the confusion. She climbed onto the table with Reverend Brown, as they had agreed she would do. "You sent me," she said simply.

"Tell us what you did there, my dear."

"What I told the men at the Farmers' Federation the other night?"

"Yes," prompted the Reverend. Some of the men from the Farmers' Federation were also members of the Gardening club, but it would not harm to tell them twice.

"I wrote down the prices people in Wellington pay for fruit and vegetables from the Splendid Isles"

"And what did you find?"

Tanisha hesitated. Perhaps this was part of a rehearsed script. Perhaps she had genuinely lost her track.

"A case of bananas sells for forty pence here—" she said in a rush. "They cost nearly three pounds in Wellington."

"The same bananas?" said the Reverend.

Tanisha nodded.

Reverend Brown fixed the men with a steady gaze. "And that, gentlemen, is why our clubhouse has been attacked."

Tom Bedall was the first to speak. "I don't see how the price housewives in Wellington pay for bananas has anything to do with what happened here."

"RW," said the Reverend, addressing the man in suit pants and white shirt for the first time. "Would you come up and explain? RW Rumsey is the new President of the Farmers' Federation, and what he has to say tonight is important." The Reverend paused. "Important for us and for everyone in the Splendid Isles."

"Good evening," began RW, with more formality than the gathering required. "I am an accountant by trade." He nodded at one or two of the men in front of him. "Last year the average farmer on the island made a loss—a loss, mind you, not a profit—of over one hundred pounds. The fruit and vegetables you labored to produce were sold in Wellington for up to twenty times more than you were paid."

"I still don't see what it has to do with wrecking our club," said Tom Bedall.

It was time to unravel the mystery. "Your rose," said Reverend Brown.

"The Independence Rose," interrupted Iwi, the first to understand. "It is a message to New Zealand, isn't it?"

"Yes, it is," confirmed the Reverend. "We are letting them know we do not want them to run our country. We do not want them to make all the profit while we do all the work."

"I still don't see—" said Tom, but the Reverend immediately interrupted.

"We were attacked by the Government of New Zealand," he said, stepping well beyond the bounds of reason. But he did not believe the farmers would see this. Moreover, he bet they would not.

"What!" cried several men at once.

"The Independence Rose is something they fear. It is the first beat of a heart that cries for freedom." The Reverend paused again. He had arrived at the pivotal moment, as he had foreseen and described it earlier to RW and Tanisha. The men could decide it was his fight, not theirs. After all, had Reverend Brown not named the rose himself? Had they not simply gone along? They knew nothing of a battle for independence, had not been consulted. The Independence Rose was a name for a flower, not a rallying point for a cause they might care little about. If that happened, if reason prevailed, all was lost because, though they did not know it, the Splendid Isles Gardening Club was critical to his plan.

Alternatively, they could be swept away by emotion, as men often are. Swept away by emotion into a moment of history.

Reverend Brown could not allow reason to prevail. In a broken, vandalized shed on a high pasture above Welcome Harbour, he now had to give the greatest sermon of his life.

"Look around you," he boomed. "This is what they have done to our club." He jumped down from the table, lithe as a man half his age, stooped and picked up a broken chair, held it aloft, then set it down again gently, as if it were a foal. He walked to the door, picked up the shattered lock, dropped it. "And this," he said, shaking with rage. He strode to the rose, which he held against his chest as though it were a kitten. He stroked the injured bloom. "This is what they have done to the Splendid Isles Independence Rose."

Possibly it was a trick of the light, but for a moment the dead rose turned a blushing pink, as they remembered marveling at it so long ago.

"This is the beginning of a fight to tell your children," he thundered.

Years later, in the bars of Welcome Harbour, they told this story, the men who had been there that night, how a simple Reverend from the rectory next to a flame tree became a giant before their eyes. How his voice cracked like lightning in the night sky. How he wept salty tears of rage.

They bounded out of the clubhouse like excited children, whooping in delight. The Splendid Isles Gardening Club would have its place in history.

CHAPTER 11
SNIFFER DOGS

In the house at Pipitea Street, Wellington, sat Prime Minister Keith Holyoake, a steaming cup of tea on his desk and, on the other side of it, 'Gallant Bill' Gilbert, the war hero Director of the Secret Service. It was their weekly review between the man who ran the open and the man who ran the secret New Zealand. Brigadier Gilbert dreaded the sessions, which he privately described as like being beaten with a rubber mouth.

"Finally," said the Prime Minister, "there is the small matter of the Independence Rose."

"Ah, yes," said Gilbert. He had reviewed a huge dossier on the topic, containing voluminous police statements of interview and a theft report from the Queen's Representative in the Splendid Isles—the only Queen's Representative, at the time, anywhere in the world. The role had been created by Buckingham Palace in 1905, as a condition to handing over the Splendids to an eager New Zealand. 'So we can keep an eye on things—together,' had been the glib explanation, though whether this had ever been properly relayed to the New Zealanders was unknown.

There was also a secret annex to the Rose report from the NZSS man in Welcome Harbour, who had 'combed through the tailings,' as they said in the service, and re-interviewed several of the more promising leads.

"The report is interesting, but I'm afraid it does not take us very far," said the spy.

"Spare the conclusions," said Holyoake, glancing at his wristwatch, a Bulova Accutron Alpha that required no winding since it ran on the latest space-age electronics.

"Beautiful watch," said Brigadier Gilbert, whose staff had informed him the Prime Minister was particularly proud of the new timepiece. It was also a gentle reminder to the PM the NZSS had arranged for the state-of-the-art electronic watch to be shipped all the way from America and onto Holyoake's arm.

"I have a few minutes before my next appointment," said the PM, "so perhaps you can take me through the story."

Gilbert looked down at his notes. "The rose was grown, so he says, by Arthur Thomas Bedall, a local farmer. No priors. He is a member of the Splendid Isles Gardening Club, which met in January and named the bloom the 'Splendid Islands Independence Rose'. Interestingly, there was a reported theft of a rosebush from the QR's residence several months earlier. It is possible the QR's rose is one of the parents of the new rose, but this has not been confirmed."

"Who came up with the name?" said the PM impatiently. "That is what interests me."

"Every member of the gardening club has been questioned. There were a number of suggested names. 'Independence Rose' was proposed by Geoffrey Graham Brown, the President of the club. It was his only suggestion. Accepted unanimously."

"What do we know about him?"

"Minister of the Splendid Isles Christian Church. Sixty-three, lives quietly with his housekeeper in the rectory near

Welcome Harbour, which is the main town on Welcome Island, the largest and most populous of the—"

"Yes." said Holyoake. Which meant 'Hurry up.'

"There are rumors about the relationship between the housekeeper and this Reverend Brown," The Chief Spy smoothly moved on. "The rumors are unconfirmed. He has no priors, no known political views. Never traveled away from Welcome Harbour, except once to New Zealand, a long time ago: February 1935. He has a telephone, but apart from several calls from his son in America, one Oxide Joshua Brown, he has neither made nor received any overseas calls as far as we know. The son is the only child of a marriage that ended before our Reverend Brown was called into God's service. Who else the Reverend might serve is not yet clear."

"Nothing to show why the name 'Independence Rose'?"

"Nothing at all. Our man interviewed the Reverend as an 'unconscious source.'" The Brigadier glanced up at the PM. As a military man he loved jargon. The intelligence community, to which he was a recent recruit, loved it more. 'Unconscious source' meant a subject who divulged information without realizing he was talking to a spy who was 'below the line'—in the jargon again—a spy under deep cover, as was Aaron Trieger, editor of the *Splendid Islands Telegraph.*

"Anything else?"

"His son came home for Christmas. Brought a friend, an older man apparently."

"Who was he?"

"That is where we ran out of puff, I'm afraid. Regrettably, there are no immigration landing cards for the period leading up to Christmas. Officer on leave. No one rostered to take his place. Things are relaxed up there. Not unusual."

"How did this older man arrive?" asked the PM irritably.

"Ship? Plane? Flying saucer?"

"Definitely not ship," said the Brigadier. "Cyclone season keeps them away this time of year. Private vessel, say, a yacht? Possible, but doubtful. We have not checked with the Harbormaster," said Gilbert, scribbling a note.

"Aircraft?" said the Prime Minister.

"TEAL flies the Coral Route from Auckland." This was New Zealand's largest city and commercial center; it lay about four hundred miles north of Wellington.

"And you have spoken to them?"

"Not at this stage, Prime Minister," replied the Brigadier, scribbling another note. "Might I ask a question? Why are we surprised? We voted in favor of decolonization at the UN, so I'd have thought all our protectorates might now be thinking independence. Not that our investigation shows anything of the sort in the Splendid Isles."

"This is about fish," said Holyoake.

"Fish?" said the Chief Spy.

"One million pounds a year, if things happen the way they should. It's our wealthiest colony. We favor independence as a broad brush policy, but we do not favor it right now—not for the Splendid Isles. Not while I am at the helm."

"Very good," said Brigadier Gilbert and rose to leave.

"Get back to me," said the Prime Minister.

"Of course," said the Brigadier, who had hoped the Independence Rose issue was closed and forgotten.

There was one thing, however, that both Gilbert and the Prime Minister did forget. Unless specifically excluded by order of the PM, the international intelligence-sharing treaty in force between New Zealand, Australia, the United States and Great Britain would kick in. The Independence Rose dossier would be distributed, as a matter of routine, to both the American CIA and Britain's MI6.

CHAPTER 12
A BUSY NEWS DAY

Aaron Trieger's office looked exactly like those of the editors he'd reported to throughout his long career. Whether this was by design or some curious, inanimate form of Darwinian evolution, was impossible to say. The office certainly fit its purpose. A black telephone sat on the newsman's desk, a well pounded Underwood typewriter rested on a side table within easy reach, piles of newspapers littered every surface. The office had glass walls so the editor could look out into his newsroom where, one day, other reporters might ply their trade. There was a door made of chipboard that could have been taken from a child's playhouse had it been better built. The door was closed. Inside the office, on a cracked, once padded chair, sat an unremarkable man in suit pants and a yellowing white shirt with armbands and a pocket bulging with pens.

"As you know," RW Rumsey began, "there has been dissatisfaction at the price our farmers receive from the Pacific Islands Shipping Company."

"We've already reported that," said Trieger, who was after a new story, not the rehash of an old one.

"As an accountant and President of the Farmers' Federation... after the unfortunate resignation of my predecessor... caused no doubt by pressure from the shipping company...." RW was nervous. He stuttered whole phrases.

"I doubt we could say that," Trieger interrupted. "I believe it would be defamatory."

"Very well," said RW. "As an accountant, a chartered account," he corrected, "with extensive experience in Wellington and Welcome Harbour ...." RW began again. "I prepare the tax affairs for a number of farmers. A good number. And I have therefore been able to put together a complete financial picture for a typical farm. Profit and loss. Balance sheet. Cash-flow. All of it."

Trieger reached for a notebook. The long-winded RW Rumsey might have a story after all.

"I call this a pro forma financial statement, since it does not represent the position for a specific farm, but an average for the industry as a whole."

"I understand," said Trieger. "What does your financial statement say?"

"The industry is going broke. Cash-flow is difficult, since there are no ships from October to March."

"Cyclone season," said the newsman. "It has always been so."

RW sailed on, if fits and starts can be described as sailing. "It is the P & L that is the real problem."

"What does it show?"

"The average grower last year lost one hundred pounds—after drawing almost nothing to live on."

Trieger made no comment. He was busy taking notes.

"The balance sheet is even worse. The return on investment is negative fourteen percent."

"I don't understand that," said Trieger, who like most journalists had only a sketchy knowledge of the accounting world and no embarrassment whatever in admitting it.

"It means they would do better to sell their land and put the money in the bank."

"What are you suggesting?" asked Trieger.

"Our farmers will not be able to survive much longer. Sooner or later they will go broke. Since this is the Splendids' most important industry, the rest of us will go broke as well."

"It cannot be as bad as you say," said Trieger.

"It is," replied RW. "Unless we can do a better deal—a much better deal—with Pacific Islands Shipping, there will be no point sending the *Jalisco Belle* to Welcome Harbour at all."

"Because?"

"There will be nothing to ship."

"Why would people not say this is a clever negotiating tactic?" probed the editor. "A way to win concession?"

"As a man might kill himself to do a better deal with the undertaker?"

Trieger retreated. "I did not mean it quite like that."

"I assure you," said RW with considerable formality, "the numbers do not lie."

"How long then, according to your submission, does the industry have until it is destroyed?" Trieger searched for a headline, and the answer to this question might provide it.

"I cannot say. Every farmer is in a slightly different position."

The editor tried again. "How long then, as an informed guess—as an expert opinion—from the President of the Farmers' Federation?"

RW stroked his chin and considered his reply. "Making some assumptions about the sunk cost, which will be different in every case... the price the land might fetch at open market... whether there are other buyers—"

"Mr. Rumsey, please!" said the newsman. "How long before the industry goes broke?"

"I understand the question, Mr. Trieger. I am simply trying to calculate an accurate answer."

"Would you say five years?" prompted the editor.

"I shouldn't think as long as that. No. Less than five."

"Three?"

There was silence as RW struggled to build a mental balance sheet. He moved his head from side to side as though he were assigning numbers to different columns. He mumbled impenetrable words like 'COS' and 'EBITDA', and puzzling initials such as 'NPBT' and 'NPV', and other terms known only to his strange profession.

Aaron Trieger sensed the man was finally getting to an answer and maybe a great headline; so like all good newsmen, he shut up.

"Not as long as three," said RW eventually.

"So we are talking one or two years before the local industry goes broke? Is that what your numbers reveal?"

"Yes," said RW firmly. "I would say the industry has two years."

"After which?"

"Farmers will not be able to carry on." With that, RW Rumsey handed a copy of his financial analysis to the newsman, stood up and left.

Across the road waited a gunmetal gray Austin A40, though Aaron Trieger did not see it. RW Rumsey climbed into the front passenger seat and closed the door. The gears grated as the old car pulled into the light traffic and headed out of town.

CHAPTER 13
A PIECE OF PIE AND THE PAPER

It was cooler on the porch than inside the rectory, so Reverend Brown and RW Rumsey sat outside on comfortable wicker chairs while Mrs. Hana brought iced tea in chilled glasses.

"I wonder," said the Reverend, before his housekeeper turned to leave, "whether there might be any of the apple pie we had last evening?"

"All gone, I'm afraid," said Mrs. Hana with a small frown.

"Pity," said the Reverend, and then turned to RW. "One of the finest cooks on the island, my housekeeper. A treasure."

"I do have a banana guava pie in the oven," relented Mrs. Hana. "I would say it is just about done."

"Mrs. Hana," scolded Reverend Brown, "I do believe you are teasing us. Please bring two slices at once."

"Will it be with fresh cream and a dusting of cinnamon?" said Mrs. Hana, playing the game.

"Off with you, Mrs. Hana. And two more iced teas."

"It went as we discussed," said RW, as the Reverend's housekeeper hurried inside.

"You did not arrive at your doomsday prediction too fast? You forced him to drag it out?"

"Oh yes!" said RW. "I made him work for it."

"And you left the financials with him?"

"Yes, but I do not think he is any expert in the accounting field."

"It does not matter," said the Reverend. "It will give him the confidence to publish exactly what you told him, and that is our purpose."

"Is it?" said RW. "I know there is far more to it."

The men were interrupted as the screen door opened and a most delicious smell wafted onto the porch.

"I believe this might be the best pie you ever had," said Reverend Brown, as large slices of the wonderful tart and two fresh iced teas were placed on the small wicker table that went with the chairs.

"I have gone along so far," RW continued, "because you are a wily ally in the farmers' fight."

"Thank you," said the Reverend. "I have much the same view of your assistance to me."

"Why could I not disclose Tanisha's shopping trip to Wellington?" asked RW. "It would have made our case to Mr. Trieger more compelling."

"Neither newspapers nor the men who work for them should be fed too much at once," said Reverend Brown. "They bloat like pigs if overfed. Public opinion is the same. It must be fed slowly. Grain by grain."

"Your purpose goes far beyond the price of banana guava pie," said RW, taking a small bite of the still warm dessert.

"I have made no secret of my desire for the Splendid Isles to achieve independence. We are aligned because independence is the only way to achieve the price your farmers deserve."

"You have no hope we may force the shipping company to a fairer position?"

"Oh, they will offer a few crumbs," conceded the churchman. "But the power lies with them. Where else can you go? Who else has a ship to carry your goods? A few crumbs is all you will get." Reverend Brown paused, licked his fingers, and then spoke again "Unless...."

"Yes?"

"Unless we gain independence. Become a nation of our own."

"We have gone full circle, Reverend Brown. I am an accountant. I would prefer a neat, straight line."

"Very well. Let us follow your straight line and see where it leads."

"A revolution requires a leader," said RW, "and this has not been discussed." There was a lengthy pause. "Also a deputy the leader can trust."

Reverend Brown nodded. "A deputy would be valuable, I agree."

"I am an accountant," said RW. "I know all the jokes—a counter of beans; a pusher of pens. But there is more in me than adding columns of numbers."

Reverend Brown nodded again. "A great deal more," he said.

"Before I die, I should like to be involved in something important. Even if I were to die because of it, I believe it would be worthwhile."

"I don't think it will come to that," said the Reverend.

"I am not stupid. There will be violence if New Zealand will not set us free. There will be blood. I have an Enfield 303, but its useful range is only five hundred yards; and we have too few guns should it come to that. Nor has this been discussed with the farmers. We cannot know what they will say, whether they will risk their lives, whether the cost of freedom will be too high."

Reverend Brown held up a hand and laughed. "Enough," he said. "We are not Mexican bandits with ammunition belts over our chests. We are too old for that, you and I. We have no need of Enfield rifles, whatever their range. And it is not my plan anyone should die." Although Reverend Brown could not have known it, Enfield rifles would be required and 'ammunition belts over our chests' was closer to the mark than he realized.

"So New Zealand will walk away? That is your hope?"

"Have you ever watched a dog that has eaten bad food? Once it realizes it cannot be digested?"

"Why, it throws up. Everyone knows that."

"That is our task—together, if you will join me. We will make the Splendid Isles so bitter, New Zealand will throw us up. It is how we will be free."

RW grimaced at the thought. "Maybe this will work," he said at last. "But revolution is a bloody business, if history is the judge. We must prepare for violence if we are to go on."

"That is exactly what we must not do," said the Reverend. "If we go to war we will lose, because we cannot possibly win against such a powerful foe. Nevertheless, I agree. We must go to the brink of it. And there is danger in that."

The afternoon sky turned crimson while the discussion raged. There was more pie, which the men gladly ate. Finally, after many more hours, they agreed. RW Rumsey, chartered accountant, formerly of Wellington and now of Welcome Harbour, would follow the sixty-three-year-old churchman down a path they would forge together. There were risks, grave risks indeed. But if the New Zealanders could be made to give up without a fight, they would have forged not just a victory for the farmers but the world's newest nation. And, though the topic did not come up, they would be its natural leaders. The Prime Minister and his loyal—perhaps brilliant

—deputy, mused RW, as the sky brightened into a magnificent dawn.

They were interrupted by a rolled-up newspaper that sailed over the fence. The sun peeped over the ocean, so the headline could be read.

SPLENDIDS BROKE IN 2 YEARS
WARNS FARMERS' BOSS

CHAPTER 14
POLICE BUSINESS AND AN UNEXPECTED GUEST

There were a hundred and twenty-four officers in Ned Tanner's Splendid Islands police, but the immutable mathematics of scheduling meant only seven were on duty this Friday morning. Four of them, including a detective, drove to the lookout above Welcome Harbour and trudged a thousand yards to the high pasture headquarters of the Gardening Club. The building was untouched, unguarded and unvisited since the club meeting several days earlier and the lodging of a police report by Reverend Brown.

The detective, recently returned from a six-month tour with the police in Wellington, stopped a few yards from the ramshackle shed, pulled a notebook and pen from his pocket and sketched the location. He marked approximate distances from trees, and noted other things he had learned from observing veteran investigators in New Zealand's capital city. He circled the building, stooping to examine a spent match and a dew-sodden brown paper bag. Whether these were important clues or not, who could say? After several minutes he approached the wrecked door, pursed his lips and peered at the shattered lock lying on the ground, which was then dropped into an evidence satchel carried by one of the officers.

Motioning them to follow, the detective stepped over the threshold and surveyed the wreckage inside. He positioned his colleagues shoulder to shoulder, in what is sometimes called an emu parade, and instructed them to shuffle forward, looking for anything out of the ordinary —'evidentiary material', as the detective called it. But evidence of what was not made clear. Was it not obvious this was the work of children from the local school? Who else would bother to break into a building where nothing of value was stored? Nevertheless, the uniformed men, used to the silliness of detectives returned from overseas tours, complied without complaint, although the day was already hot and the inside of the tin-roofed shed was particularly so. Various objects were solemnly tagged, including a recent grocery receipt and a soda can.

Meanwhile, the detective approached the overturned bar fridge as though it were a slaughtered corpse from some bloody crime. He looked at it for a long time, prodded the door with his boot, and bent to examine more closely the dead rose on the floor. This, too, was scooped into an evidence bag, along with a crushed cigar butt that lay nearby.

In Welcome Harbour, a police line—if two men can be called a line—nervously guarded the shopfront office of the Pacific Islands Shipping Company. After the inflammatory story in the local paper, as Resident Commissioner Randolph Herd had fumed to Police Chief Tanner, trouble was to be expected. Irate farmers, enlightened at last about their growing poverty—as if they had not noticed it before—might, well... what they might do was not stated. Nevertheless, police were to be on 'full alert,' and officers were dispatched to the shipping office 'just in case'.

Reverend Brown, meanwhile, drove the old Austin to the

Telegraph and asked to see editor Trieger with an 'important story'. Newspapermen love headlines the way other men love their wives, or perhaps their dogs, so the Reverend talked headlines. This suited the busy editor, since it meant little time was wasted on small talk.

The Reverend took the cracked, once-padded chair in front of Trieger's desk, waved aside offers of tea, and launched into his story without delay. "The Splendid Isles Gardening Club has been viciously attacked," he solemnly declared.

The newsman reached for a notebook as effortlessly as a tennis pro reaches for a serve. "In what way?" said Trieger, not looking up.

"The Independence Rose has been destroyed."

"Righty-oh!" said the editor cheerfully, since the arrival of a good story always improved a slow day. "Let's start from the beginning."

"The police are there right now," said Reverend Brown. "I believe a detective is in charge of the case." The Splendid Isles had only three detectives, so the assignment of such a rare resource underlined the importance of the Reverend's account.

"Whoa!" said Trieger. "From the beginning, please."

At the end of the story, the editor looked up, sucked the end of his pen and flicked back through his notes. "So tell me, who do you think did this?"

"That is what I hope the police will find out."

But the newsman was having none of that. "Perhaps you cannot name a name, but you must have a theory."

"I have a theory, of course," said the Reverend, playing the flirt. "More than a theory," he teased. "I believe the vandalism of the club, though serious in itself, was no more than a diversion from the real purpose of the attack."

"Which was?"

"To destroy the Independence Rose."

"Lot of effort to kill a flower," said Trieger drily. "Why would anyone bother?"

"Maybe not the flower itself," said the Reverend. "More what it stood for."

At this, Trieger grew very still. His public and secret worlds had just collided. "Go on," he said quietly.

"Perhaps someone objected to the name."

"And why would they do that?"

"Independence Rose," said Reverend Brown. "I think someone is unnerved by it. Perhaps they do not like the mention of the word 'independence' and the Splendid Isles together."

It is hard to know whether Trieger's next question came from the newsman or the spy. "Who?" he said, his head still down.

"Someone who had plenty to gain by the Splendid Isles remaining a colony of another power."

"Are you accusing the New Zealand Government of breaking into your gardening shed and trampling a flower? Because of its name?" said Trieger. He was incredulous—or at least did his best to sound so. Who knew what games his masters might play.

"Yes," said Reverend Brown, "and I am saddened by this hostile act."

There was nowhere for Trieger to go. He simply stopped. There were no other questions. Nothing more to learn. The newsman had a story to write. The spy did too, though the audience for this second tale would be tiny indeed.

*****

PHILIP R. ACKMAN

The Coral Route Lockheed L188 Electra came in fast over the sea and dropped quickly onto the only runway at Briggs International Airport. There was a whine of protest as the four turbo props were thrown into reverse pitch. The aircraft slowed to a sedate speed and taxied to the concrete apron in front of the arrivals hall. As the engines spun down, an airport worker pushed a set of stairs up to the metal skin of the huge plane.

There were two passengers, one of whom was met with hugs, kisses and the vigorous shaking of hands. The second, un-greeted, un-met, headed straight from the arrivals hall to a waiting cab. There were no immigration or customs officials on duty, so the whole process took less than a minute.

The cab was a 1951 Ford Custom, jet black, with whitewall tires. Its powerful six-cylinder motor idled at the curb. Along its doors, in amateur script, was painted 'Tehiri Transportation Services', as though this might be one of a vast fleet of taxis. In fact, it was the only one in the fleet, or in the whole Splendid Isles, so the weary tourist was lucky indeed. Behind the wheel sat a man in a peaked baseball cap with 'Dan' embroidered on the front in bright red thread.

*****

Mrs. Hana was the first to see the cab as it picked its way through the ruts on the long driveway up to the rectory. She had been in the kitchen making tea, so she selected another cup and put the kettle on to boil more water. Whoever arrived at nine o'clock at night meant to stay, she decided, and then wondered who it could possibly be. Oxide Brown was at school in Boston and surely could not interrupt his studies mid-term—certainly not in his final year. Nor would he arrive by taxi, as the Tehiris were renowned over-chargers; she had heard tourists were sometimes levied a pound or more for the short ride to town.

While she pondered all this, the doorbell rang. She heard voices in the hall and then Reverend Brown's wholly unnecessary announcement.

"Mrs. Hana. Tea please. We have a visitor." The Reverend was used to surprise guests, as any churchman was bound to be. He took the arrival of Professor Titus Buchanan in his stride.

By the time Mrs. Hana brought the requested refreshments, the two men were seated in the study, the cap unscrewed from a bottle of sherry.

"You remember the Professor, Mrs. Hana?" said Reverend Brown, as though she had the memory of a housefly or a gnat.

The Professor surveyed her the way a stockman might appraise a horse. His eyes moved to her breasts, traveled down her flat stomach, lingered on her slender legs.

"Of course I remember him," she said sharply. She dipped her head, mumbled something about making up the spare room, and left the two men to their business.

"Forgive the lack of notice," said Professor Buchanan. "I like to come to you unannounced so the experiment may be observed in its pure state."

"I hope it is far more than an experiment," said the Reverend. "But your arrival is timely nonetheless."

"It is underway then?"

"Oh, yes. Maybe it has already gone too far to be stopped."

"Then my trip will not be wasted. If you do not mind, I will record some notes. Have you found a social club, perhaps a union—a group to be the spearhead, as we discussed?"

"The Gardening Club and the Farmers' Federation," said Reverend Brown promptly.

"Two then. That is excellent. Are you sure they are properly aligned with your purpose? It is probably too early to ask a question such as this."

"Not at all," said Reverend Brown. "I would say alignment has commenced but is not yet complete."

"And is there anything yet from the authorities? Do they understand what is going on?"

"I would say they begin to understand it," said the Reverend, reaching for the newspaper on his desk and handing it to the Professor.

The academic read the front page article without comment, and then returned to the headline, which he read aloud: "'INDEPENDENCE ROSE DESTROYED. CHURCH BOSS ACCUSES NZ'. Has there been any reaction to this?"

"It is the first time we have landed a blow. They have not yet responded."

"We spoke of this aspect of the game. It is not a game, of course," the Professor quickly corrected. "Do not mistake latency for inaction. They are not the same. It takes time for the cogs of government to mesh and grind and turn. But when the great machine begins to move, it will be difficult to stop."

"I am sure your prediction will be proved right," replied the Reverend. "My charge surely cannot be ignored."

"Oh, it can be ignored if they choose to do it." The Professor folded the newspaper and placed it on the table beside him. "I can see in one other aspect you have made progress. You have selected an emblem, if I am not mistaken. Tell me more about this Independence Rose."

"Now we are near the heart of my concerns," replied Reverend Brown. "It is a powerful symbol, but there are some difficulties I did not foresee."

"We will see if I can help," said Professor Buchanan.

"The rose is hybridized from two parent roses. I have reason to believe both parents were stolen—one from an unconscious sailor, the other from the garden of the Queen's Representative at Government House. If this were to come out—"

"But it is not a concern," interrupted the Professor. "A magnificent rose, stolen from the Government which plunders your country? That is fair, do you not think?"

"If you look at it that way, which I have not done."

"You spoke of more than one difficulty."

"The sailor," said the Reverend. "When he returns with his ship he could lay a complaint with the police."

"Perhaps the ship will never return."

"It will," said the Reverend. "It is the *Jalisco Belle*. Cyclone season is over; it is due back soon." He stopped talking and slapped himself on the forehead with the palm of his hand. "It is not a worry at all," he cried. "The *Jalisco Belle* is the tool depriving our farmers of a living. A rose taken from one of her crew is nothing compared to what she takes from us."

"You see!" said the Professor. "Your problems are going away as we discuss them."

"I am also concerned," the Reverend resumed, "because of the shrub from which the Independence Rose comes. The rose is the symbol of our nation's hope, but the bloom dies after only a few days."

"The bush surely remains alive," said the Professor. "The Independence Rose is therefore reborn with each new bloom." He seemed to have an answer for every concern. "You also have a religious resonance in this. It maps perfectly to a man of God leading his people to a better place."

"There is one other thing," said the Reverend. "It is my deepest concern. The Gardening Club was vandalized and the Independence Rose destroyed. This was the basis of the story in the paper. It is sinister for the symbols of our independence movement to be attacked like that."

"Sinister indeed," said the Professor. "It is also what I would call 'nested symbolism'. One symbol inside another. This is a very powerful idea and not yet built into my theory, though it should be."

"It could not have been the work of the New Zealand Government, whom I accused."

"Not the Government, I agree. They could not react so quickly—even if they chose this method, which I doubt. Probably it was children, or a hopeful thief. It does not matter. Luck is with you, and you played it well."

"Professor Buchanan!" said Reverend Brown. His face was grave. "I vandalized the club myself. I destroyed the Independence Rose. I could trust no one else to do it, since they would then have a power over me."

The American visitor barely blinked. "Brilliant!" he said. "I commend you. But you are right to be concerned. If your role is discovered, independence for the Splendid Isles will be killed at the root. Could you have been seen, or left anything behind?"

"No, I do not think so," said Reverend Brown, unconsciously patting his pockets to check everything was in place.

"Then you have nothing to worry about."

The churchman seemed to relax at this, and drank his sherry. "I think we might have a cigar."

"Certainly," said the Professor. "But not too quickly on the sherry; we still have much to discuss."

THE MAN IN THE SPIDER WEB COAT

*****

The following morning the Tehiri taxi returned and Professor Buchanan retraced his journey to Briggs Field. There was no TEAL Electra or any other commercial aircraft due for almost a week. On a far corner of the airport, however, sat a new Beechcraft Travelair 95 with long-range tanks. Its twin 180-horsepower motors had sufficient range to reach Tahiti, more than a thousand miles away. The plane took off to the east, circled once, and disappeared.

CHAPTER 15
I SPY

In a manner of speaking, Professor Buchanan made two trips that week: the first to the Splendid Isles and the second, as an intelligence file, to a low-slung, five-story building in Taranaki Street, Wellington. The file was marked 'TOP SECRET SPECIAL ACCESS DSS—C', which in the arcane jargon of the intelligence world meant it had the highest secrecy classification and was to be read only by the Director of New Zealand's Secret Service and by intelligence sources denoted—for some reason lost in time—by the letter C.

The file was delivered to an aide on the second basement level of the building, which, despite a misleading commercial sign out front, was actually headquarters of the NZSS. One of the underground levels housed a private apartment for Gilbert with a simple cot and a small kitchen. The other contained a shooting range and three crude cells. Whether they were ever occupied and, if so, by whom, was probably also top secret.

While 'civilians' (as NZSS insiders referred to the public) knew from Hollywood that everything in the spy world is classified, the truth was far more complicated—as it usually is. There were actually eight intelligence classifications. 'Unclassified Uncontrolled' was the lowest. Above that were

'For Official Use Only', 'Controlled Unclassified', 'Sensitive Unclassified' and 'Restricted Unclassified'. 'Confidential', 'Secret' and 'Top Secret' rounded out the options. There were also subclassifications, including 'Special Access', restricted to an individual or office; and the alphabetic notations 'A' to 'H,' which denoted the subject matter of the relevant document, from Military through Scientific, Nuclear, National Security and so on.

The aide signed for the file, which came in a wax-sealed envelope, and pushed a button on his desk.

A few minutes later, Brigadier Gilbert caught an elevator to the ground floor and exited, briefcase in hand, to a waiting Humber Super Snipe Series II, a popular vehicle for senior New Zealand Government officials at the time. The car pulled away from the curb and headed north, where it turned into Vivian Street.

Brigadier Gilbert liked to travel fast, so the uniformed chauffeur put his foot down in the patchy mid-morning traffic. The Humber's three-liter, one-hundred-and-twenty-one-horsepower engine accelerated the one-and-three-quarter-ton limousine to forty miles per hour. It was autumn in the southern hemisphere, and though the air outside was brisk, the air conditioner in the car hummed quietly. Air conditioning was a rarity in New Zealand, and Brigadier Gilbert liked it to be operational, even if inside the vehicle was fogged with cold.

The big car turned left at Lambton Quay and eventually made a right into Pipitea Street, where it stopped outside the Prime Minister's residence at number 41. Nothing happened for a few moments, as New Zealand's most senior spy assembled his thoughts. Eventually the rear curb-side door opened and the Brigadier strode quickly up the steps to the house.

*****

"I am all ears," said Holyoake, though in truth he was all eyes as he peered over the top of a new pair of reading glasses, which he had not yet learned to balance properly on his nose.

"We have discovered quite a bit more about what may be happening in the Splendid Isles and, as you feared, Prime Minister, the news is disturbing."

"Go on," said Holyoake. Which meant 'hurry up'.

"The Christmas visitor to our Reverend Brown has been tracked through our good friends at the airline, and cross-checked with our own Customs and certain other sources." The Brigadier unlatched his briefcase and removed a buff file, which he consulted briefly. "His name is Titus Bernd Buchanan. He is an American citizen, but his birthplace is Leipzig. Behind the Iron Curtain, Prime Minister. Not far from Berlin."

Holyoake nodded curtly.

"He is an Associate Professor of Sociology at Williams College in Massachusetts. He heads a think tank, as they are called, though what he thinks about in this tank is less than clear. It is on the college grounds, but he is not a member of the Sociology Faculty and does not appear to be involved with the university in any other way. He is believed, however, to have been in Ghana before it won independence from Britain in 1957."

The Prime Minister was a clever man but famously impatient. "When do you propose to get to the heart of your report?" he asked. "Am I to be treated to a potted biography of this man for the rest of the day?"

Gilbert continued as though the Prime Minister had not spoken. "This Professor also has links to the UN Committee on Non-Self-Governing Territories, whose chairman—as you are no doubt aware, Prime Minister—is from Ghana."

"How does this Professor come to know a Reverend from a tiny church on a remote island more renowned for coconuts than intrigue?" asked Holyoake. This was the key question, of course. Its answer might expose what was happening in the Splendid Isles, and whose interests, precisely, were being served.

"We do not know," said the Brigadier.

The PM tried another tack. "What does it study, this think tank?"

"Human power structures."

"That could be anything," said Holyoake.

"Precisely, Prime Minister. Our scientific section has been tasked with answering that very question. I must say I do not like the sound of it. A great deal of this think tank's work is private. We can find nothing in the scientific literature."

"Who funds this think tank?" said Holyoake.

"Again, there is nothing public, Prime Minister. We have asked our cousins at CIA."

"And?"

"We have not heard back from them yet."

"Meaning?"

"They are taking longer than usual for a basic request."

"Has your department developed a theory to explain all this?"

"We prefer to work with facts, Prime Minister."

"Indulge me."

"Very well. By a path we do not yet understand, a well-funded Professor from the other side of the world, who specializes in 'human power structures', chose to spend Christmas in one of the most remote places on Earth with a clergyman in his sixties. There is no evidence the two men, until now, have ever met. The Professor was in Ghana immediately before its independence. We do not know why. Nor do we know where his funding comes from, or who he works for. His recent activity has occurred within weeks of a UN resolution declaring all nations must have the right to self-determination—on which New Zealand voted in the affirmative."

"And this leads where?" asked Holyoake.

"I'm tempted to say it fits nicely with the Independence Rose—a reason for the name. We cannot discard the possibility the hitherto unnoticed Reverend Geoffrey Brown of the Splendid Isles Christian Church is taking advice or is in some way involved with a man whose interests appear to center on nations pursuing self-government."

The Prime Minister digested all this without comment.

"There is another development I have not yet raised," said the Brigadier.

"Oh yes?"

"Our mysterious Professor Buchanan has returned to the Splendids. Presumably, he is with Reverend Brown as we speak."

Brigadier Gilbert was wrong about this. Professor Buchanan had already left Welcome Harbour and was dozing in the right-hand front seat of a tiny speck in the clouds as it whirred towards Tahiti at its long range cruising speed of more than a hundred and sixty miles an hour.

The Brigadier's report was also out of date thanks to Professor Buchanan's 'official latency.' A cable from spy and newsman Aaron Trieger, which detailed Reverend Brown's astonishing charge against the New Zealand Government, was still worming its way through the NZSS's labyrinthine bureaucracy and had not yet arrived on the Director's desk.

As Gilbert rose to leave, a prime ministerial aide entered the office, mumbled "Beg pardon," and whispered in the spy's ear.

"Prime Minister," said Gilbert, "if I am permitted to take a brief call, it seems we may have further news."

Holyoake waved the Brigadier away and turned his attention to the next item on his list. A few moments later Gilbert re-entered the PM's office and resumed his seat.

"Sir, I do have an update, from our people in Washington. It is of some interest. The Professor is an expert in the study of military command and control."

"Military command and control?" repeated Holyoake.

"Specifically, the ways in which it can be compromised."

"Accidentally compromised?" asked the PM with uncharacteristic optimism.

"We do not know," said Gilbert. "I can, however, answer another question."

"Out with it," said the Prime Minister.

"Actually, sir, it appears the Professor's think tank is funded by the US Navy. Also, the word in Washington—again from our people and unconfirmed at this stage—is that Professor Buchanan is graded 'Yankee White'."

"Which means, in English?"

"It is a high-security clearance granted only to Americans who have absolutely no links to other countries."

"Didn't you say this fellow was born in Berlin?"

CHAPTER 16
SOUR WHISKY

Ned Tanner and Randolph Herd drank together most afternoons at Trader Mike's. They sat at a trestle table by the water, reserved for them as a matter of custom, and sipped whisky sours, which both had come to favor. Bourbon was an uncommon spirit in the Splendids—gin and Scotch were much more popular—but the barman, and no doubt Trader Mike himself, made sure there was a steady supply of Jim Beam and a jar of maraschino cherries for their two most important customers. The cocktail, which also contained sugar, lemon juice and egg whites, was delivered to their table in a pitcher, along with a bucket of ice and two frosted glasses kept for them behind the bar. In this way, no time was lost waiting for refills.

Administering the Splendid Isles and running its police force was thirsty work, the pair had long ago agreed. It was established routine for their daily meeting to occur in the 'fresh air', as Police Chief Tanner described it, across the road from the government administration building, which soared two stories into the sky.

With a population of just thirty-nine thousand six hundred, and a climate where, except in the hills, the daytime temperature almost never fell below seventy degrees, there was not a lot of crime in the island paradise. Most of the locals fished or farmed from before sunup until long past dusk. There was neither television nor radio, and the power grid failed with regularity, so most of the islanders were early to bed and early to rise. This made for a tranquil life for the police, who were not often called to anything more serious than a minor traffic violation or an injured animal.

The tempo, however, had changed in the last several weeks, with bubbling concerns—fanned inconveniently by the *Telegraph*—that the island's key farming industry was in the soup and low prices from the shipping company were to blame. Sullen groups began to cluster at Trader Mike's, some with a pink Independence Rose pinned to their shirts. They greeted each other without banter, talked in low voices, watched spectacular sunsets without comment, and drank their beer stony-faced.

Police can smell trouble, and Ned Tanner, who had been a cop for more than fifteen years, smelled it now. His relationship with Aaron Trieger had cooled since the publication of Reverend Brown's intemperate charge that the New Zealand Government and, by extension, the local administration—and no doubt the police—had vandalized the Splendid Isles Gardening Club. It had been good luck—or a good police chief's nose—to have assigned a detective and three other investigators to what was really no more than a misdemeanor. Regrettably, the case had not advanced, despite police chewing up six months' forensic budget sending soda cans, grocery receipts and cigar butts to the Welcome Harbour Hospital for analysis by the barely post-teenage laboratory technician—the closest thing to a scientist within a thousand miles.

Randolph Herd's world was no less mournful. The

Resident Commissioner reported to Ralph Hanan, Attorney-General of New Zealand and Minister for the Splendid Isles. By a complicated path, he also seemed to report to every cabinet minister and head of department in Wellington. Ever since the flap over the Independence Rose, he had been peppered with 'requests' to run around in circles while his entire administration followed dutifully behind.

"The AG has been on the phone again," he lamented to Chief Tanner. 'AG' meant Attorney-General Hanan, who was particularly anxious to see someone charged with the Gardening Club break-in, if for no other reason than to discredit Reverend Brown and to restore the New Zealand Government's image to its rightful place as an unblemished example of everything good, just and decent in the world.

"I have been asked to facilitate a meeting with several illustrious members of the Board of Pacific Islands Shipping when they arrive on the Coral flight in a couple of days," Herd continued joylessly. "*Your* presence is required. The QR will likely also attend."

"I already have two officers assigned to guard their building," said the Police Chief. "What else do they want?"

"It's gone rather beyond that, I'm afraid. We are being asked to impose a security blanket over the entire island."

"I thought security blankets provided comfort to small children."

"Exactly," replied Herd. "Do you believe there is any prospect of an arrest?"

"Over the Gardening Club break-in? None whatever. It's clear to me—if not the idiot I assigned to the case—that it is the work of children. It's quiet up there. No one to see them. Had a bit of fun. You and I might have done the same when we were kids."

Herd considered this as he sipped his whisky sour.

"Nothing from forensics?"

"I do not expect a bloody fingerprint to be found, if that's what you mean. Or Colonel Mustard in the ballroom with the candlestick." This was a reference to *Clue*, the popular whodunit board game, invented by Anthony Ernest Pratt in 1944 and first published shortly after World War Two.

"Grocery receipt went nowhere?"

"Where could it go? It showed someone bought a can of beans a few days before the terrible crime."

"Cigar butt?"

"Sure. In the previous week someone smoked a cigar in the clubhouse and discarded the stub."

"Reverend Brown smokes cigars, doesn't he?"

"As do five other members of the club. My investigators looked into it. Can you believe it? We have conclusive proof someone smoked a cigar."

The two men recharged their whisky sours and watched the sun melt into the ocean on the other side of the reef. A fisherman in a small canoe was silhouetted for a moment, and then it was dark.

PART 2

ALL AT SEA

CHAPTER 17
WAITING FOR THE JALISCO BELLE

The *Jalisco Belle* swung listlessly at anchor in Papeete Harbor, Tahiti. Her twelve-man crew were ashore in various bars, save for the Master, who waited for authorization from Pacific Islands Shipping to set sail for Welcome Harbour.

Built at the Philadelphia yards at Beaumont, Texas in 1943, the three-hundred-and-thirty-foot freighter had a surprising turn of speed, thanks to her powerful Sulzer two-stroke diesel engine. She spent six months of the year romping across the South Pacific at her cruising speed of eleven knots, collecting produce to sell into the voracious New Zealand markets. The other six she sulked in Wellington's Port Nicholson Harbour, sheltered from the cyclones no ship dared face.

But it was now late March, and her schedule required her to be wharf-side in the Splendid Isles, loading the first produce of the season. Except, for reasons her Master did not understand, the *Jalisco Belle* had been told to remain in Papeete until further notice. It was unusual for the shipping company to do this, because it was much more expensive to meet daily port fees than to be at sea. And the crew had to be paid whether they worked or caroused in waterfront bars.

*****

At Briggs Field, meanwhile, the now weekly Coral flight had landed. Two men in suits and ties strode across the tarmac to the arrivals hall. Customs and immigration posts were fully manned. A uniformed policeman patrolled with an elderly bolt-action rifle across his chest. The 1915 World War One Enfield Mark III weighed nine pounds and had been signed out of the 'police magazine', as the Police Chief's former drinks cabinet was now called.

The men were the only passengers, and after careful scrutiny of their passports and a luggage search which revealed they carried no more than the permitted two hundred cigarettes, they were waved through. Outside the airport idled the Tehiri Ford Custom taxi.

They were taken to Trader Mike's, the only hotel in Welcome Harbour, and assigned separate seafront rooms for a small extra fee. In fact, all the rooms at Trader Mike's were seafront; but, as in so many places, local business had discovered tourist pricing in the shrewd belief anyone who could afford airfare from New Zealand could pay Dan Tehiri a pound for a short cab ride and four pounds for a seafront room that might otherwise fetch a pound, if it were occupied at all.

The following morning, refreshed after their long flight, the two men strolled to the shop-front office of Pacific Islands Shipping. They climbed the stairs to a storeroom, cleared of fading posters and old boxes and converted into the 'appropriate meeting facility' staff had been ordered to provide. The office manager, Mrs. Tiro Wiriwi, arranged coffee, and left them to discuss whatever chairmen and directors of boards discuss while waiting to meet other VIPs.

At 10 am, the Queen's Representative, Sir Jonathan O'Dowd, arrived in his official 1936 Rolls-Royce Phantom II, which he drove himself. Ned Tanner—dazzling in his ornate Police Chief uniform—and Randolph Herd arrived together a few moments later.

"Sir Brendan, Mr. Edmonds, we are honored by your presence," said the QR, speaking with effortless formality. "I believe our meeting may be short today because we think—" he nodded briefly at the Resident Commissioner and Chief of Police, "—we think there may be a quick solution to the little difficulty that has arisen."

"There better be," growled shipping company chairman Sir Brendan Court, who talked out of the corner of his mouth and had a way of looking at everyone at the same time, "because she's not coming until the 'little difficulty' has un-arisen." 'She' was the *Jalisco Belle*. Behind them, framed almost perfectly in the grimy shipping-office window, lay the starkly empty Welcome Harbour wharf with a couple of longshoremen lounging against a pylon.

"Perhaps we should begin," said the QR.

"Begin away," agreed Sir Brendan, a little more pleasantly. He was like a hangman on a sunny day.

"As you know," said the QR, "some of the farmers here on the island feel the return on investment from the sale of their produce is not reasonably optimized, with regard to the effort which—"

At this point, Sir Brendan Court raised a beefy arm like a traffic cop at a snarled intersection. "How much do they want?" he said.

"A five percent price increase might make the problem 'un-arise', as you put it," said the QR, trying to tack into calmer waters.

"How do you know?"

"Randolph asked our finance people to review the public accounts of Pacific Islands Shipping. It is their advice that the impact to your bottom line would be minimal if this price rise were offered."

"How much do they want?" repeated Sir Brendan.

"Randolph? You're closer to this than me," said the QR, throwing the Resident Commissioner what is referred to in football circles as a 'hospital pass': Here's the ball. The ambulance will be along in a moment.

"It's going to require a little finesse to answer that," replied Herd, simultaneously stalling for time and swimming for shore.

"Has anyone asked them how much they want?" demanded Sir Brendan. He looked at Ned Tanner for the first time. "You," he said. "Have you asked? Why are you here, by the way? What's this got to do with the police?"

Before the Police Chief could reply, the Chairman of Pacific Islands Shipping turned his guns on the Resident Commissioner. "Have *you* asked?"

Randolph Herd opened his mouth to speak but was immediately overrun.

"I didn't think so," said Sir Brendan. He eyed the QR silently for a few moments, but the Queen's Representative had nothing to say. "All right," the shipping chief added a little more reasonably. "The wrong people are in this meeting." He looked at his watch. "I want to reconvene at two o'clock—with the right people. None of you need be here."

Clearly dismissed, the three local officials got to their feet. There was a café across the road, where they ordered tea and scones, which were homemade, but none the better for it. Like soldiers who had stormed a machine-gun nest and narrowly survived, they were stripped of rank, joined in brotherhood by a common foe.

"Christ!" said the QR.

"Almighty!" agreed the Resident Commissioner.

"Amen!" added the Police Chief.

At 2 pm, the stern figure of Sir Brendan Court and his silent companion, Mr. Edmonds, ascended the stairs to the 'appropriate meeting facility' and resumed their places. At ten past two, when no one else had shown up, the chairman phoned the QR in a somewhat one-sided, unpleasant exchange.

At two twenty arrived a certain local accountant with the chain of a fob watch disappearing into his pants, and a once-white shirt with a pocket full of pens.

"At last," said Sir Brendan. He looked pointedly at his watch.

"Five more minutes," said RW Rumsey mildly.

At 2:25, Reverend Geoffrey Brown finally arrived. "Gentlemen," he said without apology, "let us start."

By this time Sir Brendan Court was near boiling point, and he began badly. "See the empty wharf!" He pointed angrily through the window, as if the locals might not know where the wharf was. "Your goods will rot on the vine and be worth nothing—"

This time Reverend Brown did the interrupting. "Fine by us. Isn't it RW?" He sweetly called the Chairman's bluff.

"Oh yes," agreed RW. "Our figures show the farmer return on investment is negative fourteen percent. They are better off not to plant their crops at all."

"So there is nothing to discuss," said Sir Brendan, hurtling down a dead-end street.

"Gents, we need not get to this," intervened Mr. Edmonds, speaking for the first time. "We are businessmen. We face nothing more than a business problem, a dispute between partners. Isn't that right, Brendan?"

"Yes, of course," muttered the Chairman, with nowhere

else to go.

"What we ask is a fair price for our goods," resumed RW.

"And what would that be?" said Edmonds, who seemed to have taken the lead.

"Fifty-six percent more than we are paid now."

The number hung in the air like a storm cloud at the beach. Small children would have scattered for shelter, but the four grown men remained seated on the sand.

"Fifty-six percent!" exploded Sir Brendan.

Once again he was cut short by Edmonds, who seemed smoother and more amenable as well. "It is certainly a large number. I doubt we could afford it."

"You can," said RW. "I have the figures here."

"I think I know our financials better than you," Edmonds replied.

"You buy our bananas at forty pence a case. You sell them in Wellington for nearly three pounds."

"I am not across those numbers," said Edmonds, "but even if they are right, they embed costs not only for us, but also for the distributor, the retailer and the delivery trucks." He looked closely at RW and Reverend Brown to discover their reaction, but their faces were blank. "I want to be reasonable," he tried. Still nothing. "We propose increasing our offer in any event."

The question that screamed to be asked was: How much? But RW, to his credit, did not ask it. As for the reverend, years of confessions had taught the churchman when to shut up.

Not surprisingly, it was the angry Chairman who spoke next. "For Christ's sake, Lawrence!"

But Edmonds put a finger to his lips and Sir Brendan slumped back into silence. "We were planning to offer ten percent more," he said, doubling the number he and the

Chairman had privately agreed.

"I analyzed most carefully all the price points," replied RW, "and fifty-six percent is the minimum increase we require for our industry to be viable."

"That is unfortunate," said Edmonds. "It is far beyond what we can pay."

"The Pacific Islands Shipping Line is a corporation owned by the New Zealand Government," weighed in Reverend Brown. "Surely the largest profit is not the only goal. Especially when our industry is on its knees."

"We are a business like any other," said Edmonds.

"So our position is hopeless," concluded RW. "We cannot take less and you cannot pay more."

"I'll tell you something else," said Sir Brendan, his fury no longer contained. "Until you come to your senses, get used to seeing an empty wharf."

CHAPTER 18
STARTING THE MACHINE

Once again farm trucks piled up outside the Mechanics Hall. Milky light spilled into the street. It half-lit a long line of men. They looked like miners waiting to descend for some hellish nightshift deep underground. Names were checked against a list. Inside the hall, they took their seats and muttered quietly.

On the podium sat RW Rumsey in his trademark white shirt and metal armbands. Next to him sat Reverend Brown.

RW climbed to his feet. He barked an order. "Someone close and lock the door." The hall felt like a submarine about to submerge on a dangerous mission beneath the ice. "Is there anybody who should not be here? If you are not a member of the Farmers' Federation or the Gardening Club, please stand up."

There was general murmuring as men glanced at their neighbors. There were no strangers among them. They had known each other all of their lives. Eventually, the only woman in the meeting, a pretty girl at the rear of the hall, rose self-consciously to her feet.

Before she could speak, RW said: "You have a right to be here. Your name is on the list."

Tanisha Hana gratefully resumed her seat.

"I apologize for the security," RW continued, "but what I have to discuss tonight is of the gravest importance. Have you all seen the headline in yesterday's paper?" He held up a copy of the *Telegraph*:

GROWER SHIPPER STALEMATE:
INDUSTRY FACES RUIN SAYS FARMER BOSS

"They did agree to pay us more," said one man, from near the back door.

"Ten percent," said another.

"Better than last year," offered a third.

"A pittance," complained a giant in the front row.

"What will happen to my crops?" asked a small man in overalls and muddy boots.

RW allowed this to continue as other farmers had their say. Eventually, he held up a hand. "Gentlemen! We are not here to argue about pennies. Whether they offer us ten percent more is not the point. It is a principle we stand for: the right to sell our produce at a fair price. You all know Reverend Brown. I have brought him here to address us tonight."

At this, the churchman rose to his feet. If a pin had dropped it would have been heard. "Our docks are empty. The *Jalisco Belle* has not come—will not come—until we bow to Pacific Islands Shipping and sell for the price they wish to pay."

"They can go straight to hell," erupted someone at the back of the hall, followed by a sheepish: "Sorry, Reverend. No offense."

The meeting erupted once again. Anger is an alchemist's mix of fear and defiance, Professor Buchanan had advised. Let it ferment, because without anger there can be no revolution, and without revolution there can be no change.

Emotion swept everything aside. Some—all, if they were frank—feared for their crops, their families, their farms. But no man responds well with a gun to the head. So defiance swirled through the hall. And as surely as milk churns to butter, so fear and defiance, properly churned, ferment to anger. And anger is a tool, as the Professor had said. But he had issued a warning as well, because anger, over-stoked, ferments hate, which is the brother of violence and a hair's-breadth from war. Finally, the Professor had warned, revolution turned to war was seldom won, because decisive, violent power lay with the authorities, not with a farmers' federation or a club that grew flowers.

The Reverend judged the milk to be churned. "Pacific Islands Shipping, as you all know—" his eyes darted around the room like a serpent searching for prey "—is owned by the Government of New Zealand." He paused while this sunk in. "It is therefore the Government which has decided our industry, our farmers, these Splendid Isles, should starve to death."

Whereupon RW Rumsey seized the floor. "This is why our brothers from the Gardening Club are here tonight. They, too, are under attack, from a Government which destroyed their Independence Rose, which was—and I do not use too strong a word—sacred to them."

"We are joined at the hip," said Reverend Brown, rising again. His voice rolled like thunder through the packed hall, his eyes glittered. "They have sent us a message, this colonial power from far away: we shall be broken at the wheel if we do not submit." There was uproar at this, which the Reverend silenced with an upraised fist. "There is one question I ask tonight." He trembled with rage as he punched the air. "Will you join RW and me to fight for a nation that is ours by right?"

A wave of yes crashed through the hall. Tanisha Hana glided to the stage and pinned Independence Roses to RW Rumsey and Reverend Brown. She turned and threw more pink roses into the crowd. There were cheers as men scrambled to pin them on. It was the night revolution came to paradise.

*****

Pipitea Street sparked with energy as Humber Super Snipes glided to the curb and discharged their precious cargo outside the Prime Minister's home. Harry Lake was first to arrive. He loitered on the front porch as another limousine unloaded Ralph Hanan. A third, close behind, disgorged the imposing figure of Brigadier 'Gallant Bill' Gilbert.

They heard the noise of motorbike engines and wailing sirens as the police escort for the Governor-General, famed English cricketer Viscount Cobham, rounded the corner. He nodded curtly to the men on the porch, while his chauffeur flicked a speck of dust from the great man's coat. Leaves swirled in the gutter. The Governor-General's two-ton Bentley Continental rocked gently in the stiff breeze.

All four men were ushered into the Prime Minister's empty office, where a portable table and five chairs had been pressed into service. In front of each place was a yellow pad embossed with the New Zealand Coat of Arms, which featured three ships, symbolic of the sea trade so vital to this smallest of colonial powers.

If the table had been rectangular, Viscount Cobham, official representative of the Queen of England, would have sat at its head, with the others down each side, and the foot reserved for the PM. There were some—the Prime Minister reputedly among them—who believed the head of the table should go to the elected representative of the people of New Zealand, rather than to some retired cricketer, however charming, who had spent most of his life on the other side of the world. But the table was round, so subtle issues of protocol did not arise and the men sat in the order in which they arrived.

"Bill," said Prime Minister Holyoake, "why don't you bring everyone up to speed?"

"There is further intelligence of which no one in this meeting is yet aware," began Gilbert.

"Very good," said the Prime Minister. "Let us hear it."

"As everyone knows, we have certain assets on the ground in the Splendid Isles—as we do elsewhere. I have their latest intelligence, which has been verified Persil by my Department." 'Persil' meant clean, which was a play on the name of a popular washing powder.

"Yes," said Holyoake, whose patience was thin.

"This so-called Gardening Club, and their rose, seem to have joined forces with the Farmers' Federation, which represents the interests of agricultural land owners."

"Joined forces in what sense?" said the PM.

"There was a meeting between them a few days ago behind closed doors. Our assets did not know and, regrettably, were not there."

"Surely we might do better than that," grumbled the Attorney-General.

"Nevertheless," said Brigadier Gilbert, ignoring the aside, "we have a full account of what took place. Before I go on—" his eyes swiveled like gun barrels to trap Hanan in his sights. The Attorney-General had been ignored; but no longer. "Before I go on, it might make sense for you to brief everyone here on the unfortunate, I think I would say unfortunate, negotiations between Pacific Islands Shipping and the

Farmers' Federation."

While shipping was well outside the Attorney-General's portfolio, Hanan was also Minister for the Splendid Isles, and, by a complicated path, responsible for freight to and from Welcome Harbour.

"Ah yes," said Hanan, whose tone now suggested graceful retreat. Possibly it occurred to him that incurring the wrath of the country's Secret Service might not be wise. Who knew what they might find if vengefully set loose? "There was a meeting, Bill—unfortunate, as you say—between our shipping line and the farmers. Our chap, Sir Brendan Court, and one of his executives came away very discouraged indeed."

"Discouraged by what?" said the PM.

"The farmers demanded a fifty-six percent price increase. Ridiculous! Brendan said no, of course."

"So where are we now?" asked Holyoake.

"On Brendan's advice, which we have gladly taken, our island freighter *Jalisco Belle* is still in Tahiti."

"A standoff," pursued the PM.

"And one we shall surely win," said the Attorney General. "Ours is the only shipping line, and their crops will rot in the ground if they do not cave in."

"And who was on the other side, representing the farmers?" asked Brigadier Gilbert, for the benefit of the others in the room.

"Reverend Geoffrey Brown and a Mister RW Rumsey," said the AG, reading from notes.

"And Brown is from the Gardening Club?"

"Yes," replied Hanan.

"Which I think is collateral proof the two groups have come together," said Gilbert.

"Who is RW Rumsey?" asked the PM.

"I can answer that," said Harry Lake, who had not yet said a word. "The whistleblower in my Department who caused all the trouble a few years back. Before my time, but there could have been a major embarrassment for the Government. As it was, he ruined a perfectly good career."

"His?" asked the Prime Minister.

"Of course," replied Lake.

"And he represents the farmers?" The PM sighed in answer to his own question. "What we have is the beginnings of a serious movement for independence in the Splendid Isles. I want it nipped in the bud."

"It is contrary to your vote in the United Nations last December," ventured Viscount Cobham. "Resolution 1514, I believe." The comment showed how removed the Queen's man in New Zealand was from the mainspring of power.

If there were any doubt about this, the PM laid it quickly to rest. "Just because you've lost your empire does not mean we should lose ours. At least not until we choose to do so, and we do not choose to do so yet." It was a cruel rejoinder, but accurate nonetheless. By early 1961, Britain was a slowly disintegrating world power: it had so far lost Australia, Malaya, Singapore, New Zealand, Canada, America, South Africa, Egypt, Ghana and a host of other countries, including, most recently, Nigeria, which had achieved independence the previous October. "The Splendid Isles has value for New Zealand," the Prime Minister added, "and us for them, whether they know it or not."

Viscount Cobham was wooden-faced; but the others nodded their support.

"I want to return to this Farmers' Federation," said the PM to his Attorney-General. "You believe their demands are ridiculous?"

"Fifty-six percent is a ridiculous demand."

"And you believe they can be forced to a more reasonable claim?"

"I do," said the AG.

"What if they have no interest in a reasonable claim?" asked the PM softly.

"But their financial interests—" protested Hanan before he was rudely cut off.

"I am not talking financial interests. I am talking politics," said the Prime Minister. "A rally point for their real objective."

"Sovereignty in their own right!" added Brigadier Gilbert, boarding the train.

"I agree with the Prime Minister completely," said Finance Minister Lake, which was no news to anyone, since he and the PM always agreed.

Holyoake turned to his Director of Intelligence. "Bill, I want a complete vet of our rabble-rousing Reverend up there."

"A positive vet," replied Gilbert, "will take some time, as I am sure the Prime Minister understands." In the spy world there are two kinds of vet. Negative, to establish what a person is not. And positive, to determine what somebody is. The answer to this curlier question requires dozens of interviews going back as far as childhood friends; as well as the assembly of documents, typically starting from before the subject was born.

"As fast as you can," coaxed the PM. "But a thorough job. Audit his taxes, the Church, who he sleeps with, the books he borrows from the library. What he eats for breakfast." The Prime Minister was looking for leverage, and the best leverage was often indiscretion. Nothing snuffed out an enemy faster than reputational threat. Put simply, the PM looked for dirt.

"I understand," said the Chief Spy.

"Ralph," said Holyoake, addressing the Attorney-General, "I think we should beef up the Splendid Isles police. Subtle show of force. How many do we have up there?"

"I don't have the information to hand," said Hanan.

"Well, beef it up."

"By how much?" enquired the AG.

"Fifty-six percent sounds a good number to me," said the PM, choosing this moment to show his rare sense of humor. "Ask your man up there for his view, of course."

"Of course," echoed Hanan.

"Finally, the boat—"

"The *Jalisco Belle*?"

Holyoake nodded. "Leave her right where she is."

And so in early April 1961, the great machine of Government, as Professor Buchanan described it, began to move at last.

CHAPTER 19
SAILING IN ROUGH SEAS

The twenty-three-foot outrigger canoe crested the wave, shivered like a wet dog emerging from a bath, and accelerated to its full twenty knots as it cleared the harbor entrance of Welcome Island and sniffed the sea.

In the stern sat physicist and sailboat enthusiast Dr. Hendrik Wade Bode, who was also a mathematician, weapons whiz-kid and NASA space expert. In front of him sat a much younger African man, resting on a paddle which he held out of the water. Near the bow of the simple craft sat a third man. He wore a military crewcut and a T-shirt upon which were the faded words 'Brown & Root'.

It is little known outside nautical circles, but outrigger canoes are among the fastest sailboats ever built. Invented by the Southeast Asians over three thousand years ago, they have sailed the great oceans of the world ever since. Like thoroughbred racehorses, they are also difficult to control. In the arms of an expert like Dr. Bode, however, the tiny craft effortlessly rode the waves and surged forward until it was a shimmering speck in the sunset.

"Tell me something, Wade," said Alex Quaison-Sackey, the thirty-six-year-old Ghanaian Ambassador to the United Nations, Chairman of the UN's Committee on Information from Non-Self-Governing Territories, and future two-time President of the all-powerful UN Security Council.

"No problem," said Dr. Bode, whose Dutch name belied his Madison, Wisconsin origins and Midwest American accent.

"Exactly what is the advantage of launching a space rocket from a place like this?"

"You want to answer that, Wil?" said Dr. Bode, calling to Wilson Tuttle, who described himself as a command and control expert who freelanced for the US Navy and represented the interests of the National Turtle Research Foundation of Washington DC—and maybe others; it was difficult to say.

Tuttle trailed a muscled arm in the water and did not seem to show much interest in replying, so for a moment all that could be heard was the roar of the wind in the sails and the steady hissing of the hull as the outrigger powered ahead. "Nah," he replied. "You're the rocket scientist, Wade. I defer to you."

"How deep do you want to go?" asked Bode. By popular tradition, scientists were supposed to be absent-minded and self-effacing. Bode was neither. He was one of a handful of American physicists awarded the Presidential Medal for Merit, and had invented both the Bode Phase Plot and the Bode Magnitude Plot—two crucial developments which would lay the foundation for modern telecommunications for decades to come. He wore his brilliance like a jewel, forgot nothing, and knew he possessed one of the great minds of his time.

"Just enough to be dangerous," said the African diplomat, as the tiny vessel crested another wave and slithered down its back.

"Objects on the surface of the Earth have an eastward

velocity," began the scientist.

"Of course," agreed Quaison-Sackey, as though everybody knew this was so.

"The velocity required for orbit is about twenty-five thousand feet per second," continued the scientist. "At the equator, of course."

"Naturally," the diplomat said equably.

"The velocity of the Earth at the equator is faster than anywhere else."

Quaison-Sackey nodded. He was accustomed to hearing things for the first time as though he had known them all his life. It is part of a diplomat's skill. The information was locked away, to be recalled at a scientific convention, or a cocktail party. His mind was filled with arcane facts, which he played as cleverly as a gambler tabling an ace.

"The net impact," resumed Dr. Bode, "is a boost, a helping hand, of around two hundred and fifty miles per hour by launching at the equator."

"As much as that?" said the diplomat. "It is a calculation I cannot do in my head." Sometimes it is wise to tell the truth.

"Compared to, say, Canaveral," added Bode, referring to NASA's already famous facility near Titusville in Florida. "Means less fuel, more cargo."

"And the Splendid Isles is fit for this purpose?" pursued Quaison-Sackey.

"Wil?" Dr. Bode deflected the question to the freelance naval engineer. But Tuttle was in a different conversation: "You know what a feedback command and control system is?" he asked.

"I am afraid I do not," confessed Quaison-Sackey. Credibility comes from knowing some things but definitely not all. "Should I?"

"Sure," said Tuttle agreeably. "You are President of a

country. You issue commands. Naturally, you want to control the will of the people."

"Naturally," echoed the diplomat. He thought for a moment. "Provided it is lawful and proper to do so." If he sounded like an official communiqué, it was down to years of training: an intemperate quotation, an off-guard remark, could destroy a career.

Much like the outrigger, Tuttle sailed on. "If the will of the people was greater than the command of the President, nothing would be achieved."

"I see that," said Quaison-Sackey.

"The purpose of command and control, viewed through the eyes of a politician, is to defeat that will, or to shape it correctly."

"This is your field?"

"A lot of folks work on this stuff," parried Tuttle.

"Who?" pursued Quaison-Sackey.

"Navy. Brookings." By which he meant the Brookings Institute, which was close to the Kennedy White House, which would soon announce their plan to put a man on the moon. "That Professor," added Tuttle, "up at Williams College."

"Titus Buchanan?" replied Quaison-Sackey. "We're old friends."

"Everyone knows Titus Buchanan," scoffed Tuttle, as though the old Professor was a household name. In certain rarefied circles, perhaps he was. "Going to be the wave of the future. Change the way countries get run. Yes sirr-ee. Command and control."

"So the Splendids is satisfactory for your purpose?" asked Quaison-Sackey, doubling back to his original question.

"What purpose?" said Tuttle, although the question had been directed at Dr. Bode.

"Launching rockets into outer space."

"Oh that!" said Tuttle, as if it were no more than a minor item on a long list. "Sure. No problem."

*****

At Trader Mike's, meanwhile, sat Randolph Herd and Ned Tanner. They were at their usual table on the waterfront, at their usual daily meeting. Between them rested a pitcher of their usual whisky sours, whose contents were being consumed at their usual brisk clip. If they had bothered to look up, they would have seen the outrigger framed in the sunset like a Gauguin painting. But they did not look up, and the tiny vessel vanished behind the point.

In front of Commissioner Herd lay a folder containing the draft report of the 'broad, vigorous, and discreet' enquiries the Splendid Islands Police had been instructed to launch into the 'affairs and person' of Reverend Geoffrey Graham Brown. He lifted the report, rifled the pages, thought better of it, snapped the cover shut and dropped the heavy document back onto the table. "Which says what?" he enquired.

"Which says our beloved Reverend Brown... No! I'm going to give you the facts. You decide."

"Very well," agreed Herd. He summoned the waiter for more ice.

The pitcher and the ice bucket were both empty by the time Ned Tanner finished talking.

"My first reaction," said the Resident Commissioner, "is it is highly speculative."

"Like life itself," replied Tanner with a sigh.

"I'd hoped for something more—" Herd searched for the best way to describe the report's deficiencies "—more solid."

"These things never turn out like that, Randolph," counseled the Police Chief. "We've been taught by detective novels to expect neat endings, everything in its proper place. But real detective work hacks its weary way through a thicket of question marks. Many of them are never answered because, well, there is no answer. Certainly none that's cut and dried. It is our lot as police to get to the best explanation we can. Others must decide what happens next."

*****

What the two men discussed that afternoon may or may not have been incorporated into the final report that lay before New Zealand Prime Minister, Keith Holyoake. They did not know because they were not further consulted. With the Prime Minister were Harry Lake, Ralph Hanan and 'Gallant Bill' Gilbert, the final report's final author, although in truth the report had been crafted by spies far below him.

"Bill?" said Holyoake pleasantly. "Perhaps you might open the bowling." Batting, pitching, bowling: Gilbert was to go first.

"Indeed, Prime Minister," said the NZSS Chief. He picked up the report and rifled the pages, much as Randolph Herd had done at a certain sunset bar in the Splendid Isles several days earlier. "If I may go straight to the conclusions." He paused while the others found the place. "It is likely Reverend Brown vandalized the Splendid Isles Gardening Club himself," he began explosively. Like American movie mogul Samuel Goldwyn, Brigadier Gilbert seemed to believe in starting with an earthquake and building to a climax.

There was a lengthy silence, eventually broken by the Prime Minister. "And you get there how?" said Holyoake quietly.

"Three converging paths," said Gilbert. "The Reverend

had the motive, because the attack could be laid at our feet, in furtherance of his so-called independence movement. He had the means, because as president of the club he had the keys and unquestioned twenty-four-hour-a-day access. Finally, he had the opportunity, because we can place him at the club—alone—on his own admission, several times during the week when the break-in occurred."

There is not much raw good news in a Prime Minister's day; true, unfettered good news was a thing to be treasured.

"Excellent!" said Holyoake, eyes now twinkling. "Motive, means and opportunity. If we can prove, as you say, this Reverend vandalized his own club and falsely blamed us, I am afraid the Splendid Isles independence movement is at an end."

Unfortunately the prime ministerial mood did not last, because Brigadier Gilbert realized he had overstated his case. "'Prove' is a strong word, Prime Minister. I prefer 'balance of probabilities'."

"Present your case," said Holyoake grandly. "I shall be the judge."

The Brigadier paused to gather his thoughts. "Among the collateral found at the break-in were a cigar butt and a grocery cash-register receipt," he said, using the intelligence jargon of which he was fond: 'collateral' in one world is 'evidentiary material' in another.

"Yes," said the Prime Minister, who had read this in the original report.

"The cigar butt had a band around it. The band had a code, still legible, on the inside."

The Prime Minister nodded.

"We traced it from the shipper in South America to a tobacconist here in Wellington."

"But I am guessing its journey was not yet complete," said

Holyoake.

The Brigadier went on, "Every year the congregation of the Splendid Isles Christian Church buys Reverend Brown the same Christmas gift. It has become a tradition."

"Let me guess again: a box of cigars?"

"Exactly, Prime Minister."

"Sounds tenuous to me," the PM replied. He turned to the Attorney-General for back up, but Ralph Hanan had already crossed bureaucratic swords in the past with Brigadier Gilbert, and chose not to do so now. "I think we should hear Bill out," he said graciously.

"Thank you," said Gilbert, acknowledging the support with a nod. "We asked the local police to interview every member of the congregation to see if any of them visited Wellington in 1955. It's the year the box was sold."

"Proves nothing," said the Attorney-General, whose legal training in the laws of evidence defeated the battle to stay silent. "They could have been mailed to the Splendids."

"We located the parishioner," continued Brigadier Gilbert smoothly. "Man called Iwi. Confirmed he visited New Zealand in November that year, and, as President of the Parish Council, purchased the cigars in question. Even had the receipt."

"So, we have a chain of evidence linking the cigar to our crusading cleric," said the AG, scrambling to recover. "Very good."

"As an aside," said the spy, "Reverend Brown is notorious for his stale cigars. If he gets a box every year, he probably has rooms full of them."

"So you've proven he smokes, which we already knew," said the Prime Minister. "And you've proven the butt at the Gardening Club was probably his."

"We also know our Reverend attended the weekly

meeting of the club where the break-in was discovered," said Brigadier Gilbert. "Two days before he reported the crime. And we know no one smoked a cigar that night, or at the previous club meeting held exactly one week earlier."

"I am keen to see where this is heading," said Holyoake.

"If I could turn to the grocery receipt which was found a few feet away," said Brigadier Gilbert, bowling, batting and pitching all at the same time.

"Ah!" said the Prime Minister.

"A 'feature article', as I believe they're called, recently appeared in the local paper in Welcome Harbour. A dull story," said Gilbert, "but it required the paper's editor—his name escapes me—to discover who did the household shopping."

"Foregone conclusion, I would have thought," said Finance Minister Lake, already falling behind.

The spy ignored the interruption. "One of the interviewees happened to be the Reverend's housekeeper and unconfirmed lover, Mrs. Piata Hana. Four days before the break-in was reported, Mrs. Hana asked Reverend Brown to buy a can of beans on the way home from town. The receipt from the transaction—"

"Was found on the floor of the Gardening Club with the cigar," interrupted the Prime Minister, galloping ahead. "So what we have, by a clever path, is proof our independence-loving churchman was at the Gardening Club in the days before the break-in was discovered. And the cigar butt and grocery receipt might have been dropped at the time. Is that right?"

"Yes," said Gilbert. "So we asked the police to re-question every member of the club."

"Why?" asked Harry Lake.

"To see who admitted visiting the clubhouse around the

time of the attack."

"And?" said the PM.

"None did. Except for the Reverend Geoffrey Brown."

"Pity!" said the Attorney-General, who understood immediately, and was for once ahead of the pack.

"I'm lost," said Finance Minister Lake. "He admitted he was there. We have him cold."

"Not at all," said the AG. "If he denied it, we'd have him. We could prove he lied. It is what we lawyers call a 'consciousness of guilt'."

"Ralph's right," said Brigadier Gilbert. "It was a clever admission indeed."

"Why?" said Lake, still mystified. As a former small-town accountant he liked facts the way he liked his numbers—neatly in rows and easy to add.

"Every instinct would be for the Reverend to deny it, especially if he did the break-in," explained the spy. "It was our bet. To agree he was there 'every day or so'—I think they were his words—makes our evidence irrelevant. Unless we can prove exactly when the break-in occurred, and he was there at that moment. Which we cannot."

"I still don't see," said Lake.

"We cannot synchronize the evidence with the break-in," said Brigadier Gilbert, mildly annoyed

"So we are where?" said the Prime Minister with a sigh. "What of the rest of the investigation?"

"Not quite complete," said Gilbert, "but I want to return to the break-in. Admissible evidence to one side, it is reasonable to conclude this man staged his own attack on the Gardening Club and blamed us." He paused for effect. "Gentlemen, I believe we are dealing with a formidable foe. Either that, or he is brilliantly advised."

"Do we have any more on this mysterious Professor?"

asked the Attorney-General, as if on cue.

"No and yes," said Brigadier Gilbert, for whom the sowing of confusion was a natural part of what is referred to in the secret world as 'tradecraft'. "We have heard back from our CIA cousins regarding Professor Buchanan's think tank."

"And?" asked the PM.

"'No information available at this time.'"

"'What the hell does that mean?" said the Finance Minister.

"Our own people in Washington know more about this think tank than does CIA, which is, of course, preposterous."

The Prime Minister waited for the spy to go on.

"It means it's black," said the Brigadier. 'Black' meant secret—Officially unofficial. "There is something else," said Gilbert. "I am disturbed by the security clearance 'Yankee White'. We got nowhere with CIA, but our excellent relations with MI6 in London proved fruitful. Evidence, yet again, that it is worth the money to maintain our intelligence liaison in Britain, despite the cost."

"Yankee White?" prompted the Prime Minister.

"Is their highest security clearance," replied Gilbert. "It is held by fewer than one hundred Americans."

"Meaning what?" said the PM.

But Brigadier Gilbert was still on his own path, 'bowling', as instructed by Holyoake, and would not be hurried along. "Foreigners can never qualify for such a clearance," he said. "It is unprecedented."

"And this Professor is German?" said the PM.

"East German," corrected Brigadier Gilbert. "Leipzig. Which is now behind the Iron Curtain. Even if the Americans bent the 'no foreigner' rule, I cannot believe they would do so for a man whose background is impossible to verify."

"Who are these one hundred trusted men?" asked Holyoake.

"So far as MI6 can ascertain, there is only one job category requiring Yankee White clearance."

"Which is?" prodded the PM.

"Mr. Prime Minister, Yankee Whites work directly for the President of the United States."

"Jesus Christ!" said Holyoake, a religious man who almost never swore.

"What the hell has the Splendid Isles got itself into?" said the Attorney-General.

"What the hell have we got ourselves into is more the question," said Brigadier Gilbert, returning the Reverend Brown report to the attaché case beside his chair.

CHAPTER 20
A PALATIAL OCCASION

Sir Jonathan O'Dowd's arrival in London was exhausting after such a long flight, humiliating because he arrived as an ordinary passenger, and puzzling because his boss, New Zealand Governor General Viscount Cobham, was most definitely out of the loop. The Queen's Representative to the Splendid Isles held a diplomatic passport, which provided a smooth path through Her Majesty's Customs and Immigration at the tranquil Heathrow Airport. But there was no protocol officer waiting to meet him. No official car. No message. No anything. All highly irregular and intriguing at the same time. It was springtime and raining, but not particularly cold when he finally arrived at the head of the taxi line.

"Where to, governor?" said the driver in a rich East End London accent.

For a moment Sir Jonathan thought he had been unmasked as Governor of the Splendid Isles, but then he realized this could not possibly be the case. The cabbie was already fiddling with his meter as he pulled into the afternoon traffic. He seemed interested only in the destination, and therefore the size of the fare.

"Buckingham Palace," said the QR.

"Going to see the Queen?" joked the driver, who was very nearly right for the second time.

"Something like that," said Sir Jonathan, but the driver had turned up his car radio—a novelty at the time—and did not hear the answer.

After a brief delay, the QR was met at a side entrance to the Palace, and was steered past many of the ninety-two offices housing the Queen's private and household staff. He felt like a tramp steamer towed through a magnificent harbor by some grand ship of state. Priceless paintings hung on the walls. Huge chandeliers, twice the length of a man, dangled from high ceilings. Reception rooms—there were nineteen in all—glittered with vast and ornate mirrors. Everywhere were antique furniture and magnificent rugs. Staff of various kinds—florists, catering officers, coffee-room maids, stewards and palace attendants—glided by, or disappeared through a maze of doorways and halls linking the fifty-two guest bedrooms, seventy-eight bathrooms and hundreds of other rooms that filled the eight-hundred-and-thirty-thousand-square-foot Royal home of the British monarch.

Lieutenant Colonel Sir Michael Adeane, Principal Private Secretary to the Sovereign, and the most powerful man at Buckingham Palace, sat behind a modest desk in an office in the north wing, not far from the private apartment where the Queen resided when she was in London. But a Union Jack, rather than the Royal Standard, flew from the flagpole on top of the Palace, which told Sir Jonathan O'Dowd—and the whole of London—that the Royal family were not in residence.

"I have asked Commander Colville to join us. He will be along in a few moments," said Adeane, half rising from his chair to greet Sir Jonathan. Commander Richard Colville was the Queen's Press Secretary, and reported directly to

Adeane, along with the heads of Archives, Research, Travel, Correspondence and Anniversaries. Colville was also the former employer of Sarah Sarnow, the young press attaché whose telex to Sir Jonathan had started the flap over the Independence Rose. 'Former' because Miss Sarnow had been quietly released from her duties shortly thereafter. "One lump or two?" asked Adeane, glancing at a solid silver tea set on a side table.

"Please," said Sir Jonathan. "One lump."

"I want to thank you for coming such a long way to see us. Sorry about the rush."

"Anything to be of service," said Sir Jonathan. A maid appeared at his side and poured the tea.

"And for putting you into a difficult position with Viscount Cobham," continued the Monarch's Private Secretary.

"Anything to be of service," Sir Jonathan heard himself say again.

"No fuss is always the key to discretion, as we say at the Palace. Particularly important not to have a fuss at the airport."

It occurred to the QR his boss's boss was actually apologizing. Perhaps Sir Jonathan was not such a tramp steamer after all. "I quite understand," he said graciously, although he still had no idea what was going on.

The door opened and a tall man popped his head into the office. "Room for another?" he asked brightly in what might have been a faint Scottish brogue.

"Perfect timing," said Adeane. "Sir Jonathan and I were just having tea."

"Richard Colville," said the new arrival, introducing himself. He grabbed a chair and pulled out a Royal crested notebook, which he flipped open to a fresh page. "So there is no misunderstanding," said the Press Secretary. "We like to have an accurate record. If it ever blows up—in the press, I mean—we know exactly what was said. Official record, if you understand my drift." The Press Secretary looked at the QR for some kind of reaction. There was none, so he continued. "Excluding material that is *sub rosa*, of course." 'Sub rosa' meant 'secret' in the strange language of diplomats.

"Naturally," said Sir Jonathan

But Colville seemed keen to avoid any possibility of a misunderstanding. "Confidential," he added. "Material that does not form part of the official record. Of course, we are not planning for any of our discussion today to actually be in the public domain."

"I suppose we might start with Viscount Cobham," said Adeane, who had sat through the exchange without comment. "It's awkward, you see. The problem is, we created the unique oversight role of Queen's Representative of the Splendid Isles as a condition to handing them over to New Zealand sixty years ago—"

"Fifty-six," interrupted Commander Colville.

"Fifty-six years ago," agreed the Queen's Private Secretary, unruffled. "Anyhow, it made sense at the time, so we could keep an eye on things. The point is, you represent Her Majesty in the Splendid Isles but report through an intermediary, the GG in Wellington." 'GG' was palace jargon for Governor-General: Viscount Cobham was GG of New Zealand. "And Viscount Cobham travels in the pack with the Prime Minister down there."

"Prime Minister Holyoake," added Commander Colville.

"I understand," said Sir Jonathan, mystified.

"I'd be surprised if you did," said Adeane, who had migrated from discreet to blunt in a single sentence. "This concerns the relationship between Britain and the Splendid

Isles. Nothing to do with New Zealand at all. Your primary responsibility is to the Queen. That was the deal agreed in nineteen oh—"

"Five," supplied Commander Colville. "Nineteen oh five. "Not the Queen then, of course," he added pleasantly. "Edward Seven." Which was palace jargon for His Royal Highness, King Edward the Seventh.

"Quite," said Adeane, who did not seem to mind being corrected. "The King, who was on the throne at the time." A brief silence. "The Queen now."

"I understand," said Sir Jonathan, who seemed to be stuck for a better answer.

The Queen's Private Secretary fixed the QR with a long look before he went on. Sir Jonathan O'Dowd had the feeling he was being sized up for something, and was not doing well. "You are familiar with Resolution 1514 of the United Nations?" asked Adeane.

"Viscount Cobham briefed me on it," said the QR. "In case things got awkward."

"'Devil does that mean?" said Adeane.

"In case things between New Zealand and the Splendid Isles become attenuated by some push for independence," replied Sir Jonathan. "Which there is, from that blasted Reverend and his Independence Rose."

"Ah! The report we requested," said Adeane, referring to the six-thousand-word document Sir Jonathan had sent the Palace, after the now-departed Miss Sarnow's alarming telex several months earlier.

"Yes," agreed the QR, trying hard not to look at Commander Colville, who would have worn the blame for the fuss.

"This is where it gets tricky," Adeane continued. "Her Majesty's Government abstained from voting on Resolution

1514."

"Yes," said the QR.

"New Zealand voted for it."

"Yes," said Sir Jonathan again.

"The problem is, we're all the wrong way around."

"Now I am a little lost," said the QR, whose confusion must have been plain to see.

"I'll make it easy," said Adeane. "Her Majesty's Government now supports Resolution 1514, particularly as it relates to independence in the Splendid Isles."

"Four months after abstaining from voting at all?" said the QR, struggling to stay up.

"As a favor to the Americans." Adeane smiled.

"Who also abstained, isn't that right?" asked the QR, his mind now racing ahead. Stripped of diplomatic jargon, the British and the Americans were apparently wriggling. Sir Jonathan had the sinking feeling he was to be instructed to wriggle as well.

"The Resolution was actually sponsored by that Russian chap. Behind the scenes, of course," said Adeane.

"Nikita Khrushchev. The Russian Premier," supplied Commander Colville.

"And the Ghanaian fellow from the decolonization committee at the UN," continued the Queen's Private Secretary.

"Alex Quaison-Sackey," Colville amended.

"That's the fellow," said Adeane. "He took the lead. But the Americans were never going to vote for a motion sponsored by the Russians. We went along with the US, of course."

Sir Jonathan nodded. "Of course."

"It's a funny old world," said Adeane.

Sir Jonathan nodded again.

The Queen's Private Secretary took a sip of his tea. Possibly he also gathered his thoughts for the remainder of his convoluted diplomatic journey. "New Zealand is actually against independence for the Splendid Isles, in spite of voting in favor of it," he resumed.

"I don't quite understand why they would vote for it and be against it," said the QR.

"Occurred in the middle of the elections down there in Wellington. Political decision not to turn independence into a possible issue among their native Maori. Over-cautious and needlessly paranoid if you ask me, but there you have it."

"I see," said Sir Jonathan.

"This is why you're in London today. Her Majesty's Government is in favor of independence for the Splendid Isles, and also strongly supports the Government of New Zealand, which is against independence."

"The two positions are contradictory," said the QR.

The Queen's Private Secretary produced a bleak smile. "Not necessarily," he said.

"What do you want me to do?" asked the QR.

"On behalf of Her Majesty, you are instructed to do everything possible to assist the New Zealand Government in their private determination not to grant independence to the Splendid Isles."

"Assist New Zealand?" asked Sir Jonathan.

"That is correct," replied Adeane. "You are to provide every assistance." There was a brief pause. "Every assistance —short of actual help."

It took a moment or two for Sir Jonathan to process this instruction, but eventually he nodded.

"On the other hand," continued Adeane, "anything you might do to assist—and help—the Splendids on their path to independence... Utmost discretion, of course."

"Sub rosa," added Press Secretary Colville, no longer taking notes.

"I think I understand," said the QR. "I am to assist but not help New Zealand; and to assist, and help, the Splendid Isles."

"Exactly," replied Adeane. "Her Majesty's Government would be most grateful." He flashed and then extinguished a radiant smile. The telephone rang on his desk. "Have a pleasant airplane flight home," he said, cupping the mouthpiece.

"Thank-you for the briefing," said the QR.

But the Queen's Private Secretary did not hear him. With effortless charm he had simply moved on.

CHAPTER 21
CHESS AT SEA

There was no accounting for owners, thought Emmet Fullmore, Captain of the *Jalisco Belle,* as he read the message from Pacific Islands Shipping:

WEIGH ANCHOR SOONEST STOP SET COURSE WELCOME HARBOUR STOP DO NOT BERTH STOP AWAIT FURTHER ORDERS STOP

'Weigh anchor soonest' meant visiting every bar and bordello along the ocean front to round up the *Jalisco Belle*'s eleven crew, who had been ashore for more than five weeks. The task took two days, and in the end only nine could be located.

'Set course Welcome Harbour' was easier. The three-hundred-and-thirty-foot World War Two freighter sniffed the breeze as it exited Papeete Harbor. Its seventeen-hundred-and-fifty-horsepower diesel coughed once, as though clearing its throat, and then settled into a throbbing purr as the ship set sail for the Splendid Isles, four days or about eleven hundred miles by sea to the northeast.

'Do not berth' was more painful. It meant to drop anchor sufficiently off Welcome Harbour to avoid the reef, which could slit the hull of the five-thousand-ton vessel in a few terrifying seconds, but not so far offshore the anchor could no longer reach bottom. The compromise meant that from the fo'c'sle Trader Mike's, and men drinking jugs of foaming beer, could be clearly seen. The tinkle of music could be heard across the water, accompanied by the smell of freshly fried fish. It also meant the *Jalisco Belle* rocked queasily at anchor, as the long Pacific swell reassembled into short, steep waves for the brief march ashore. Finally, there was no breeze because the ship was stationary, so her iron decks shimmered in the tropic afternoon heat.

*****

The Prime Minister of the Splendid Isles and his Deputy, as Reverend Brown and RW Rumsey joked to each other, sat on the front porch of the rectory, cigars burning side by side, as they discussed the latest developments. In a way they were trying on their new jobs for size, though neither would have explained it quite like that.

"We know two things," said Reverend Brown. "The *Jalisco Belle* has returned, even though we have made no concession. And the Chairman of Pacific Islands Shipping is on an airplane headed to Briggs Field."

"The arrival of the ship and her owner mean either a lot, or nothing at all," said RW.

"I disagree," said the Reverend. "The *Jalisco Belle* has not berthed and shows no sign of doing so. On the other hand, if there was no intention to dock, then why send her here at all? Do you play chess?" he asked, and then answered the question himself, "They have moved a piece on the board. No more than that."

"And Sir Brendan Court?" said RW, referring to the cantankerous Chairman of Pacific Islands Shipping. "They have also moved the king."

"He is not the king," said Reverend Brown, "merely a pawn in the game. The king remains safe in Wellington, where he has always been. Nevertheless, we shall have to see what is wanted by this pawn who thinks he is the king."

"With the *Jalisco Belle* so close and the Chairman here to talk, the pressure may now be on us instead of them," observed RW.

"It is what troubles me," said Reverend Brown. "A small increase in the price they pay, but the end of any hope for self-government in these Splendid Isles. And they have sent us the hard man, and not the more amenable Mr. Edmonds, with whom some progress was made."

*****

They filled the Mechanics Hall that night. Almost every farmer on the island had come. Word had spread quickly the freighter was back, sweating at anchor a few yards offshore. Word also spread the big boss of the shipping company was on his way. The men smelled victory: their crops would be sold, and the price would be handsome, as was only fair.

The hall quietened as RW Rumsey rose to speak.

"Gentlemen," he said, raising a hand. "There are developments, as some of you know."

"We have won!" interjected a man from the front. "They have returned with their tail between their legs."

Several others began to clap, but RW again raised a hand. "On the contrary," he said. "They have fashioned a clever move. Everything is at risk. Reverend Brown and I—" He glanced at the churchman, who sat beside him, "—need your most solemn advice."

At this, there was a lengthy silence. A clever move?

Everything at risk? How could it be when the *Jalisco Belle* was now so close, when the big boss of Pacific Islands Shipping was on his way?

"If they planned to meet our price they would have done so by now," said Reverend Brown, as he climbed to his feet.

"Still, they will offer something," said one of the men, "or why come at all?"

"You have found the cleverness," said the Reverend. "They will offer something, but RW and I fear it will not be large. They hope we will collapse and accept a small win."

There was further silence as the men took this in. What would a small win look like? Would it be enough? If so, would they be fools not to take it? And independence, if it were the greater prize, might not be so simple. Why risk more for a fanciful goal they might never achieve? Slowly the fervor drained away. Reverend Brown could feel it seeping out of the hall and into the street. It was as he expected. It was as he feared.

"Gentlemen," he addressed them in his quietest voice, acknowledging the force of the outflowing tide. "The Chairman and the *Jalisco Belle* are pieces they have moved on the board. No more than that. But as RW has said, we need your most solemn guidance."

"See how much they will offer," said a voice from the rear of the hall. "Once we know it, we can decide."

"We should make a concession," said someone else. "Less than we want, but more than we might expect to get."

"Invite the big boss to a meeting with us," said another. "He will see we are reasonable folk."

This went on for many minutes until a good number of men had had their say. When the fervor wanes, Professor Buchanan had warned, let it bleed away. Only then, when all is seemingly lost, can you build again. Eventually, as

Professor Buchanan had predicted, the hall fell silent. The farmers waited once more to be led.

"RW and I have an idea to put to you, but it requires your help. Do I have your consent to go on?" Again, he stuck to the Professor's counsel. When you are leading them back, be humble. Do not spook them in any way. A stampede could be started and all would be lost. He repeated the question. "Do I have your consent?" He spoke in hushed and reverent tones, a churchman gently guiding his flock.

"Yes," came the reply from the hall.

He returned the farmers' expectant gaze. To look away now might break the spell. He motioned to RW with a flick of one hand. "They have moved one of their chess pieces," he said as the island accountant came alongside. "It is reasonable, in the spirit of cooperation, for us to move one of ours." Possibly a few of the men understood the Reverend's thinking. Most did not. They were farmers, tired from their fields. "It is time now to harvest your crops," he counseled. "They are dying, and the holds of the *Jalisco Belle* are hungry for our food."

"But it would end the strike," said one of the men, "before we achieved a better price."

"I did not say they could load their ship. Merely that we would harvest our crops." The Reverend paused. "As a sign of goodwill."

"But they can only be stored on the wharf itself," someone said from the front of the hall.

"Exactly," said RW Rumsey. "We must harvest the crops and store them in the warehouse on the wharf."

"Why should we do that?" asked a man from the very back row.

"It is a question of balance," said the Reverend. "They tempt us with the *Jalisco Belle*. We shall tempt them with the crops she has come to load."

"Yes!" someone called from the back of the hall. It was seductive. Others joined in.

"Can I have a show of hands," shouted RW above the din.

Afterwards, when the meeting was over, Reverend Brown cradled his head in his arms. He looked gray, pale, and sixty-three. "Every ounce of energy has left me," he said. "I doubt I can even stand."

"Then I shall help you," said RW.

Together, the two men hobbled outside and into the street.

CHAPTER 22
THE WAREHOUSE AND THE BEACH

Maybe a few of the residents of Welcome Harbour heard the howl of the T56-A-9 turboprop engines, but it was nearly three o'clock in the morning when the two giant Lockheed C-130A Hercules planes landed at Briggs Field and pulled up at the deserted arrivals shed. Their rear cargo doors dropped to the ground. The planes looked like lizards about to drink from a puddle. Within a few minutes, the bellies of the beasts disgorged two trucks. They filled with disembarking passengers who filed out of the Hercules once the engines spun down. Half an hour later, each aircraft took on twenty-eight tons of fuel, their combined thirty-thousand-horsepower engines spun up to take-off power, and they disappeared into a jet-black sky.

*****

The telephone at the bedside of Police Chief Ned Tanner rang shrilly. Tanner fumbled for a light and noted the time at ten minutes past three.

"They're here."

"Get them into the van to Trader Mike's," said Tanner. "Then we can all go back to bed."

The voice on the other end of the phone hesitated for a

moment. "I don't think that plan is going to work."

"Why not?" Tanner yawned.

"Sir, we were expecting twelve?"

"I requested twelve," said Tanner. "God knows what we will do with them. 'Security blanket' my ass."

"Sir," said the voice. "I counted sixty-two."

At this, Tanner sat bolt upright. "Sixty-two?"

"Yes sir," the voice confirmed.

The entire Splendid Islands Police Force comprised one hundred and twenty-four men. And there wasn't enough work for them, if the truth were told, which in the civil service it frequently was not. Now Tanner had half that number again. He didn't have enough patrol cars, motorcycles, desks, chairs—coffee cups, if it came down to it.

"We can't billet all that lot at Trader Mike's," said the Chief, addressing his most urgent concern.

"Sir, they have their own trucks, tents, everything, as far as I could see. I believe they're going to pitch camp on the far side of the island, by the lagoon."

Tanner regrouped. "Did you say sixty-two?"

"Yes, sir," said the voice.

"Christ!" muttered Tanner and quietly hung up.

*****

"So bring me up to date, excluding the wild rumors I am hearing of an enemy invasion," said Randolph Herd, sipping his breakfast cocktail of brandy, milk, sugar syrup and nutmeg.

"There is no invasion," began the Police Chief. "But the wild rumors—"

"Are balderdash, I hope."

"Are actually wild fact," corrected Tanner. He had not

slept a wink since his pre-dawn phone call, and had just returned from the campsite of Welcome Island's latest visitors. "Our masters did not send twelve police as we recommended."

"What did they send?" asked the Resident Commissioner.

"Sixty-two men from Six Parachute Regiment."

"Military?" said Herd incredulously.

"There is no sixth parachute regiment in the New Zealand Police so far as I know," said the Police Chief with sullen humor. "Some Major chap is calling the shots. They're wearing steel helmets and carrying guns. They've set up guard posts on the sand."

"What are they doing here?" demanded the Resident Commissioner.

"I asked them that," said Tanner. "'Waiting for orders,' was the Major's reply."

"From you?"

"I was a sergeant in payroll; de-mobbed after the war. So no, I don't think the Sixth Parachute Regiment of the New Zealand Army is waiting for orders from me."

"Who then?"

The Police Chief shrugged his shoulders. "I believe we deserve another round of breakfast."

The Resident Commissioner motioned impatiently to the barman, who hurried over. "I'm afraid I have more bad news," he said grimly.

"Not the air force is it?" replied Tanner. "Fleet of destroyers? A thousand natives in war canoes?"

"Worse," said Herd. "Sir Brendan Court, distinguished Chairman of Pacific Islands Shipping, speeds to us in an airplane as we speak. He intends to make a final offer to the farmers."

"Explains the military then," said Tanner, showing not the slightest trace of a smile.

*****

On the fo'c'sle of the *Jalisco Belle*, the brooding crew sipped tea from stained mugs, sweated in the heat and wished they were ashore at Trader Mike's as they watched a waiter deliver drinks to the only customers so early in the day. Among the sailors was a certain junior seaman, whose wallet and a potted rosebush had disappeared during his last trip to the Splendids after a wildly drunken game of darts.

The business district of Welcome Harbour is not normally a busy place, especially when the sun is fierce, and the men are still in their fields or asleep in the shade. So the hissing steam tractor, ridden by tiny Tom Bedall, could not go unnoticed. Nor could the procession of diesel tractors and battered trucks piled high with produce of every kind. People drifted into the street as the clattering procession stopped on the wharf in a chorus of brakes.

Not much is missed in the Splendid Isles. Everyone knew the strike was deadlocked since neither the farmers nor the shippers had budged an inch. But the arrival of the *Jalisco Belle* suggested the shipping company had just blinked. And the arrival of the farmers suggested they had blinked too. Was the strike now over? The ruinous impasse finally resolved? How could that be, since the big boss of the shipping line had not yet arrived?

At Government House, tea and scones were being served. Sir Jonathan O'Dowd and his guest sat on uncomfortable garden chairs. Why, thought Aaron Trieger, doesn't the old boy get decent furniture? Still, the visits were usually fruitful, since many a front-page story had come from afternoon tea meetings like this in the Governor's conservatory. He waited patiently for the QR to begin. Eventually, he obliged.

"I trust you are abreast of the latest developments?" asked O'Dowd.

"Try me," said Trieger, one professional to another.

"Sir Brendan Court is on his way."

The newsman nodded but did not reply.

"He is here to negotiate with the Farmers' Federation on behalf of Pacific Islands Shipping and, indirectly, the New Zealand Government."

Trieger nodded again. The QR had so far said nothing he did not know.

"The negotiations may not go well."

"Righty-oh!" said Trieger, sucking on the end of his pen. Perhaps the old boy had a story after all.

"You've missed what I am saying," said the QR.

"Have I?" asked Trieger.

"Your own position contains a risk."

"I simply report the news."

"More tea?"

"Please."

Sir Jonathan pushed on. "The *Telegraph* is sympathetic to the current administration."

"Thank you," said Trieger. "The administration here does a good job. Wellington as well. They pull the strings. Not yours, of course," he added.

But the QR ignored both the slight and the apology. "This is my home," he said, indicating the magnificent grounds and the rambling residence. "I do not wish to retire to Wellington, or anywhere else. Your home too. Ten years, isn't that right?"

"Almost," said Trieger.

"You are betting the independence movement will fail."

"I do not sense New Zealand favors it," said Trieger,

navigating between what he knew as editor and what he knew as spy.

"What is favored by New Zealand may not matter," said the QR. "It is a question of what will happen, and how you and I shall fare in a changing world."

"Ah!" said the newsman. "You believe the independents will win?"

"Perhaps," said the QR. "These things are less predictable than you think."

Aaron Trieger did not respond. His newsman's brain whirred with possibilities. His spy brain charted a separate course.

The QR was speaking again. "Take some advice from a man who has your interest at heart."

"Are you saying the *Telegraph* should back the independents?"

But now it was Sir Jonathan's turn to remain silent. It seemed he had nothing further to say at all.

On the drive back to his office, Trieger wondered what had happened. Essentially, the QR was New Zealand's man. Had he switched camps? If so, should Aaron Trieger follow suit? There were other issues also to ponder. What should he report to his master? What if he said nothing and was then found out? Was the conversation some kind of trap, a test to confirm where his loyalty lay? What of the looming negotiations between the farmers and the shippers—were they programmed to fail? Did that explain the presence of sixty paratroopers, which had set Welcome Island abuzz? Was New Zealand expecting a civil war? Or planning one? The questions swirled in the editor's head as his pickup hurtled along the road. What has the Splendid Isles got itself into, he wondered. He was not the first to wonder that.

CHAPTER 23
PLANE SPEAKING

The unpleasant Sir Brendan Court was first down the stairs, first into the arrivals shed and first into Dan Tehiri's black Ford Custom cab, when the plane's only other passenger cleared immigration and sauntered across to the rank.

"Do you mind?" said Tehiri, for whom two passengers meant twice the profit.

"Very well," replied the Chairman of Pacific Islands Shipping without grace.

Though the two men had sat within a few seats of each other on the flight from Tahiti, each had been engrossed in his own world, and they had neither spoken nor met.

"Thanks," said the second man, who opened the cab door and climbed in. "Titus Buchanan." He stuck out a hand, fashioned a smile.

Court nodded imperceptibly as the cab accelerated away from the curb.

"What brings you to Welcome Harbour?" Buchanan asked.

"Official business, which I am not at liberty to discuss," "And yourself?"

"Oh, a day or two in the sun. Warmer than Boston,"

replied Professor Buchanan.

"Never been there," said Court.

It was the kind of discussion strangers had in the back of cabs: polite but guarded, nothing given or taken away. Professor Buchanan was wondering what to say next when they were interrupted by the driver, Tehiri. "Trader Mike's coming up on the left."

"My stop," said Court, turning to the Professor. "Have a nice vacation."

"Where to?" asked Tehiri, but Professor Buchanan did not reply until Sir Brendan Court was out of the car. Tehiri nodded when he heard the address. "Just a few minutes more, then. Newspaper's in the seat pocket."

Piata Hana was baking an apple and butterscotch pie when she saw the black Ford pull into the drive. She watched as the Professor paid that greedy man with the awful wife, which is how many people on the island viewed the Tehiris and their pretentious Transportation Services, when everyone knew they had only one cab, and that on borrowed money. She heard the Reverend answer the door and gave them a few minutes to settle into the study and light their cigars, before wheeling in the trolley with a pot of tea and two slices of pie swimming in thick Bavarian cream.

"Mrs. Hana, perfect timing as always," said Reverend Brown. "Professor Buchanan will be staying with us tonight. Will you make up the spare room?"

"Certainly," said the housekeeper through the tight smile she hoisted when Professor Buchanan was within range. The smile said 'stay clear'. On this occasion she did not need to be concerned; the Professor paid her not the slightest attention.

"You have come to check on your experiment," said the Reverend when the door had closed. "Let me bring you up to date."

THE MAN IN THE SPIDER WEB COAT

*****

"Why, I shared a cab with him on the way from the airport," replied the Professor, once he learned negotiations were about to resume. "You are right. He does not look like a man in a mood to bargain. I would say the offer from him will be small."

"My thinking entirely," said Reverend Brown.

"It is planned, of course," said the Professor. "The show of military, the arrival of the freighter, my fellow passenger in the cab. They mean to scare you into a lousy deal."

"That is my dilemma," said the Reverend. "It is why I moved the crops to the warehouse on the wharf. It is not so hard for the farmers when the dying is behind closed doors rather than in the fields they see every day. The pain subsides a little. That is my hope at least."

"I agree with this step," said Professor Buchanan, "and its cunning disguise as a gesture of goodwill, as I read in your local paper."

"It is the Chairman's offer that worries me," the Reverend continued. "If it is fair—even faintly so—I do not believe I can hold the line."

"You are right," agreed the Professor. "Your farmers would get a better price, but the independence movement would die, as their crops do now."

"But if the offer is poor we lose in a different way," said the Reverend.

"How so?"

"I have created fear and defiance, as you advised."

The Professor nodded. "They are required to foster anger, which is required for revolution, as my thesis states."

"You also advised that anger, unless properly steered,

turns to hate."

"And hate to violence and violence to war," said Professor Buchanan, completing the thought.

"There are sixty soldiers camped on the beach," said the Reverend. "They are more violent, I will wager, than a gardening club and a federation of farmers."

"This is exactly my point," said the Professor. He dipped a finger into the melting cream. "You cannot win if violence prevails."

"So we accept their offer. Independence is at an end. Or we lose because our battle becomes violent, as if a fight between our poor farmers and the New Zealand Army is any kind of battle at all. Whichever way we go, the outcome is that we lose."

"Now I see why you have not touched your delicious pie," said the Professor, chewing and talking at the same time. "You have arrived at the hard place where victory can no longer be seen. Every revolution comes to this. You think others are easy? Only yours is hard? The pressure of power we have not yet discussed. But you feel the power. It is within your grasp."

"It is a lonely power and likely to die like our crops," said the Reverend.

"Not so lonely as you might think," said Professor Buchanan. "There is support you cannot yet see."

"Support that cannot be seen does not sound like support to me."

"Reverend Brown," said the Professor, irritated, "you are not alone. Do you imagine I am no more than chalk on a blackboard, adding numbers? I am here because the Splendid Isles will achieve independence. And you will lead it. Now tell me your plan."

There was a long silence before the Reverend replied. "I

have said we must accept their offer or lose at war. Maybe there is an alternative."

"I am keen to hear it."

"To accept their offer—because the alternative is—"

"Unwinnable?" guessed the Professor.

"It is a matter of lives, not victory," said the Reverend in a flash of anger. The alternative has to be to accept their offer and win in peace."

"As a play on language this is clever indeed. But as a practical plan? I do not see how it can be achieved."

"Nor do I," said Reverend Brown. "But there must be a way." After a long time the old churchman took a bite of his pie. "There must be a way," he repeated as if to himself.

*****

It was late April, 1961. A few days earlier, twenty-seven-year-old Russian cosmonaut Yuri Gagarin had become the first man in space. Standing just five feet two inches tall, Gagarin's one-hundred-and-eight-minute flight triggered official congratulations from the United States. Privately, however, President Kennedy and the Pentagon chiefs were dismayed. The stakes had just been raised. The space race was no longer a matter of beeping satellites, but of manned missions.

*****

As the Reverend munched his pie, a clock chimed nine at the Prime Minister's residence in Wellington, which was precisely twenty-two hours ahead of Welcome Harbour.

"Bill," said Prime Minister Holyoake, turning to NZSS Chief, Brigadier Gilbert, "you requested the meeting this morning. Why not bring us all up to date?"

Harry Lake and Ralph Hanan nodded in agreement as

the country's most senior spy unlatched his brief case and extracted a folder marked: TOP SECRET SPECIAL ACCESS DSS-C.

"Before I begin," said Gilbert, thumbing through the pages of a long report, "perhaps Ralph might tell us the security situation in the Splendids."

"Certainly," said the Attorney-General. "I believe we are now in a position to nip this Independence Rose in the bud, Prime Minister."

"Excellent, Ralph," said Holyoake. "How does this nipping occur?"

"We have reinforced the island police with a substantial force, as you requested, Prime Minister. Unfortunately the aircraft were configured to carry only a total of sixty-two men, so we were unable, by a small margin, to bolster the locals by the fifty-six percent you requested. They are bivouacked on a remote beach on the far side of Welcome Island but could be ordered to town in less than an hour."

"Bivouacked?" asked the Prime Minister.

"Camped," said Hanan.

"You have sixty-two police in tents on a beach?" pursued Holyoake.

"Paratroops," replied Hanan.

"You have sixty-two paratroopers camped on a beach?" There was a lengthy pause as Holyoake digested the information. "In the Splendid Islands?" he said at last.

"My word," said Hanan. "I think we are fully prepared for all developments."

"I told you to reinforce the police, not send the bloody army," blasted the Prime Minister.

"We had insufficient police available at such short notice," said Hanan. "Six Para, thanks to my colleagues at the Ministry of Defence, were ready to deploy. Discreetly," he added as an afterthought.

"I fail to see how we can *discreetly* deploy half a company of armed paratroopers on a tiny island in the South Pacific," said Brigadier Gilbert, repaying the swipe he had received from the Attorney-General at their previous meeting.

"We flew them in at three o'clock in the morning," said Hanan. He seemed prepared to march on, even as the bullets flew.

"Not TEAL then," said the PM, referring to New Zealand's national carrier. "I suppose that is something, although I agree with Bill. It is a long way from discreet."

"We used a couple of Hercules," said Hanan. "Borrowed from the Australians. The Brits had aircraft only a few hours away but, regrettably, they could not be provided. Same with the Americans, who have a squadron of Hercules in Honolulu. Still," he said, "the Australians came through."

"Alright," said Holyoake. "We have an army in the Splendid Isles, and military aircraft buzzing their tiny airfield in the middle of the night. But we were discreet and no one noticed."

There was silence at this rebuke. Neither Brigadier Gilbert nor Finance Minister Lake was in the line of fire and Hanan could think of nothing to say.

"If I may be allowed?" said Gilbert. "We have come up trumps with our investigations into this Geoffrey Brown."

"Out with it, man," said the PM, from whom all good humor had now vanished.

The Chief Spy thumbed through his folder to find the place. "Our Reverend has fiddled the books. Larceny as a servant; fraud maybe.... It will be for others to say." He cast a glance at the crestfallen Attorney-General, who was ultimately responsible for all matters at law.

"What did he do exactly?" asked the PM.

"The Reverend Geoffrey Brown misappropriated ninety-one pounds from the account of the Splendid Isles Christian Church, of which he is chief custodian."

"For what purpose?" said Holyoake.

"To purchase an air ticket for Miss Tanisha Hana, the daughter of his live-in housekeeper, Piata Hana, who we suspect, but cannot prove, is his lover."

"Where did this girl go?"

"She flew from Auckland to Welcome Harbour on the Coral flight in January this year."

"How did she get to Auckland in the first place?"

"We do not have that information, Prime Minister. She was in New Zealand to visit her father, who is divorced from her mother."

"So," said Holyoake, summing up, "Reverend Brown pilfered ninety pounds of church money to fly his lover's daughter—but we cannot prove the lover bit—back from Auckland to the Splendid Isles, after a private visit to a relative. Do I have it?"

"Perfectly, Prime Minister."

"Mr. Attorney-General," said Holyoake, turning to Hanan, who seemed to have only a title now and no name, "have your Department look into this and recommend what charges, if any, might be laid."

"I have noted it already," Hanan replied. "There is one other matter. Sir Brendan Court has arrived in the Splendids and is preparing to meet the Farmers' Federation, and presumably Reverend Brown. And, as you ordered, the *Jalisco Belle* is anchored a few yards offshore."

"What of the fellow who traveled with your man last time?" asked Harry Lake.

"Lawrence Edmonds," said Hanan, "was not required."

"Why not?" asked Lake.

"A bit soft. Gave away too much without a fight. In Brendan's view, anyway."

"What is his brief, your man up there?" enquired Holyoake.

"He is to offer fifteen percent. And dragged kicking to that."

"They asked fifty-six?" said Holyoake.

Hanan nodded.

"We offered what? Remind me!"

"Ten percent, Prime Minister. Fifteen is generous indeed."

"They will take it? That is your best advice?"

"The farmers are starving. I do not believe our troublesome man of God will be able to stop them. Once they do, their independence movement is dead. A flickering candle of defiance, if I may say it, snuffed out by a few more pennies for their coconuts."

"And if they say no?"

"Six Para is on the beach less than an hour away."

"I do not want it to come to that," said Holyoake.

"The farmers have moved their crops to the wharf," said the Attorney-General. "They need a deal. They shall have one."

CHAPTER 24
A NIGHT TO REMEMBER

Clouds sailed across a moonlit sky. The lagoon rippled with tiny waves. Big seas pounded the reef beyond. Not a living or man-made thing moved along the roads, or in the fields, or on the mountain, or in the air. At least it seemed that way.

On the far shore snored sixty-two men in camouflage tents. They dreamed of battle, or a night on the tiles in some vanquished city. A pair of guards dozed beneath a coconut palm, their rifles propped snugly, one against the other.

At Government House slept the Queen's Representative, washed by an icy breeze from an air conditioner set high on a wall. If he was troubled by his Palace brief—all assistance to New Zealand, short of actual help—he failed to show it. Perhaps it is the role of the top man to function with orders that cancel out. Perhaps it troubled him not a jot.

On a sofa above a newsroom snoozed Aaron Trieger, editor, reporter, clandestine spy. He lived inside a dilemma too: favor his master in Wellington, or support the churchman his master opposed?

Police Chief Tanner sweltered beneath a noisy fan. Asleep at last, he dreamed of shootouts and gallant acts—or parking tickets and early retirement, as his men would more likely have said.

Resident Commissioner Randolph Herd had drunk too much. Slumped in a chair, he dreamed of nothing at all.

Trader Mike's was silent, too. Sir Brendan Court, shipping magnate and government pawn, slept like a rock. His four-pound-a-night seafront room may as well have faced a fence for all the attention he'd paid to the view.

Independence Rose grower and farmer Tom Bedall slumbered in his three-room shack, nuzzled by a goat that had so far dodged the pot.

Titus Buchanan slept in a guest room bed. What he dreamed was a mystery to all. Perhaps he ran math in his head, or reworked the edges of his thesis, as he called it, on which the fate of the Splendid Islands now rested.

Reverend Brown was wide awake, deep in thought. The door cracked open. Between the moon and the darkened hall stood Piata Hana in a white chemise. She was no spring chicken, but beautiful to him as she glided over the floor and into his bed.

"What of our rule?" he whispered into his housekeeper's ear. It is true lovers take risks, and they took one now, neither believing Professor Buchanan would find out, nor caring if he did.

A hand fluttered down the Reverend's chest. The rest was a blur. Afterwards, as she lay in the crook of his arm, she listened. He talked.

"He must be driven to anger," said the Reverend, "of that I am sure."

"This shipping man who has come to see you?" She nuzzled his neck.

"It is the team, as always: RW and me. Between us lies the greater chance of driving Sir Brendan Court to some point of honor he will have to defend."

"If two are better than one," she said, and nibbled his cheek. Her perfume roared in his ears. Her hair tickled his nose. Her voice delighted his eyes. "If two are better than one," she said again, "then why not three?"

"Now that," he conceded after a lengthy pause—he was after all distracted—"is an excellent idea. Our case might seem larger, even though our actual strength was completely unchanged."

"Randolph Herd?" she tried.

"No," he said. "It could not be him. He is almost a stranger to me."

"The newsman?"

"We want Sir Brendan Court angry, not gushing sweetly for the press."

"Explain why it is better for the man to be angry," said Piata Hana, whose skills went well beyond making apple pie, housekeeping, and being a secret lover.

"Angry is less likely to be fair."

"Every farmer prays for fair."

"It would end our movement," he said gruffly. "Of which unfairness is the glue."

"If there is no fair offer, the farmers may revolt."

"Yes," he agreed. "They may do that."

"Which your professor has said will lead to violence." She ran her tongue along his chest, looked up into his hazel eyes. "And violence to failure. You have told me this."

He nodded, but otherwise did not respond to her saucy attack.

"So," she resumed, suddenly sad, "independence is lost every way you turn."

"I think I have it!" he announced. "If two is better than one, and three is better than two, might not the reverse also hold true?"

"It rhymes," she said, delighted as a child. "But you have lost me with your clever way."

"What if we sent one man alone?" said the Reverend.

"To negotiate with your belligerent shipping tycoon?"

"Rough-hewn. Simple perhaps. But sly as well."

"Better than three?"

"Possibly so," said the Reverend, lost in thought. "There must be no fair offer and we must avoid violence at any cost. But, after we have teetered on the edge of it, victory must lie within our grasp."

"That is your whole purpose these last months—though it seems like years to me."

"It is what happens before that I cannot unlock."

"The violence must be diverted," she said. "That much is clear."

"Diverted?" he said.

But Piata Hana grew suddenly quiet. Her hand fluttered down the Reverend's stomach and the moon sailed slowly across the sky.

CHAPTER 25
TALKING TURKEY

In the first move of several that day, Sir Brendan Court decided to be unreasonably late. He adjusted his tie, sipped the tea he made for himself, glanced at his watch, paced, sipped more tea and sat on the edge of his unmade bed.

The upstairs room at Pacific Islands Shipping was readied again, an 'appropriate meeting facility' as local manager, Mrs. Tiro Wiriwi, had been brusquely informed, for the second time in two short months.

The first to arrive came at three-thirty on a steam tractor, which he left hissing in the street below. He wore a jacket, misshapen and torn at one sleeve, a long-ago-white shirt missing a button, trousers a little too short, and farm boots, polished if not until they gleamed, then at least until they were passably clean.

Sir Brendan Court sauntered as slowly as he could, but arrived only a minute later and followed the disheveled Tom Bedall up the stairs.

"Who the hell are you?" he said, mistaking Bedall for a workman gone to the wrong door.

"I'm here to meet the big boss," said Tom, whose rough-hewn language matched his rough-hewn look.

"What happened to the Reverend and the fellow from the

Farmers' Federation?"

"Held up," said Tom sweetly and selected a chair.

"The meeting's important to you people, or it's damn well not," said Sir Brendan.

"We need a better price for our crops."

Sir Brendan dismissed this with an impatient wave of his hand.

"Are you going to give us what we want?" Tom pursued.

"I'm negotiating with you? Is that the plan?"

But the simple island farmer simply ploughed on. "We want thirty percent." He laid out the number, as he had been told to do.

"Who wants it?" asked Sir Brendan. He had spotted many an opening in life and saw one now. Like a truck on a steep hill, he also changed down to a slower gear. "The Reverend and RW Clancy?"

"Maybe," said Tom, innocent as a teenage girl at a high-school dance.

"Why do they think that?" probed the tycoon, careful not to tug the line.

"His name's not Clancy."

"Fine. Why do they think we can pay thirty percent?"

But Tom had nothing else to add.

"Now I want you to tell me, son," said Sir Brendan Court at his wily best. "How much do you think they might actually take?"

"We brought our produce to the wharf so you can load up fast."

Sir Brendan Court knew this, of course, but played dumb. "You'd like us to do that?"

"Uh-huh," said Tom, the simple fool.

"We can go fast. Would that be good?"

"Sure," said Tom. "We don't want our fruit to spoil."

"We could give you nine percent and go extra fast."

"Maybe," said Tom, who had been told to accept any number less than fifteen; and to leave immediately, saying "I have to go and ask them," if the number offered was more than that.

"Is this a decision you could make?"

"Maybe," said Tom.

"You can tell me, son," Sir Brendan purred. "I'm not really the big boss." At heart I'm a farmer just like you." Sir Brendan Court owned a cattle station in Australia, which he never visited, and a piece of a meat-processing plant near Wellington, but 'farmer' was a flamboyant stretch. "I'd have to ask my big boss if it was all right to give you nine percent. Why aren't the Reverend and Mr. Clancy here?"

"Bit of a fight," said Tom, who had learned his lines and stuck to the script.

"So they're not really delayed at all?"

"They sent me," said Tom.

"And you act with full authority? On their behalf?"

"Uh-huh!"

"This fight," said Sir Brendan, who cooed like a dove and swooped like a hawk, "you don't know how it started, do you?"

"Maybe," said Tom. Once again the slow and simple island boy followed his lines.

"Perhaps I could help if I knew what it was about," pressed Sir Brendan with a lover's touch.

"Reverend Brown wants thirty percent," said Tom quickly. Speed is sometimes associated with indiscretion, the Reverend had said. Go fast when you want him to believe you.

"I see." The powerful chairman did not blink. "What about Mr. Rumsey?" he said, now effortlessly retrieving

RW's name.

There was a long silence. If it gets to this—a following lie —the answer must be wrenched from you or will not be believed. Go slow. Like pulling teeth. "OK," Tom replied. But now he was there, he wasn't sure how slow to go. "I shouldn't say," he tried at last.

Sir Brendan Court looped an arm over his tiny fellow farmer's un-broad shoulder. "You don't have to tell me anything you're not supposed to—" the shipping tycoon paused for a moment "—unless you really want to."

"Reverend Brown—" said Tom, and suddenly stopped.

"Yes," said Sir Brendan patiently.

There was another silence before Tom resumed. "He's not a farmer." But Tom stopped again. A slow pulling of teeth, they said, and he meant to obey.

"So the farmers want to sell their produce at a price that is fair?" said Sir Brendan, playing Tom like a fish on the line.

"Uh-huh!"

"And, as their authorized representative—" Sir Brendan looked for any sign of a blink, and saw none. "As their authorized representative," he repeated firmly, "you think nine percent is fair."

"Sure," said Tom. "We got that far."

"But this preacher," said the tycoon, working to distance his foe, "this preacher, who spends his life indoors, thinks you should hold out for a price no one could pay?"

"Maybe," said Tom, hiding again.

"And that is why they sent you?"

"I don't know," said Tom, wily and artless both at once.

"I need to leave the room to make a call," said Sir Brendan.

Tom looked out the window at the empty wharf. A few yards beyond, he watched the *Jalisco Belle*'s anchor chain flex in the swell.

When he returned after a long time, the Chairman smiled. "I spoke to my boss and I've got some really terrific news, because you have been so fair, because you have been so reasonable. Such a skillful representative of the farmers' interests!" He was like a child over-trimming a Christmas tree. "My big boss has decided to pay you more."

"How much?" said Tom, fearing the new number may be more than fifteen and, if so, he would have to leave.

"Eleven percent," said the Chairman. "We are giving the farmers of the Splendid Isles eleven percent more for their crops than we did last year. Isn't that great?"

"Sure!" agreed Tom, as the Chairman looped an arm over his shoulder again.

"And Mrs. Wiriwi has typed up something for us both to sign."

"I don't know if I can do that," said Tom.

"Why not?" asked Sir Brendan. "You represent the farmers. You've told me that."

"Yes," said Tom, according to his instructions: if the number is less than fifteen, and they want you to sign.

"Now if you'll just attach your signature here." Court produced a sheet of paper, which Tom signed in his spidery script.

"Congratulations, son. We have a deal."

*****

It was after eleven when Reverend Brown nosed the hood of his tiny car into the drive and up to the rectory beside the church. The lights were on, so Mrs. Hana was surely awake. But it was Professor Buchanan who answered the door and ushered the Reverend into the study, as if it were America's Williams College, where the Professor worked, or did not, depending on your point of view. He steered the Reverend into his churchman's chair, as if the Reverend, not the Professor, was the guest. He poured him a sherry from the Reverend's own stock and passed him a cigar from the exhausted Reverend's inexhaustible supply. "Now tell me everything," he said. "I am dying to know."

"It went well," said Reverend Brown, drinking his sherry and savoring the smoke from his stale cigar. "I think it would be fair to say it went well."

"The meeting with the shipping man, or at the Mechanics Hall?"

"Both, I would say. But I would benefit from your point of view."

"And you shall have it," said the Professor who was security graded Yankee White, although he was neither on the staff of the President of the United States—so it seemed— nor born in America, which was always required. "I cancelled my flight because you are nearing the time."

"The time?" said Reverend Brown.

"My dear fellow, the time when the fight will be won or lost."

"We are so close?"

But the Professor waved the subject away with a flick of the wrist. "Tell me about the meeting with the shipping man, since this was your first concern."

"Sir Brendan Court offered eleven percent. Our man accepted it on the spot."

"An unfair offer, as you had hoped."

"Yes," said Reverend Brown. He could not resist an impish grin.

"And the farmers at your Mechanics Hall?"

"Offer rejected, as I dared to pray."

"So," said Professor Buchanan, as he took this in, "the

independence movement is alive and well?"

"Finely balanced, as you said it would be. Sir Brendan Court thinks the deal is done. He has an agreement signed and sealed. But the meeting said 'no', so it is also undone."

The Professor paused while he considered this. "You are right," he said. "The balance is fine."

"Yes," said Reverend Brown. "And Sir Brendan Court is an intelligent man."

"It is common to overestimate a foe."

"Not of our man, Tom Bedall. I would wager that."

"Perhaps you are the clever one who is underestimated."

"I do not believe," said the churchman, "that you see what I am saying."

"Then say it again." Tersely spoken.

"Sir Brendan Court offered nine percent. Our man agreed. But when he returned—"

"Yes! Yes! They raised their offer to eleven," interrupted the Professor. "My dear fellow, he wanted to be sure your man signed off. They are trapped by wanting the produce, which I would say is more important to them than you think."

"Once again you have missed the point," said Reverend Brown. "They care less for the produce than the deal itself."

"Because a deal destroys the independence movement of which they are so afraid? I did not miss your point; we merely circle it from opposite sides." The Professor refilled his glass, relit his cigar, puffed hard until the end glowed like coal in a fire. Then he leaned closer to Reverend Brown. "There is still a knot that remains fast."

"The *Jalisco Belle* will come to the wharf?"

"Yes," said Professor Buchanan. "The ship will come."

"If it loads unopposed then we have lost," said Reverend Brown.

"Because the farmers would boil over and could not be stopped?"

"They would boil over," agreed the churchman. "They could not be stopped."

"It is one risk," conceded the Professor. "A bad one at that."

"If the deadlock is broken, our momentum is gone."

"Finely balanced," the Professor replied.

"But if we picket the warehouse, as we voted tonight, war will hang by a thread that could easily ignite, and peace by a thread I cannot control."

"Approached from a different angle," said the Professor, "but the knot remains fast."

"Professor Buchanan, if you can offer me nothing more, not ever again, then offer me this: when the lines are drawn as tightly as now, what does your thesis say should be done?"

"My dear fellow," said the Professor, "you worry too much. A solution will occur. You can be sure of that."

The two men finished their sherry, smoked their cigars to the stub. Eventually, in silence, they went to bed.

'A solution will occur. You can be sure of that,' the Professor had said. Maybe so, fretted Reverend Brown. On the other hand, what if there was no solution at all?

Sir Brendan Court slept drunk in his oceanfront suite. He smelled of Scotland's Spey Valley, where whisky is made.

Tom Bedall drank beer in his three-room shack, pausing only to stir goat stew.

Reverend Brown tossed and turned. He did not manage to sleep a wink.

Piata Hana, housekeeper, cook and secret lover, slept alone. Of them all, she slept the best.

CHAPTER 26
A QUICKENING PULSE

The message arrived in the radio shack shortly before 9 am, and in Captain Fullmore's cramped cabin a few moments later. He was shaving at the time.

DOCK WELCOME HARBOUR IMMEDIATE STOP LOAD FASTEST AGAINST COMPANY PO STOP NIL REPUDIATION STOP PREPARE SEAL LOG STOP TRIM FOR SPEED STOP ADVISE WHEN LOADEN STOP

Translated into English, Captain Fullmore was instructed to berth his ship as soon as possible, notwithstanding he and what was left of her crew—two men had been left behind in Papeete—had been cooling their heels for several weeks.

'Load fastest' was clear, even to a layman.

'Against Company PO' meant his authorization to load would be a Purchase Order from the Pacific Islands Shipping office in Welcome Harbour, prepared presumably by the charming and efficient Mrs. Wiriwi. This was unusual. There would normally be a swathe of documents, including several from the Farmers' Federation. But it was none of the Captain's business and he did not much care.

THE MAN IN THE SPIDER WEB COAT

'Nil Repudiation' was odd. Ignore any dispute the cargo was improperly consigned. Actually, any dispute at all. But again, Captain Emmett Fullmore was little concerned with what happened on land, since his chosen life was to be at sea.

'Prepare Seal Log' meant to wax-seal each hold and to record its number in a log. The purpose was to prove that what was loaded was also unloaded, down to the last coconut, if it came to that. There was nothing extraordinary about this, except seal logs were not usually required unless the goods were of high value. A missing gold bar was one thing. A missing potato, thought Captain Fullmore, surely another.

'Trim for Speed' was also strange, especially for the parsimonious Pacific Islands Shipping Company, which ran like a plodding government department with clerks at the helm. Freighters usually trimmed for the optimal balance of speed and fuel. 'Trim for Speed' meant pedal to the floor and damn the cost.

'Advise When Loaden' was no more than nautical terminology for: 'Tell us when you are ready to sail.'

Captain Fullmore read his orders and hurried to the bridge.

There was no tug at Welcome Harbour, so the *Jalisco Belle* crept to the wharf like a schoolboy sneaking home after dark. A five-thousand-ton ship hitting a pylon at even a knot or two would do enormous damage to the wharf; and more importantly, thought Captain Fullmore, to the ship itself.

A gang of longshoremen watched with professional disinterest as the three-hundred-and-thirty-foot freighter inched alongside. They sprang to life when uncoiling ropes were flung ashore, and they looped them expertly across steel bollards. When the lines were secured, the *Jalisco Belle* was officially docked—which was the message sent from the radio shack, as required by company rules.

A man climbed a ladder to the foredeck derrick, which coughed black smoke and swiveled around as the boom swung ashore. The gooseneck was lowered and fastened, so it could not swing further and injure or kill. Such things were common on working wharves, even in Welcome Harbour, where the breeze was sweet and warm, and from where two men could be observed at an outside trestle table at Trader Mike's.

*****

"The usual," said Ned Tanner. The waiter nodded and scurried away. "Mission accomplished," Ned continued. "Although God knows why they sent the village idiot to deal with that awful man."

"Maybe the Reverend and Rumsey were too scared to go," offered Randolph Herd, who remembered his own encounter with the shipping boss and shuddered at the thought.

"I don't think it's that," said Tanner. "Their fruit and vegetables were rotting on the vines. I imagine they decided a small offer was better than none."

"And what's it to do with a Reverend from the local church?" posed Herd. "They had everything to lose. He risked nothing at all."

"Maybe it was smart to send the village idiot," mused Tanner. "'Yes, sir, no, sir. Three bags full, sir.'"

"Crates," corrected Randolph Herd. "Three crates full."

"Also decent of the shippers to offer a little more," said Tanner. "Maybe the idiot Bedall did better than we thought."

"Signed, sealed and delivered," added Herd. "You should have been in the bar last night. Our beknighted lord of the seas, Sir Brendan Court, got quite drunk, bought whisky all round. Dancing on the tables, he'd have been, if he'd had any more."

"What happened at the Mechanics Hall?" asked Tanner.

"Short meeting, I would think. 'All those who'd rather take eleven percent than nothing, say aye.'"

Which goes to show resident commissioners, police chiefs, newsmen and spies can sometimes miss what is happening by their own front door.

"When do you expect the loading to start?" asked Herd.

"An hour or so," replied the Police Chief, checking his watch.

"And your men?"

"What does one do with a security blanket?" said Tanner. "Fold it away? Stow it neatly under the bed?"

They clinked glasses and toasted each other.

"I shall be glad when the ship sails," said Herd. "The farmers happy. Sir Brendan Court back in his master's cave. Six Para out of our hair." He turned to Tanner. "I hope that's right."

"Packed and ready to go," confirmed the Police Chief. "As surely as we enjoy our breakfast in the sun."

"And the soon to be un-independent Reverend Brown?" asked Herd. "Your detective still on the trail?"

"No," said Tanner. "Action no longer required."

"Sounds like peace is returning to Welcome Harbour," said the Resident Commissioner.

*****

At the village idiot's shack were fifty men, and more arrived. Pickup trucks and tractors lined the path. An untethered goat chewed thistles and surveyed the scene.

"When should we go?" asked one of the men.

"Give RW and me fifteen minutes, then follow us out.

And remember," said the Reverend, as he climbed into his car, "no violence. This is our most important rule." It was the third time the Reverend had repeated this, although he said nothing of Titus Buchanan, or the dangerous thesis that had got them this far. The gears grated as he over-revved the tiny engine. He turned onto the main road. Welcome Harbour lay just minutes away.

CHAPTER 27
A TRAP IS SET

"I believe, Prime Minister, our ducks are lined up," said Ralph Hanan, who had been mauled at their last meeting, and did not intend to be so again.

"Run through it, will you," said Holyoake. He picked up a pen and a sheet of paper, as if he might note something down, though he rarely did.

"Their man, one Arthur Thomas Bedall, signed the agreement," said Hanan.

"Witnessed?" asked the PM, probing for holes.

"Sir Brendan himself."

"Hmm!" said the Prime Minister. "A neutral witness would have been better."

"Sir Brendan seized the moment, after a skillful negotiation on our behalf. Their fellow was ready to sign the agreement, and did so."

"Agreement to what?" said Holyoake, still circling.

"Two parts, Prime Minister. To sell their produce for eleven percent more—"

"Not fifteen?"

"No, Prime Minister," said Hanan with pride.

"Very good."

"Also," resumed the AG, "for sea freight to New Zealand."

"That is all the documentation required by the shipper?"

"Normally not," conceded Hanan, "but the agreement was crafted by members of my own Department, who worked under pressure while Sir Brendan kept this Bedall fellow rocking on his muddy heels."

"So, the documentation is solid?" pressed the PM.

"I am advised it is robust. Robust enough," said the Attorney-General.

"What happened to your whistleblower and the churchman?"

"A falling-out," said the Attorney-General, "which Sir Brendan uncovered."

"A falling out?" said Holyoake.

"The Reverend wanted a price rise of thirty percent."

"And the whistleblower?"

"Far more reasonable, Prime Minister. Happy to settle for what he could get."

"And this fellow, Bedall, had the authority to sign?"

"We get there by a defensible route."

"Do we?" said Holyoake, who doubted everything until it was proven, and even then, until it was done.

The Attorney-General held up a hand and peeled back a finger. "One. He attested he had the power to sign."

"Hmm." said the PM.

"Two. His status has not been challenged."

"Yet!" said Holyoake.

"Three." Another finger. "Intention to proceed."

"Meaning?"

"The produce was transferred to the wharf to load."

"Days ago," said Holyoake. "As you lawyers would say, *a priori*." Which meant 'before the fact'.

"It is a point nonetheless," replied Hanan. "I am so

advised."

"Very well," said the PM.

"Four," said Hanan, who was well rehearsed. "There is a non-repudiation clause. The contract cannot be undone."

"That would never stand up in court, unless the bush lawyer in me is wrong," said Holyoake. The Prime Minister was seldom in error.

"And five," said the AG, ignoring the objection, "they can do nothing to stop us."

"Has the loading begun?"

"A small hitch," said Hanan, who had hoped this question would not be asked. "A forklift is required. The keys, unfortunately, could not be found."

"Which means?"

"Another forklift is on its way."

"Good," said the Prime Minister. "The farmers are where?"

"Working their fields. Drinking beer. Swimming on the beach. They are not at the wharf, if that is your worry. It is peaceful as a Sunday afternoon."

"And if they do come, even at this stage?"

"Prime Minister," said Hanan, "we have a binding agreement at law."

*****

At the office of Pacific Islands Shipping, a Reverend in a clerical collar and a slightly younger man in a once-white shirt with metal armbands waited patiently for Mrs. Tiro Wiriwi to return. A fan swung slowly overhead. A fly buzzed loudly across the room.

"She may be some little time," said an assistant. "She has gone to the wharf."

"Sir Brendan Court is not about?"

The assistant shook her head, and then smiled brightly at an attractive figure in a floral skirt. "Here is Mrs. Wiriwi now." Behind them, the street grew unusually noisy as a line of farm vehicles rattled by.

"Mrs. Wiriwi," said Reverend Brown, "I have come to you on a misunderstanding of the gravest kind."

"Then let us sort it out," she said. It was a cheerful reply, but hopeless nonetheless.

The agreement was withdrawn, she was politely informed. Thrown out by the meeting at the Mechanics Hall. A duly constituted meeting. In strict compliance with the bylaws of the Farmers' Federation. A properly registered body. In New Zealand, added the Reverend, still hammering nails.

Down on the wharf, the farmers filed through the huge sliding door and into the warehouse, which was piled to the rafters with coconuts, breadfruit, guavas, and a dozen other varieties of fruit and vegetables coaxed from the native soil. A forklift moved between the rows. Cases were stacked ready to load.

"Oy!" said Tom Bedall, who had become a spokesman for the men. Perhaps no one else wanted the job. The forklift driver fixed him with a wary gaze. "Hands off them crates," said the island's fool.

Nothing happened for a moment. Fifty farmers on one side. A gang of longshoreman on the other.

The wharf foreman shrugged "Come on," he said. "Nothing to do with us. Someone else can sort it out."

The forklift stopped. The longshoremen ambled back into the afternoon sun.

The *Jalisco Belle*'s derrick halted mid arc. Even the breeze had gone away. All that could be heard was the occasional tinking of the ship's steel deck and muffled voices.

It took ten minutes to find Ned Tanner. He and the Resident Commissioner were found together. "Here's a curly one," he said to Herd. "The bloody farmers have changed their mind."

*****

By the time Reverend Brown, RW Rumsey and a worried Mrs. Wiriwi set off for the dock, two patrol cars and a police motorcycle had already arrived. 'Wait for further orders,' the police had been told, and they did so without complaint. It is the policeman's lot to spend most of their day doing nothing, and their reward that they do not have to look busy while doing it.

The longshoremen repaired to the shade and sat cross-legged on the ground, smoking. If a year had passed they wouldn't have cared.

On the *Jalisco Belle*, Captain Emmett Fullmore waited as well. His orders were clear, but it was up to others to load the sling. Captains were paid to sail from place to place, and to avoid union trouble when tied up in port.

Aaron Trieger arrived with a newsman's camera on a leather strap. "Righty-oh!" he said to the Sergeant dozing in the closest cruiser. "What's the drum?"

"Farmers refusing to let her load," said the Sergeant, without opening his eyes.

"Refusing because of why?" said Trieger, working to get the lie of the land. The officer opened one eye, shook his head and turned away. So the newsman strolled to the longshoremen who sat in a clump. "Nice work if you can get it," he joked. But that didn't play either, so he relaxed even more and ambled across to the warehouse, as if it were by chance in his path. He made a show of knocking on the wide-open door. "Knock! Knock! Anyone home?" He put his hands in his pockets, and produced a sigh. "I'd kill for a beer," he said, while studying the label on a crate of fruit.

"Me too," said Tom Bedall.

"Let's get this lot sorted and you're on for a drink."

"We're not sorting nothing," Tom replied.

It is the art of a newsman to sometimes not immediately ask the question a layman would ask, and Aaron Trieger was a newsman right to the tip of his editor's pen. "Mind if I get the weight off?" He hitched himself onto a stack of crates. First of all, stake out a space that is yours.

"No problem," said Tom.

Outside, meanwhile, was the sound of sirens as more police arrived.

"Something's stirred up. What's going on?" said Trieger, playing dumb.

"I'm not authorized to say," said Tom.

"Why's that?" Trieger fiddled with a lens cap, so the question seemed idle, not important at all.

"Official business," said Tom.

"Everything's official these days," complained Trieger with a good-humored frown.

"They're not loading our stuff," said Tom, relenting a bit.

"Thought they upped the price and you guys were happy?"

"Nope," said Tom. "Who told you that?"

But Aaron Trieger, fine newsman that he was, headed down a different track. "Why don't you tell them to leave?" he asked.

"We already done that."

"Well, they seem to have stopped, so what's the drum?" Which put him right back where he had started.

If things ambled along inside the warehouse, a few yards away they picked up speed. Ned Tanner and Randolph Herd arrived together in a government car.

A pair of army trucks rumbled down the street and turned onto the dock. A policeman climbed from the front seat of a patrol car and waved them through. Soldiers poured over the tailgates. Their boots squeaked. Their helmets glinted in the tropic sun.

The Major hurried across to the Police Chief and the Resident Commissioner. They talked softly so they would not be heard, even if the paratroopers or the police had tried to listen, which they did not. Cigarettes were smoked. There was whispered banter and the stamping of feet.

Reverend Brown and RW Rumsey arrived stony-faced. They headed straight to the warehouse. Mrs. Wiriwi was with them, but peeled off like a fighter jet breaking formation.

"Fine afternoon for a standoff," said Herd, as brightly as he could.

"Sad day," said Mrs. Wiriwi. Which put an end to that.

"I'm the bloody Chairman of the company," they all heard, as a large figure stomped towards them.

"Jesus!" muttered Ned Tanner. "That's all we need."

Sir Brendan Court had bloodshot eyes and smelled of Scotch. But like the others he could do nothing else but stand and wait.

Neither the churchman nor Rumsey emerged from the warehouse.

Captain Emmett Fullmore clattered down the gangplank and joined the huddle. "Gentlemen," he said, and then noticed Mrs. Wiriwi. "Madam. I have been told to proceed to load. I also have a message for Sir Brendan Court." The Captain looked quizzically at each of the men. It was clear he had no idea which was his boss.

"I'll take it," said the Chairman, grabbing the note. He read it with a poker face. "Inspector, you are authorized to use your men if there is any attempt to impede loading by these—these farmers," he said finally, but one had the feeling he had selected a crueler word and then reluctantly discarded it.

"Chief of Police, not Inspector," corrected Ned Tanner. "Authorized by whom?"

"The Attorney-General," said Sir Brendan. And then unnecessarily: "Your superior."

"May I see that?" said Tanner.

"Certainly not," said the Chairman. He turned to the officer in charge of the waiting soldiers. "Colonel!" he barked.

"Sir! It is Major, sir!"

"Your orders are to provide full support."

"Beg pardon, sir, but you are outside my chain of command."

A soldier quick-timed over to join the huddle. He saluted the Major. "Radio message, sir."

The Major read the note and saluted the Chairman. "My orders are to comply," he said.

Events over the next few minutes moved swiftly indeed. The longshoremen were escorted by police to the warehouse, where a picket of farmers now guarded the door. Behind them, although the police did not glance back, thumped sixty-two pairs of combat boots.

CHAPTER 28
READ ALL ABOUT IT

They stood like this for a short while, the farmers trying not to slouch, avoiding eye contact; the police searching for it, hard eyed; the soldiers with their thousand-yard stare, looking at nothing at all.

Islanders poured onto the wharf as word spread the farmers were making a stand. They watched wide-eyed, like children at a circus parade. The battle of wills swept back and forth. At one moment the farmers seemed to have the upper hand. Their line stiffened. Their confidence soared. Maybe a policeman had blinked, or a soldier switched weight from one foot to the other. And then they crumpled before their eyes. They were simple farmers, after all. How could they withstand the will of the army, the police and the all-powerful shipping company combined?

The *Jalisco Belle* rocked empty at the dock.

It is dangerous, this swirling of power: one way one moment, another the next. At any instant the police or the army could be told to advance. As Reverend Brown considered this, there came a dreadful sound, a rasping squeal and a heavy, thudding diesel breath.

"Finally," said Sir Brendan Court, as a bright orange Allison-Chalmers HD-5 bulldozer crawled into view. Its thirteen-inch steel tracks edged the six-ton beast towards the picket line; a slow bullet at an unstoppable one-and-a-half miles an hour. At the front of the dozer, which had been brought to Welcome Harbour for some project years earlier and left behind, was a six-foot blade. Curved and shiny, it arced four feet above the ground and could push a five-ton weight—fifty farmers, perhaps—into the sea.

In its rattling wake, half a dozen farm trucks slewed to a halt. Doors were flung open. Twenty figures spilled onto the dock. The first impression was they were unnaturally fair; but then could be seen bobbing breasts and dark pubic hair. Some were older, Rubenesque, with pudgy knees and pillowed bellies. Others had trim legs, narrow waists and muscles rippling as they strode along. At the front, Piata Hana, radiant, nude, determined, and striking, in the way middle-aged women can often be; and Tanisha, who had swapped bashful for defiant, modest for some kind of magnificent island goddess. It took a moment for the crowd to absorb all this. Their mothers, daughters, neighbors, unblushingly unclothed as the day they were born. So much was happening all at once.

The women elbowed past the soldiers, who did not resist, and scolded the police, who, without orders to do anything else, stepped back. Then they turned and stood spread-eagled, their backs to their men, protecting the burly farmers, as if twenty stark-naked women could do just that.

No one moved and no one spoke. The bulldozer fell silent. More than that: everything stopped. Everything except Aaron Trieger, who darted like a bumblebee; but instead of buzzing, he ker-klunked. The motor drive of his Nikon F went ker-klunk, ker-klunk, as it fired the shutter and advanced the film. There is something about a camera that makes that noise: determined, like a chugging train on a mountain pass.

What went through the Major's mind could not be guessed, but after a few moments, he cried, "Fall back!"

Police Chief Tanner followed suit. "Sergeant!" he called. The voice was enough.

"Well—" started Sir Brendan Court, as the police line melted away. But the Chairman could think of nothing else to say.

The motor drive stopped and Aaron Trieger hurried off, which changed the balance because media absence remakes the rules. But the bulldozer, the soldiers, Ned Tanner's police, Sir Brendan, the farmers, the *Jalisco Belle* and twenty buck-naked women had changed them so much already, no one was sure what might happen next.

The police stood in a huddle. The soldiers returned to their truck, which they drove across the entrance to the wharf, although whether to stop people coming or going could not be known.

The women and their men retreated into the sweltering warehouse. If the showdown were scored it would be nil-all.

*****

Aaron Trieger made a long-distance call to his old stomping ground in Fleet Street, London. He asked for the news desk at the *Daily Mail*. It was the third largest newspaper in the world, and reached a million people every day, including, no doubt, the Queen's Private Secretary, Sir Michael Adeane, and Her Royal Highness's press attaché, Commander Richard Colville.

It was 3 am in London, but the call was answered by a retired reporter, happy for a few crumbs on the graveyard shift. There was no rush. It would be twenty hours before the next edition of the famous broadsheet hit the street.

*****

The Splendid Islands Telephone Company had recently acquired a Muirhead-Jarvis picturegram machine, which enabled photographs to be reduced to electronic beeps, transferred across phone lines, a beep at a time, and reassembled into grainy pictures at the other end.

The technician took the black and white photo from the newsman and told him to wait. "Mr. Trieger," asked the technician, when he returned, "London, you said? The cost will be four pounds and twenty pence."

Trieger gulped and paid the fee. Then he went to Trader Mike's, exhilarated by his sale to the big-time newspaper. He got methodically drunk, returned to his sofa bed above the newsroom, drank some more and fell asleep. It was six hours later when his peace was punctured by a ringing phone.

A voice identified itself as picture editor of the *Daily Mail*. "Say, old chap, you haven't sold the story anywhere else?"

"No," said Trieger.

"A hundred pounds then, for the international exclusive, until our first edition hits the street."

*****

The front-page headline in the *Splendid Isles Telegraph* read:

THEY BLINKED!
NUDE ISLAND WOMEN SEND ARMY,
POLICE PACKING

It was illustrated by a large photograph, of course. The paper sold well that day.

THE MAN IN THE SPIDER WEB COAT

But it wasn't until one o'clock in the afternoon, 11 pm London time, that all hell finally broke loose when Aaron Trieger received a call from Agence France-Presse, the huge European news agency in Paris, France. Ten minutes later, a flat American accent was on the line. The Associated Press wanted his picture. The *New York Times* phoned after that. Aaron Trieger imagined a newsroom high above the fabled city. Then the *Toronto Globe*. Within the next few hours he heard from newspapers in Madrid, Rome, Los Angeles and Sydney.

New Zealand's most important newspaper, the *New Zealand Herald*, phoned last of all. The story was moving on the global wire services, Aaron was told. They wanted an exclusive 'from our man in Welcome Harbour', as they proposed he become.

'NUDE WOMEN PROTEST ON TROPICAL ISLE' screamed the *Daily Mail* with a front-page picture to prove the point. 'INDEPENDENCE MOVEMENT BARES THE FACTS' tried the normally sedate *New York Times*. 'SNATCH AND GRAB FOR INDEPENDENCE' blared the racy Sydney *Daily Mirror*. Over the next twenty-four hours, photographs of the nude protest appeared in more than two hundred newspapers, from Vladivostok in Russia to Copenhagen, Denmark and to Lima, Peru. The story was reported by countless radio stations, including the BBC World Service, and WRAP in Nashville, Tennessee. It made the six o'clock news on all three of America's giant television networks. The Splendids were famous for a moment in time. Where was this idyllic place? And what was their beef? an American commentator wanted to know. Were the women always dressed—well—like that?

Late that night, a certain Allison-Chalmers HD-5 bulldozer inched serenely off the end of the wharf and settled on the bottom of the harbor, forty feet below. Who had driven it, none could say.

Half a century later, it would still be a minor tourist trap, eliciting such remarks as, "Can you believe they did that?" from an Australian woman in orange shorts.

"No respect for machinery," replies her husband, peering down at the still-yellow dozer on the harbor floor. "Poor savages," he added. "Probably didn't even know what it was."

A horn beeps and they hurry back to their bus.

*****

British race-car driver Stirling Moss won the Monaco Grand Prix that month. Alan Shepard rode his Mercury Redstone 3 rocket from Cape Canaveral, becoming the first American, and the second man, in space. Shepard's spaceship climbed to an altitude of one hundred and fifteen miles, but his nineteen-minute ride did not achieve orbit. "Perhaps," remarked NASA rocket scientist Dr. Helmut Wade Bode, "we should have launched the damn thing from a pretty little island I know down in the South Pacific."

CHAPTER 29
STOP THE PRESSES

It is a requirement of prime ministers and presidents, when all about them is in flames, that they remain calm. Panic at the top is weakness, and is looked for eagerly by others keen to take their place.

Keith Holyoake was furious, but famous for his 'grip', as it is sometimes known. The *New Zealand Herald* lay on the table before him. Ralph Hanan, Harry Lake and Brigadier Bill Gilbert sat waiting for the Prime Minister to speak, a position none of them seemed to relish.

Holyoake picked up the paper and read aloud:

"'SPLENDIDS DEMAND END TO NZ RULE. NAKED PROTEST JUST THE START.'"

Like the famous boast of Rolls-Royce, the only sound that could be heard was the ticking of a clock.

The Prime Minister peered over the top of his glasses at the three men and continued: "'Welcome Harbour, Wednesday. Farmers in the New Zealand protectorate of the Splendid Isles want an end to colonial rule, and demand immediate self-government, local church leader Reverend Geoffrey Brown said in an exclusive interview with the *Herald* last night. Reverend Brown said his tiny country had been "raped by New Zealand" since the Splendids were handed over as a protectorate by the British in 1905.' Raped by New Zealand!" repeated Holyoake in disgust. No one spoke, so he continued to read.

"'Referring to the dramatic showdown between heavily armed New Zealand paratroopers, riot police, a peaceful gathering of unarmed farmers and a handful of naked female protesters at Welcome Harbour on Monday, Reverend Brown said it was a shameful display of aggressive colonial power.'" The Prime Minister skimmed the next few lines, then resumed: "'A former top New Zealand diplomat, who did not wish to be identified, told Aaron Trieger, our man in the Splendids—' The *New Zealand Herald* has a correspondent in Welcome Harbour?" asked Holyoake. He looked up. "If that's what he is."

"Editor of the local paper," said Hanan, widely missing the PM's meaning. "Freelancing on the side, I would say."

Holyoake ignored the Attorney-General and fixed Brigadier Gilbert with a blistering gaze.

The Chief Spy's face became a blank. He waited for the focus to move away from Aaron Trieger, his undercover man in the Splendid Isles. And he wondered whether the Prime Minister had guessed Trieger's nocturnal role.

"I'm not going to say more," said the PM, although to the trained ear of the spy, he had already said it.

"No, Prime Minister," said Gilbert, deflecting the question that had not been asked.

Holyoake cleared his throat and resumed: "'—told Trieger he was disappointed but not surprised that New Zealand had recently voted at the United Nations in favor of self-determination for all nations, but, within a few months was trying to crush a lawful independence movement in one of its own protectorates. The diplomat—'" Holyoake read the word slowly, as if further emphasis were required, "'warned that the Government's unwarranted and heavy-handed actions in Welcome Harbour could have ramifications at home, once the New Zealand Maori community realized what was happening to their brothers in the Splendid Isles.'" Holyoake looked up and surveyed each of the members of his Splendid Isles kitchen cabinet, as it was known to the wags in his civil service. "'Top New Zealand diplomat who does not want to be named?'" he said again.

"Sir Leslie Knox Munro?" ventured Spy Chief Gilbert. Munro was a former New Zealand ambassador to the UN, between engagements at the current time, and at a loose end in America. The relationship between Sir Leslie and the PM was cool, to say the least.

"Well, gentlemen. What do we do?"

"About the unnamed diplomat?" asked Hanan hopefully.

"About the whole damn mess," said Holyoake.

"We could make a case," said Hanan. He imagined he argued it before the Supreme Court, instead of the kitchen cabinet, whose deliberations were far more rubbery. "One: The farmers acted unlawfully. Two: Reneged on an agreement they signed the day before. Three: After a generous and sympathetic offer from Pacific Islands Shipping, an independent body, outside government control. Four—"

"There's that word again," interrupted Holyoake.

"Prime Minister?"

"Independent!"

"Indeed!" said Harry Lake, chipping in for the first time. "There are two issues, it seems to me. Public relations, as I believe it is called: the impact on our reputation overseas— and the domestic implications if the Maori become involved."

"Exactly!" said the Prime Minister.

Ralph Hanan weighed in again. "I think we should hold the line."

But he was promptly interrupted by Lake, who had not often shown such confidence in the past. Possibly he had been prepped for this meeting by the PM himself. They were in accord, as usual, but uncharacteristically it was Lake who led. "Maori make up ten percent of the electorate," reminded the PM's man.

"If I might say something?" said Brigadier Gilbert.

Holyoake nodded his gruff consent.

"The center of things is this Reverend Geoffrey Brown. The Independence Rose! The farmers' revolt! His leadership has always prevailed. I wonder," said Gilbert, "whether Ralph," he looked at the hapless AG, "might have formed an opinion, by now, as to what charges might be brought against this man, who stole ninety pounds from his own church to buy an airplane ticket for his lover's daughter?"

"Why certainly!" said Hanan. He ignored Gilbert and looked straight at the PM. "Reverend Brown might be charged as a thief, for which the penalty, upon successful prosecution, is up to seven years' jail. Alternatively, if he were convicted of theft while a servant of his employer—"

"Which do you recommend?" said Holyoake.

"If we were to proceed, I imagine charged as a thief would be easier to prove."

"I sense some reluctance on your part," said Gilbert, pressing for weakness.

"There is a small difficulty," said the Attorney-General.

The Prime Minister pounced. "Difficulty?"

"A minor technical matter, which is not an issue."

"Can he be charged with theft or not?"

"Oh yes!" assured Hanan.

CHAPTER 30
DOCTOR'S ORDERS

By unspoken agreement, Welcome Harbour returned to calm. Ned Tanner's police returned to their lazy routine. Six Para returned to their pleasant campsite. Reverend Brown, RW Rumsey, Tom Bedall and the Farmers' Federation returned home to the attention of their wives, their empty beds, their lovers, or their goat stew, as the case may be.

One of Piata Hana's famed banana guava tarts came out of the oven and onto a plate as the Reverend's Austin A40 clattered up the drive. Professor Buchanan was out walking, Mrs. Hana advised him. Perhaps she might join the Reverend for a piece of pie? She had whipped Bavarian cream, which she spooned onto his plate. Cinnamon was sprinkled over the heavenly dessert.

"Piata," he said, waving a finger in mock anger.

"You need fattening," she replied.

"I am not talking of that," he said, patting his generous belly.

"You did not approve of the visit we made to your showdown—or was it a stand-off? I am not sure how it would best be described."

"On the contrary," he said, hugging her, like the older couple they had long ago become. "It was brilliant. A master

195

stroke."

"You did not mind we were naked?" she teased.

"I would prefer to keep you for myself," he answered, squeezing her hand.

"Still," she replied, "it was effective? Diverted the violence, as we discussed?" She popped a piece of pie into the Reverend's mouth. At that very moment, the telephone rang. She moved to answer it.

"Piata?" he called, once she had hung up.

"You will never guess," she said. "You are invited to Government House for afternoon tea."

"That is curious," said Reverend Brown. He glanced at his watch. "Considering it is nine o'clock at night."

*****

Jonathan O'Dowd came crunching down the pathway in Wellington boots as the Reverend's car lights picked the main gate out of the darkness. There was almost no moon. It was the first time Reverend Brown had visited Government House, a rambling, whitewash mansion set in extensive grounds, and flanked by a certain rose bed, which guarded the drive.

"The tea is ready," said the QR, rubbing his hands. "And I asked cook to make some cakes." They settled into uncomfortable chairs in the conservatory. The perfumed air smelled of frangipani and other flowers mixed with a slight sea breeze. They sipped tea and ate tiny cakes filled with cream and adorned with pastry wings, so it looked as though they might actually have fluttered onto the plate.

"Reverend," said the QR, touching the churchman on the knee, "I want us to have a chat, you and I. A private discussion between two grown men. But I require your promise that what we discuss remains between us."

"You have it," said Reverend Brown. "But I should like to understand why I have been invited for afternoon tea at nine pm?"

"The Government," began the QR, "is interested in finding a way to settle the current difficulties."

"That is most—"

The QR raised a hand. "I should like to be allowed to finish," he said. "I am talking to you because you have emerged as the natural spokesman for the farmers. They follow what you say." The QR did not mention the supposed falling out between the Reverend and his chief cohort, RW Rumsey, or the Government's thinking that, since the farmers had rejected shipping chairman Sir Brendan Court's offer, the churchman—who wanted more than RW Rumsey—must be the man in charge.

It was a fair analysis and an accurate conclusion; but Reverend Brown chose to muddy the waters, if for no other reason than to keep the Government guessing. "Sometimes, I may seem to be their spokesman," he allowed, "but they are their own men. I can put a case. They must decide."

And cupcakes might fly, thought the QR. Perhaps held aloft on their pastry wings. "It is all anyone can ask," he said. "The Government would like to find a way in which these—difficulties—can be resolved." He paused and assembled his thoughts with meticulous care. "Without violence," he added. "Not that violence is threatened in any way."

"Come," said Reverend Brown. "There are a hundred soldiers camped on the beach."

"It is unfortunate and a mistake," agreed the QR. He had no idea why troops had arrived, or what fool had sent them.

"If violence were not a possibility, they would not be here," said Reverend Brown.

"Let us move on," said the QR. Metaphorically speaking,

he unfurled a white flag which he waved once and quickly withdrew. "I am instructed to sound you out, informally, on an offer we would like to make."

"I am keen to hear it," said Reverend Brown.

"Your produce is rotting on the wharf. At least forty percent is spoiled, even if the ship could load tonight."

"I don't know I would agree that—"

Once again the QR cut him off. "Whether it is forty percent, or thirty, or seventy-five, does not matter. The Government is sympathetic to your claim for greater payment, so your farmers might extract a more pleasing return."

"That is our case," said the Reverend, dreading what might come next. If the offer were to be greatly improved, the independence movement would be in ruins; the bullet un-dodged after all. "Am I bargaining with the shipping company or the Government?" he managed to ask.

"It is the same thing," said the QR. "You are not naïve. The Minister himself is sympathetic to your position. I believe I could arrange a much more generous offer—subject, naturally, to certain conditions."

"And what are they?"

"Pacific Islands Shipping will be instructed to almost triple—you have heard me correctly—almost triple its offer, to thirty percent."

The figure can have been no accident, thought Reverend Brown, since this was the number he and RW Rumsey had concocted to underpin their falling out. "Well," he said, "on the face of it—"

Again the QR interrupted. "I have not finished. The offer is for the entire contents of the warehouse—" he paused, "—for everything you have grown. Whether it is rotten or not."

'Gentlemen,' thought Reverend Brown, playing out the

meeting in his head, 'the Government has tripled its offer. For everything you have grown. Whether it is rotten or not. Even if it has spoiled on the wharf. You shall earn thirty percent more than you received last year. Nevertheless, RW and I urge you to reject this offer, because, well, because we think independence is more important than money.'

"Take the money!" someone would shout. Others would join in. "Take the money! Take the money!"

"You mentioned conditions?" he heard himself say.

"The independence movement must be at an end," said the Queen's Representative. "The farmers win. Everything else as it was."

"I see," said Reverend Brown.

Every help to New Zealand short of assistance, thought Sir Jonathan O'Dowd. Every help to the Splendid Isles with assistance thrown in. Discreet assistance. Sub Rosa.

Take the money! Take the money! thought Reverend Geoffrey Brown. The farmers have won. It is only I who cares for independence. And Professor Buchanan, he corrected. Whoever he is.

There was a long silence before either man spoke again.

"I shall miss Welcome Harbour—" said the QR. But Reverend Brown was lost in thought, and did not respond. I will cast the line again, thought the QR. "—when my term is up in a few months' time."

"You are retiring?" said the Reverend, taking the hook at last.

Gently, now. "My term will not be renewed. Just when we were getting to know each other," he sighed. "It cannot be helped."

Reverend Brown wrenched himself back to the present. There was a purpose here he could not detect. "That is unfortunate," he heard himself say.

"Not for Sir Brendan Court," said the QR, jerking the line.

The hook bit into the Reverend's mouth. "Sir Brendan Court is the new QR?"

"And a splendid fellow," said the QR. He made a small joke. "A splendid fellow for the Splendid Isles. You must agree?"

"The Chairman of Pacific Islands Shipping?" said Reverend Brown, sinking his teeth into the bait.

"He would no longer be that," conceded the QR. "It would not be allowed. He would still be a large shareholder, of course. The largest after the Government, as I recall."

Reverend Brown processed the new data. "I can also say," he imagined telling the farmers in the Mechanics Hall, "our bitterest foe, Sir Brendan Court, will be the new QR. An owner of Pacific Islands Shipping will represent the Queen and the New Zealand Government on behalf of the Splendid Isles. So, it will go badly for us in the next dispute." They would listen carefully. They owed him that.

Then someone would say: "Cross that bridge when we get there." And the chanting would resume. "Take the money! Take the money!"

Still, it was a small weapon he had been handed. Maybe it would be of some use. He was dimly aware the QR had started to speak again. "I am sorry?" he said.

"I said you look not at all well. If I were you, I should confine myself to a day in bed."

"I have to convene a meeting of the farmers," said Reverend Brown.

"It can wait a day. Our offer is not yet public. You need to rest." The QR looked hard at the Reverend. "A lot can happen in a day. As your doctor—" he smiled—"I order you to bed."

CHAPTER 31
TURTLES AT THE READY

On Sicard Street, SE Washington, DC, a few minutes from the White House, lay the headquarters of the National Turtle Research Foundation. In the second-floor boardroom, five men sat around two card tables pulled together and covered with cloth.

Harvey Wesner rose to his feet as if he had been called to propose a toast or make an after-dinner speech. He glanced at the Chairman, Wendell Steinbeck, cleared his throat and began to speak. "There is nothing official, but we may have found a home for our new turtle research station."

"Navy still good for the money?" asked one of the men, referring to the previous board meeting where the US Navy had earmarked two hundred and eighty thousand dollars towards the cost of a turtle watching facility, which might be allowed to connect to an American satellite.

"I would say most definitely, yes. Isn't that right, Mr. Tuttle?"

Wilson Tuttle, a lean, middle-aged Navy contractor, sat directly behind the Chairman. He stood up. "Sure," he said. "I have visited, on behalf of Navy, and certain other clients, a destination which appears to fit the bill." He sounded as though he were testifying before a court.

"Where is this destination?" asked one of the others.

"I'm not at liberty to say."

"Not even a hint?" prompted the man.

"I can say the proposed location is somewhere in the Pacific Ocean."

"Anywhere near our other facilities at Paihia or Punta Galera?"

"Uh-huh!" said Tuttle, resuming his seat.

"If I might say something here, Harvey," said the Chairman. "The reason for all the secrecy is that the people at the proposed location are not yet in a position to negotiate terms. That's the heart of it, isn't it Wilson?"

Tuttle nodded but did not reply.

"Why not?" asked another of the men.

"Their status is somewhat in flux at this moment," said the Chairman. "But there is good—I would say excellent—reason to believe their status will be favorable in the near future." He turned to Tuttle. "Right, Wilson?"

"Right!" Tuttle allowed.

"Wilson has actually surveyed the proposed location."

"I was there with two friends," said Tuttle. "We sailed around the island to get a look."

"At last we are learning something," said one of the men. "We are talking of a small island, somewhere in the Pacific?"

"Not Australia, is it?" asked one of the others. Australia is the largest island in the world, almost the size of the United States, and nearly sixteen thousand miles in circumference.

"I would call Australia a medium island," said Tuttle, who appeared to have some sense of humor after all; by his standards at least, he had also became more talkative. "I would say the island in question is fine for our—for your—purposes," he corrected.

"Why is that?" asked one of the men.

"It is surrounded by water, which is where your turtles spend their lives flopping about," said Tuttle.

"I would not put it like that," said the man. "Their migration patterns are complex and not well understood."

"Sure!" said Tuttle, holding up an arm in defense. He tried a different tack. "The island is well suited from an engineering perspective. And excellently located for satellite radio communications if Navy agrees to lend you the necessary tracking transmitters."

"Your friends thought so as well?" questioned the man.

"Yes," said Tuttle.

"They are also engineers?"

"In a manner of speaking. One of them is an eminent scientist."

"Wildlife?" said the man.

"No."

"And the other?"

"Expert in government-to-government communications is how I would put it."

"So your report back to Navy on this location is favorable?"

"Yes."

"Very good," said the Chairman, drawing a curtain on the discussion. "I think it is as far as we can go."

"The money?" mouthed Harvey, rising to speak again.

"Of course," said the Chairman. "As I have been reminded by our able Treasurer, Navy proposes to advance us the first tranche of cash. Ten thousand, is that right?"

"It is a facilitation fee," said Harvey.

"Payable to whom?" said one of the men.

But the Chairman did not answer the question. Once again, he reined in the discussion and the meeting adjourned.

*****

Aaron Trieger had played things as carefully as he knew how, and given his long experience as a journalist and editor, that was very carefully indeed. He reported the showdown between the farmers and the authorities 'right down the middle', as they liked to say in his trade when the reportage leaned neither one way nor the other.

He could easily have sermonized: 'shameful display', 'against all Christian decency'—or found an outraged citizen to sermonize for him. He did not. His reportage demonized neither the farmers—which might have been suicidal for a newspaper in such a small place—nor the authorities, who could have been attacked for bringing in the troops: 'heavy-handed', 'jackbooted', 'complete over-reaction'. But the authorities were his secret paymaster and he dared not bite the hand that fed him.

Either of these positions could have been argued through articles, editorials, or carefully orchestrated letters to the editor from tame mouthpieces, of which every newspaper has its share. Trieger could have dashed out an opinion piece to support the side of his choosing. Such was the power of the *Splendid Islands Telegraph*, the only newspaper in a tiny colony without television, radio, or competition of any kind.

The moment for choice, however, had finally come—via telephone from the Queen's Representative.

"You recall our conversation?" said Sir Jonathan.

"Oh, yes," said Trieger.

"The independence movement is balanced on a knife edge."

"The troops and the police are withdrawn," said Trieger, "but our farm produce rots on the dock, so I agree. Someone will blink."

"The New Zealand Government has already blinked," corrected the QR. "It is now no more than a matter of time."

"You know something I don't?" asked Trieger.

"Without doubt," said Sir Jonathan. "There are two things I believe would be wise for you to do."

And so began an arduous day for the editor. He phoned the news desk of the *London Daily Mail*, where it was already 8 pm. Then he phoned the *New York Times* and the *Toronto Globe*. It was mid-afternoon in both cities. Other calls were made to newspapers in Paris, Madrid, Rome, Los Angeles and Sydney.

He also called the home of Turi Carroll, who had risen to prominence among the New Zealand Maori, and who would shortly be knighted for his services to the community. Was Turi aware of the struggle for independence in the Splendid Isles? He was. Like most New Zealanders he had followed the story in the paper.

"Do the Maori in New Zealand feel a particular kinship for their brothers in the islands?"

"They do," allowed the seventy-one-year-old elder statesman, devout Christian and returned soldier.

"Would the Maori in New Zealand favor independence for their brothers in the Splendid Isles?"

"If it was best for them," replied the canny Turi, choosing his words with great care.

Trieger tried again. "Would you agree all peoples should have the right to self-determination?"

"In principle, of course," came the answer. Careful again.

"Including your brothers in the Splendid Isles?"

"Yes," Turi Carroll had finally agreed.

Which goes to show a patient newsman can get to almost

any answer he desires, if he is skillful enough to ask the right questions. Aaron Trieger had his 'quote', as these things were called in his world. Finally, he phoned the news desk of the *New Zealand Herald*.

Two other events occurred on this most unusual day, though neither was within thousands of miles of Welcome Harbour. The Zealand High Commissioner in London received a handwritten note from Sir Michael Adeane, and the New Zealand Embassy in Washington DC reported an unusual encounter with a junior State Department official, who had attended a cocktail luncheon at the embassy on Observatory Circle NW the previous afternoon.

Professor Buchanan received a telephone call from America, but did not otherwise emerge from his room.

Reverend Geoffrey Brown took the advice of the Queen's Representative and stayed in bed, under 'doctor's orders', as Sir Jonathan O'Dowd had playfully put it. His briefly famous housekeeper, Piata Hana, happily joined him.

PART 3

THE ALMOST WAR

CHAPTER 32
CONSTRUED AND MISCONSTRUED

The battle-hardened Splendid Isles kitchen cabinet of the New Zealand Government was around the table in the private office of Prime Minister Keith Holyoake. Ralph Hanan sat next to Brigadier Bill Gilbert, who sat directly opposite the PM's one-man cheer squad, Finance Minister Harry Lake.

Before the PM was a file which contained a tear sheet of an article from the *New Zealand Herald*, and a swathe of telexes. Holyoake reviewed the file while the others waited in silence.

"Let us start in London, shall we?" he said calmly. No one spoke, so he went on. "I'm going to read the telex so we are all on the same page." He cleared his throat. "'My dear George, just an informal note to say how impressed we are at the Palace over your Government's restrained handling of the secession movement in the Splendid Isles.'" 'George' was George Laking, Acting New Zealand High Commissioner to the United Kingdom, former head of the wartime Organization of National Security, and soon to be New Zealand's newest ambassador to the United States. "It's signed Michael," said the PM. "Handwritten on the personal stationery of Sir Michael Adeane, Private Secretary to the

Queen. Any comments?" The PM looked at each of them in turn.

"I think the meaning is clear," said Spy Chief Gilbert, whose world and Laking's regularly intersected.

Holyoake grunted and went on. "I also have an account of a luncheon conversation at our embassy in Washington, between our Second Deputy Cultural Attaché and the subject of interest to us." 'Subject' was jargon for 'person', not 'topic of conversation'.

Gilbert nodded but did not speak. The young diplomat in the PM's crosshairs was an 'above the line' member of the New Zealand Secret Service, which meant official Embassy cover, as opposed to 'below the line'—'black'. The NZSS, like all security organizations, deployed both 'black' and 'above the line' spies into target countries, friend or foe, since today's friend could just as easily be tomorrow's enemy.

The PM was still speaking. "The subject is a junior US State Department officer, according to the telex. Subject— details supplied—said, quote: 'the secession movement in the islands you guys own out in the Pacific is being watched by State' unquote."

"Bill?" said Holyoake, turning to Gilbert. "The embassy asked you to run this chap down for them."

"Certainly," said the Chief Spy. "The embassy captures details of everyone attending official events. This fellow said he worked for the Bureau of East Asian and Pacific Affairs, which he explained was a small piece of the empire of the Under Secretary for Democracy and Global Affairs."

"So, this fellow's patch, then?" said the PM.

"Not necessarily," said Gilbert. "He's got it scrambled, you see. East Asian and Pacific Affairs does not report to the Under Secretary for Democracy and Global Affairs. Either this chap doesn't know who he really works for, or he doesn't want us to know."

"Meaning?"

"I would say 'spook'."

"Makes two of them, then," said Holyoake. "Did you notice anything else?" The PM looked directly at Attorney-General Hanan as he asked the question.

"Not immediately," replied the AG. He wondered what he might have missed.

The PM rummaged through his file for the two telexes, which he placed side by side. He cleared his throat for dramatic effect. "'... over your Government's restrained handling of the secession movement in the Splendid Isles.' That was Adeane's note. Now here's the American chap: '... the secession movement in the islands you guys own out in the Pacific'." Holyoake looked up. "Got it?"

"I would say we're getting the message that Buckingham Palace and the US State Department are watching the Splendids," said Hanan. "Curious, though, they should both use the same term."

"Precisely," said the PM, as though he were a headmaster encouraging a dull student. "'Secession movement.' We've never used that phrase. Nor has the press, as far as I know." He retrieved the tear sheet of the story that had appeared in the *New Zealand Herald* and read aloud: "'MAORI SUPPORT SELF-RULE FOR SPLENDID ISLES BROTHERS'. It's an interview with Maori leader Turi Carroll. Written by 'our man in Welcome Harbour', the paper proclaims. So this fellow, 'our man' in Welcome Harbour—"

"Aaron Trieger," supplied Brigadier Gilbert.

The Prime Minister fixed the Brigadier with a skeptical eye. "This man, Aaron Trieger," he said slowly, "interviewed Turi Carroll in New Zealand, by telephone from the Splendid Isles. The *New Zealand Herald* hasn't got any reporters in

New Zealand of their own, have they?"

"I would say they plucked the story straight from the paper in the Splendids," ventured Gilbert, defending his man to the last. "Doesn't mean anything in itself."

The others said nothing, happy, perhaps, that someone else was under the gun.

The PM paused while he located another telex from the file. "Got you," he said, as though the document had been trying to escape.

"*Splendid Islands Telegraph*. Front-page lead. 'WORLD EYES ON SPLENDID ISLES INDEPENDENCE MOVEMENT'. Accompanied by artist's impressions of the international coverage of the Welcome Harbour standoff." He looked around the assemblage once more.

"So?" said the Prime Minister, "who will pull all this together for me? Harry? You haven't said much."

"This is far out of my field," said the Finance Minister, ducking for cover.

"Ralph?" said the Prime Minister. He swiveled his gaze to the Attorney-General.

Hanan was determined to say something useful. The last meeting of the kitchen cabinet had been personally disastrous, and he was keen to return to the PM's favor. "America and Britain are sending the same message," he said.

"Yes," said Holyoake, the headmaster again. "And our loyal allies seem to have discussed it between themselves: the Queen's Private Secretary and this fellow from State, if that's where he works, which Bill says not."

At least he was still 'Bill'. "Excellent timing, as well," said Gilbert, who had a spy's mistrust for what others might dismiss as coincidence.

"My thoughts, exactly," said Hanan. "The QR meets the

Reverend. Offers thirty percent, provided the independence movement is consigned to the depths. Chap takes a dive for twenty-four hours. Pardon the pun. In bed with the flu, while Buckingham Palace, US State, the *New Zealand Herald*, the local paper and the Maori community all give us a nudge."

"Can I add something, Prime Minister?" said Brigadier Gilbert. "Immigration records up in the Splendids are finally in some kind of order. Our American, Professor Buchanan, is back in town."

"Surely the airline could have told you that," said Holyoake.

"Only if he flew in on a scheduled flight," said Gilbert. "Which he did not. Private plane. Beechcraft twin-engine job. Ex Tahiti, I believe."

"You believe?"

"Flight plan said 'Tahiti' is all we know."

Holyoake sat up, as though he were now the schoolboy and about to answer a question in class. "We are getting a great deal more than a nudge, and we cannot afford to ignore Britain and America. Nor can we afford public opinion to be whipped up at home. Ralph, your man in the Splendids?"

"The QR, Sir Jonathan O'Dowd."

"Time he had another meeting with our troublesome Reverend."

"We discussed this, Prime Minister. We are looking to replace the QR when his term ends in a few months. What about Sir Brendan Court? After all, he's going to be the new man once O'Dowd is gone."

"And therefore completely wrong," replied the PM. "We need someone who is not going to be around after the dust has settled. Tell me, does O'Dowd know he's on the way out?"

"Of course not," said Hanan.

"Ralph," said the Prime Minister, as though Hanan were again the dunce, "they always know. Drop him the word there could be a role in Wellington once he's done."

*****

"So that is the new offer that will be made to you," said Sir Jonathan O'Dowd. He and the Reverend were sitting in the conservatory at the rambling Government House. They sat on uncomfortable metal chairs, which for some reason are favored in garden settings. A squadron of butterfly cakes landed between them, followed by fresh pot of tea. It was as though the meeting were starting, not ending. The cook turned and departed.

"And this is official?" managed Reverend Brown.

"It can become official, of course. But I do not yet have instructions to make it so."

"And you are waiting for me to say... what?"

"That is a matter entirely for you to decide," said the QR, pouring the tea. "Sugar?"

"One lump," said Reverend Brown, patting his stomach. "Are you recommending another bout of twenty-four-hour flu?"

But the Queen's Representative seemed more distant than at their previous meeting. He smiled but did not reply.

"Very well," said the churchman. "You have given me a lot to ponder."

*****

The little Austin drove itself back to the rectory. It very nearly missed the turn, skated for a moment on the gravel, and threw up a cloud of dust. The vehicle behind braked sharply, but its driver waved when he saw Reverend Brown at the wheel.

Mrs. Hana, firmly back in housekeeper mode, had baked a brown sugar, peach and honey pie, which emerged from the oven as the Reverend hurried inside.

Professor Buchanan was in the study, with a glass of the churchman's wretched sherry and a stale cigar. "My dear fellow—" He let out a small puff of smoke, and eyed the dessert and Piata Hana at the same time. "I am keen to hear what the Governor had to say."

"And you shall hear it." The Reverend helped himself to a slice of pie and a scoop of fresh strawberry ice cream, which was one of Mrs. Hana's greatest accomplishments. "The short of it is, the thirty percent offer is withdrawn."

"So that is the stick," said the Professor. "What is the—?"

"Carrot?" said Reverend Brown. "I am not sure it could be called that. We are to be offered what they describe as 'limited independence'."

"There is no such thing," said Professor Buchanan. "Limited by what?"

"There is to be a Parliament for the Splendid Isles, in a disused construction facility, near the airport."

"Very well. There is a building, suitable or not."

"A Parliament of nine. Duly elected by the people of the Splendid Isles."

"Duly elected to do what?"

"The Parliament is to have an advisory role."

"Advisory?"

"To the Government of New Zealand."

"So this Parliament would have no powers of its own?"

"None whatsoever," said Reverend Brown. "They imagine I will lead it—assuming I am elected, which they would not oppose."

"So you would advise the New Zealand Government to, let us say, raise taxes."

"Perhaps," said Reverend Brown, "we might advise that."

"But it would be up to New Zealand whether to do so or not?"

"Also when or how these taxes might be imposed." The churchman sighed.

"So the Parliament they propose has no purpose at all?"

"The farmers have lost," said the Reverend. "The Splendid Isles is to have a sham government and a pretend nation."

Professor Buchanan sat for a long time smoking his cigar. A slice of pie sulked on his plate, a shortbread island in a strawberry ice cream sea. "They cannot give the farmers nothing," he said at last.

"Perhaps the eleven percent offer could be reinstated," said Reverend Brown, referring to the offer accepted by Tom Bedall and repudiated by the farmers at the Mechanics Hall. "Without some kind of deal there will be riots. The Splendids will go broke."

"And a sham government, powerless to act," the Professor reminded. He drew deeply on his pungent cigar. "But my dear fellow," he said, blowing a perfect smoke ring into the room. His eyes twinkled. "It cannot possibly work. Can you spot the flaw?"

"I confess I cannot," the churchman replied.

"Why, all of the problems would be in New Zealand's lap, not yours!"

Reverend Brown slowly smiled. "You are right," he said. "New Zealand could live with a generous deal for the farmers, and limited independence—"

"That is correct," interrupted Professor Buchanan. "The farmers would be happy. Independence dead. Wellington in charge, as they are now."

"Or," said the Reverend. His smile broadened. "A poor

deal for the farmers, and full independence."

"Precisely," agreed Professor Buchanan. "New Zealand would be free of the headache, which would be yours to solve."

Reverend Brown dipped a finger into his pie while he considered the impact of the logic. "No deal for the farmers; and a sham government cannot work for either side."

The Professor stood up. "Reverend Brown, I have a most marvelous thought. One day you will build a statue of me for this."

CHAPTER 33
MIS-UNDER-ESTIMATED

"I think I have a story for you," said Reverend Brown, settling into an uncomfortable chair. They all seemed uncomfortable of late.

"Tea?" asked the editor of the *Splendid Islands Telegraph*. An electric kettle by the side of his desk had just come to a boil, and was surrounded by a collection of badly chipped mugs.

It occurred to the Reverend, as he selected the cleanest cup, that he should shout at the kettle: 'Come out with your hands up!' but he resisted the temptation. "Thanks. One lump," he said instead.

"The farmers and the shipping company have kissed and made up?" ventured Trieger facetiously.

"In a manner of speaking," said the Reverend, "but there is far more to it than that. I am going to offer you the biggest story in the history of these Splendid Isles."

"Righty-oh!" said Trieger, whose notebook appeared as smoothly as a Colt 45 into the fist of an American cowboy.

"The New Zealand Government," the Reverend lied, "has offered the Splendid Isles full independence."

"Wow!" said Trieger. "Starting when?"

"Naturally, there will have to be elections and the

217

formation of a Parliament."

"Naturally," agreed Trieger. "Who, precisely, made this offer?"

"The Queen's Representative, Sir Jonathan O'Dowd, at a meeting at Government House yesterday afternoon."

"This is official?"

"It is not yet in writing. But it is official. 'Full independence' were Sir Jonathan's own words." So this is how the quest for power works, reflected Reverend Brown. Distortion, misinformation, outright lies. Pressed into service for the greater good. Or what I believe the greater good to be.

"Who else attended this meeting?" pursued Trieger.

"It was described to me as a meeting of principals. He and I met together, at Sir Jonathan's request."

"I suppose the question is a formality, but what do you intend to do?"

I intend to run these Splendid Isles, thought Reverend Brown, free of the yoke of New Zealand. And I will do anything within my growing power to achieve it. "I am consulting with my colleagues, he heard himself say, "but we will certainly accept this wise and just offer from the New Zealand Government." Lay it on, the Professor had counseled. It will make it more difficult for them to say 'no'.

"So who will be the candidates for this historic first Parliament?

"The plan calls for nine MPs."

"I am asking how candidates will be selected?" said Trieger.

I shall select candidates of my own choosing, who are loyal to me and capable of doing the job, though if they are one or the other, I will have to discover the virtue I better prefer. "It is not yet decided," the Reverend said. "There will be wide consultation, since it will be critical for our nation to be represented by the best people for the task."

"You will lead it?

Who will stop me? I have fashioned the independence movement, and I am its natural head. "I am a man of God. If called upon to do so, I will shoulder that grave burden," replied Reverend Brown, sipping his tea.

"So I am interviewing the future Prime Minister of the Splendid Isles?"

Yes, you fool! And I shall have the power to bring you to heel, if I choose to do it. "That is not for me to say," he replied. "We shall see what the people demand."

"The Splendid Isles has been a colony of New Zealand for..." Trieger looked up, while he calculated the number, "more than half a century, if I am not mistaken. So why this dramatic turn?"

We shall shortly discover whether it is a dramatic turn, thought Reverend Brown, or whether my ploy has failed, and there is no change whatever. "The New Zealand Government is wise and just," he heard himself say.

"You already said that," reminded the editor.

No harm in restating it. Sugar-coat the pill, the Professor had advised; it will be bitter for them nonetheless. "We have had our differences, of course," the Reverend began again. "This is only to be expected of close family. But" —he held up a hand as Trieger was about to interrupt— "they have come to see, these past months, our people are mature and ready to make our own way in the world."

"Does this mean the farmers' dispute is also resolved?"

"Oh, indeed yes!" lied Reverend Brown with a beaming smile. "The farmers of the Splendid Isles have been offered thirty percent more than they were paid last year."

"You are aware of the claim you already accepted eleven

percent?" said Trieger.

It was part of our plan, which I am glad you have not discovered. Accept nine percent, or accept eleven percent. Then reject eleven percent. Run them in circles, until the dog bites its own tail. "Rumors abound in such a small place," he said. "Many numbers have been discussed and considered."

"This offer," the one I have just invented, the Reverend thought, but did not say, "was made to me officially as part of the warm and forthright discussions I had yesterday with Sir Jonathan."

"So..." said Trieger, licking a thumb and flicking back through his notes.

"So..." echoed Reverend Brown, "I want my admiration and deep respect for the New Zealand Government to be 'on the record', as you newspaper fellows like to say. It is a relationship we will cherish and maintain, as these Splendid Isles take our place among the free nations of the world."

*****

The telephone rang at Sir Jonathan O'Dowd's office almost before Reverend Brown left the newsroom. It is the journalist's way. Double-check the facts; who knows what might turn up? The Queen's Representative heard the story without comment. He weighed his options. Confirm the Reverend's preposterous account? He could not do that. Reject the account as absurd? Tempting at a human level, but poor diplomacy, since denials set like concrete and kill the diplomatic preference to duck and swerve. Besides, he had the authority to neither confirm nor deny. This was a matter for his Minister, the sometimes moody Ralph Hanan; or, more probably, the Prime Minister himself. Sir Jonathan O'Dowd did what all officials do when asked to make a tricky call. He immediately kicked it straight upstairs.

"Aaron," he said smoothly into the phone. "No comment, and don't quote me. I refer you to the Attorney-General's office in Wellington."

*****

Reverend Geoffrey Brown settled into a chair in his study. He drank his sherry, lit a stale cigar, and turned to Professor Buchanan, who paced, smoked, and drank, all at the same time.

"It is done," said Reverend Brown. "Though there was no pleasure in it."

"He will go immediately to your Governor for confirmation," said the Professor.

"Queen's Representative," corrected the Reverend distractedly.

"Who will not dare deny it without instructions from his master in Wellington? Nor can he confirm it, since it is untrue."

"According to your thinking, that is the case," said Reverend Brown. He swirled the sherry around his glass.

"You are too impatient," said the Professor. "The power is coming to you sooner than you think."

"I am uneasy with what I have done. I have breached the confidence of a man whose sympathies, I suspect, we had won."

"My dear fellow," replied Professor Buchanan, "you must learn to live in the zone between moral decency and the demands of power. You have no choice. As I have said, the power is coming to you sooner than you think."

"Unless the New Zealand Government issues a denial," countered Reverend Brown. For a moment he seemed to brighten at the thought.

*****

Aaron Trieger pondered the 'no comment and don't quote me' response from the QR. Interesting, he thought. He phoned the office of Ralph Hanan in Wellington and asked for the Minister's Press Secretary, who came on the line. Then he placed a call to the news desk of the *New Zealand Herald*. "Your man in Welcome Harbour," he parodied himself. "I have a rather good story I would like to file."

*****

Within half an hour, three Humber Snipe limousines conveyed their important passengers through the city's narrow streets and along Lambton Quay to the Prime Minister's residence in Pipitea Street.

Five minutes later, three men stirred their tea, while an aide whispered in the PM's ear. Presently, the great man looked up. He searched the faces of his colleagues before his eyes finally came to rest on the Attorney-General. "Ralph," said the PM, "your man took the call from our Mr. Trieger."

"Indeed," said the Attorney-General, and quickly brought the others up to date.

"Questions?" asked the Prime Minister.

"I should like my Department to confirm the impact on Pacific Islands Shipping," began Harry Lake, "if this thirty percent price hike were to occur."

He is cautious, thought the Prime Minister. But at least he is loyal. "Noted!" he replied. "Much more pressing is our response to the main question. Are we confirming full independence for the Splendid Isles or not?"

"The story is patently untrue," said the AG. "I have spoken to Sir Jonathan O'Dowd and no such offer was ever made. The Reverend's account is a monstrous lie."

And this one sometimes misses the point, thought the Prime Minister. He is quite bright, but not quite so loyal. "Anyone dispute that?" said Holyoake, looking at each of them in turn.

"I have a question," said Spy Chief Gilbert. He turned to face the AG. "Ralph, you told the QR he could count on a pleasant job in Wellington after he had been of service to us?"

"Absolutely!" confirmed Hanan.

"Because if the QR saw nothing for himself back here. Or if he saw something in London with his masters there. It has never been clear to me which is his boss."

"If the choice is between Ralph and Her Royal Highness, Queen of England and all that she sees, including New Zealand and the troublesome Splendid Isles," offered Harry Lake, "I think I know who would win that."

"Are you accusing this loyal diplomat?" replied the AG.

The PM raised a hand. "Gentlemen, we have a simple choice. We either confirm the account, or we deny it."

"Deny," said the Attorney-General.

Holyoake swatted the advice away. "Whether it is true or false is not the issue. I am talking here of politics." He looked squarely at the Attorney-General. "It has nothing to do with right or wrong. We have little time. The paper in Welcome Harbour must have a statement, and the *New Zealand Herald* has been on the phone."

"I also say 'deny'." Harry Lake's bravery seemed to grow. "It is better for our budget if these Splendid Isles remain in place."

"But survivable if they do not," said the PM.

"There is the matter of fishing rights," said Lake. "As we have discussed, they could be valuable indeed."

"And if they could somehow be preserved?"

"Subject to reconfirming the impact on the shipping company?"

"Subject to that," allowed the Prime Minister.

"The cost would not be great," conceded Lake. "An impact; but modest, as these things go."

"Ralph?" said the PM. "Do you care to revise your view?"

"We are considering whether to allow the Splendid Isles to shrug us off?"

"We are."

"Without regard to the truth of the discussions between our man and this blasted churchman?"

"Yes," said the Prime Minister. "You are thinking too much like a lawyer, too little like a politician." Hanan was a trained lawyer, but had been a politician for fifteen years.

"Perhaps it is a fault," agreed the Attorney-General, "but I do not see why we should do nothing while a liar hijacks a country we have magnificently governed." Governed by himself, he meant, since as Minister for the Splendid Isles he was ultimately responsible for the remote protectorate.

"Bill?" said the PM.

"From an intelligence perspective," said the head of the NZSS, "it is of value, but no great jewel."

"I think that is right," said the PM.

"I am worried, however, on several fronts," continued the spy. "This Professor Buchanan and his so-called think tank, about which CIA is unusually coy. The fact he is graded Yankee White, which is deeply troubling. Back-channel messages from Buckingham Palace and the Americans."

"It is worrying," agreed the PM.

But Brigadier Gilbert was not yet finished. "This independence movement, and its unlikely head. We are missing something. I do not yet know what it is."

THE MAN IN THE SPIDER WEB COAT

"The newspapers, here and in the Splendid Isles, will carry the story whether we deny it or not," said the Prime Minister. "Denial puts us into a tug of war for the truth to emerge, if it ever does. Also, we voted for this Resolution 1514. It was right at the time, since we dared not risk the Maori vote. Now we must live in the house we built."

He peered over his reading glasses as each of the others nodded agreement. "And we have received the word, as Bill reminds us, that both Washington and London would look kindly upon independence—'secession', as they describe it— even though they abstained from the vote at the UN themselves. There is also the question of Harry's thirty percent." He looked straight at the Finance Minister. "We know we can live with this, so it is not a bone in our throat. Finally, this Reverend Brown has lavished praise on us. 'Wise and just', I believe were his words. If we do not confirm his account, we will lose in the court of public opinion. Sooner or later, we may be forced to a position we can adopt today. So that is the choice. Wise and just now, or—probably, I would say—an uncomfortable retreat, later on."

"Your reasoning cannot be faulted," said Finance Minister Lake, climbing immediately aboard. "There is another issue. The Maori in New Zealand must not be drawn in."

*****

The *London Daily Mail* was pumped onto the streets and was read over breakfast by countless households, as were the *New Zealand Herald*, the *Toronto Globe*, the *New York Times*, and later, the *Sydney Daily Mirror*. People in Rome, Madrid, Mexico City and Los Angeles also read of independence for the world's newest nation. In the Splendid Isles, the *Telegraph* came off the presses and onto the trucks. Naturally, the photographs of Piata Hana were run again, since there were not many excuses for nude pictures in 1961.

On Radio WRAP, in Nashville, the story came between the traffic report and the weather. "Remember those crazy folks down in the South Pacific?" the announcer hyped. "Where all the women took off their clothes and protested naked? Well, I'll be blowed if they ain't won independence and become their own country." Then the punchline: "Maybe if we take our clothes off, we can become our own country down here in Tennessee."

"If'n you take your clothes off, I'm leaving the state as fast as I can," deadpanned the traffic reporter as they cut to the forecast. She was young, and tired of fighting off the advances of the middle-aged announcer, but she knew how to play the game.

*****

In Wellington, USDAO NZ, known otherwise as the local United States Defense Attaché, informed his counterpart in the New Zealand Military of a happy development. A brace of C130A Hercules aircraft, as earlier requested, were now suddenly available. The aircraft were at Barbers Point Naval Air Station, a few miles from Honolulu in the recent American state of Hawaii, and could be at Briggs Field within a day.

CHAPTER 34
POWERFUL THOUGHTS

The explosive front-page story in the *Splendid Islands Telegraph* was greeted with a mix of joy and trepidation: joy that the farmers had won, and that the collection of five tiny islands was to become a nation; trepidation from a natural fear of the uncharted. Would the new country be too small, too weak to survive? Would New Zealand, shortly to be spurned, react as a kindly uncle or a spiteful neighbor? Of more immediate concern, who would comprise this new Parliament? How would it work? And the biggest question of all, what kind of leader would a church reverend make when his flock was an entire country, rather than a few pews on Sunday morning?

This last question preyed most on the mind of Reverend Brown, as he sat in the afternoon sunlight, on the porch, at the rectory, next to the Splendid Isles Christian Church.

"My dear fellow," said Professor Buchanan, "you have identified your concerns, and it is crucial each one be addressed. There are a number of things you must do."

"So many things," Reverend Brown sighed. "I do not know where to begin."

"The most important is always a good place to start. Do you remember when we spoke at your lookout above

Welcome Harbour many months ago?"

"Remind me."

"I said every revolution required a clear opponent to the current regime."

"Was that before or after you offered the job to my son?"

"You are the leader. You have not come this far to crumble now. This is a dangerous time, which you can sense," remarked the Professor. "Many a revolution is lost when victory is within reach. In accordance with my theory, I am going to tell you what to do. Which do you prefer? From the center of things moving out, or from outside the center, moving in?"

*****

Over the next ten days, Reverend Brown traveled to the four outer Splendid Islands, where he sat one by one with the Chiefs. Would each of them consent to serve in Parliament as the elected representative of his people?

At Tarakapua—'cloudy peak' in English—they sat on a mountain top. There were no clouds. They gazed across the sandy beach far below, where a native fisherman dragged a net. "I am already their representative," said the Chief gravely, "but I will come."

At Ranginui, which means 'big sky', they shared the shade of a coconut palm with an island dog suckling a pup. "What is your plan for my people?" asked the Chief. The mother dog lifted her head and watched through soft and gentle eyes, as if the question had been asked for her.

"We shall make a plan together," said Reverend Brown.

The Chief smiled and nodded his head.

At Aowai, the most distant of them all, they huddled beneath a tin roof while fat drops of rain fell to the ground. Aowai means 'world of water', and seemed well named. "You want everything to be on Welcome Island," said the Chief after a long silence. "Yet we have the best soil."

"Your soil is fertile indeed," agreed Reverend Brown. "I am asking you to help plant green shoots on all our islands so one day they will be as rich as here."

At Koura, famous for its seafood, and which meant 'crayfish' in English, Reverend Brown dangled a line over the side of a boat and watched as his baited hook plunged straight to the ocean floor. "As a fisherman, you are not so skilled," observed the Chief, casting his own line far out to sea.

"It is a high standard you set," said Reverend Brown, casting again.

Very well," said the Chief. "I will serve with you."

*****

\Tom Bedall arrived at the rectory on his steam tractor, which hissed like an angry snake. He wore his best boots, and Sunday pants, a little too short, but freshly washed.

"I am assembling my team," said Reverend Brown, "and I want you on it."

"What would I do?" asked Tom cautiously.

"Be part of the Parliament. Make the law."

"I don't know nothing about that," said Tom. "You would have to give me a lot of help. Like when I met the man from the shipping company. Help like that."

"Why, of course," said Reverend Brown, throwing an arm over his comrade's shoulder. "We have come this far toward success. We must not give up now."

Tom's face lit up like an urchin handed a golden coin. "Very well," he said quietly, but there was joy in his step as he climbed back on his tractor, which towered ten feet in the air. For the first time in his life, Tom Bedall felt tall.

Finally, the Reverend sat with RW Rumsey, who wore his once-white shirt, with the chain of a fob watch disappearing into his pants. "RW, you are my most trusted ally. We have spoken informally but now I want your most excellent oath."

"Oath to what?" said the accountant, farmers' president and whistleblower, though who the whistle was blown for, or why, was still unknown.

"You will serve with me to run these Splendid Isles."

"I will swear to that," said RW Rumsey. "I will gladly swear to it."

"My friend and Deputy," said Reverend Brown. "Together we will make this nation great."

*****

In Pipitea Street, in the study of the Prime Minister, sat Keith Holyoake and Ralph Hanan. They stirred their tea and picked through a plate of cookies, no doubt supplied through some government tender designed to favor the cheapest and therefore least tempting fare.

"What I would give for a chocolate macaroon," said the Prime Minister, unusually mellow after an opinion poll showed more than sixty percent of New Zealanders felt he was doing a good job. "Come, Ralph," he said, "take me through this draft constitution your experts have toiled on these past weeks."

"With pleasure, Prime Minister," said the Attorney-General, dipping into his briefcase for a large file.

"I am sure your draftsmen have done an excellent job," said Holyoake, "but will you remind me why we cannot leave this task to the Parliament of the Splendid Isles, once their churchman has won?"

"Prime Minister, they cannot start a nation in a vacuum

with no law. There is also a safeguard for us, since it will be more difficult to change a law once it is already in place."

"I understand," said Holyoake. "Please proceed."

The Attorney-General picked up the file and began to read. "'Part One'," he said, "'Queen's Representative.'"

"Just the highlights," prompted Holyoake.

"Of course," said Hanan, skimming the document. "Let me see. Constitution of the Parliament. Powers. Judiciary, including right of QR to appoint judges. Right to impose taxes."

"Yes," said Holyoake, rummaging hopefully through the cookies.

"Transitional provisions. Existing New Zealand law to continue, until, or unless they make changes."

"Uh-huh!" said the PM, his mouth full of crumbs.

"Qualification of electors. Qualification of candidates."

"What qualifications?"

"Completely standard," said the Attorney-General. "Cannot be a bankrupt, convicted felon, proscribed lunatic."

"Anything else?"

"How the Public Service works. Fundamental rights and freedoms."

"And all of this comes from?"

"Great Britain, Prime Minister. The ramshackle constitution they handed us." New Zealand, in fact, had no supreme constitutional document, just a collection of Acts of Parliament, treaties, decisions of the Courts, and unwritten conventions swept into a unified document for the Splendid Isles, for the very first time.

"Try one of these cookies with red jelly," said Holyoake. "I rather think they're the best."

*****

Trieger answered the phone, a reporter's habit, on the first ring. Few calls to the editor of a newspaper, even as tiny as the *Telegraph*, are a complete waste of time. Powerful people call, wanting to receive or bestow favors; ordinary folk—more of them had phones these days—with stories that might make a front page; officials briskly—or sometimes unhappily—responding 'for the record' or, evasively, off it; others begging for a story to be run, or not, depending on their point of view.

Contrary to spy novels, which were popular at the time, there was not much cloak and dagger about Brigadier Bill Gilbert's call. He identified himself clearly, asked politely how the paper was doing, and issued orders—which, as Aaron Trieger's spymaster, paymaster and boss, he was entitled to do. "What do you know about opinion polls?" he asked, after the pleasantries had been dispatched.

"We did a few in London," replied Trieger, who on reflection thought better of his admission and quickly added: "Not much."

"No matter," said the head of the NZSS. "I want you to knock on doors. Reporters are good at asking questions, and there are some answers I'd like to have."

"Can I publish the results?" asked the editor.

"It depends," said Gilbert. "I will let you know when I have seen them myself."

"People might ask questions if nothing is published."

"I will bear that in mind. By the way, Aaron?" This was followed by a distinct pause.

"Yes?" replied Trieger, immediately wary.

"You haven't gone native on me, have you?" 'Going native' was a risk for intelligence agents and diplomats alike, at least in the minds of their masters. Over time, it was feared, they might more strongly identify with the land of their posting than the land of their birth. In short, they might forget which team they were on.

"Heavens no!" said the editor, now fully alert.

"Wouldn't do for the bank to get spooked, if they thought your policies had changed for the worse." If this was a pun, Brigadier Gilbert did not mention it. The spymaster paused again. "There is no change, is there?"

"None at all," said Trieger, confronting the spy's nightmare, where all truths are suspected as false, and all denials as masking the truth. 'A wilderness of mirrors' as a legendary American counterspy would one day say. Aaron Trieger's loan to buy the *Telegraph* had been arranged in return for what the NZSS described as 'an understanding of the bigger issues from time to time'. The real message was clear: what the NZSS gives, it can also take away.

Aaron Trieger noted the questions to be asked, grabbed his keys and headed out. Over the next few hours he knocked on many doors. "Hi," he said. "The *Telegraph* would love to hear your thoughts about the elections we are to have, and the future direction of these Splendid Isles."

*****

In his study at the rectory, Reverend Brown had concerns of a different kind. "How are we to fight an election campaign against no one?" he asked.

"What do you mean?" said Professor Buchanan, stirring his tea.

"We have no opponent of any kind."

"My dear fellow," said the Professor. "Opposition from New Zealand is not enough?"

"They oppose us still?"

"I am reminded of a quotation from a famous American abolitionist. I have forgotten his name. 'Power concedes nothing without a demand. It never did, and it never will.'" For a moment, the Professor was back at the Beekman Tower Hotel in New York, a stone's throw from the UN, with a certain Ghanaian diplomat in a spider web coat.

"Come," said Reverend Brown. "I need some air."

Mrs. Hana watched from the kitchen as the Austin disappeared down a dip in the driveway and turned at the main road. She heard a crunch of gears, sighed, and went back to her scones.

The car struggled uphill, into the heat of the unpaved parking lot, high above Welcome Harbour. The two men watched from the lookout as waves smashed onto the reef and dissolved into foam.

"A few yards offshore—" began Reverend Brown.

"I remember," interrupted Professor Buchanan. "Five thousand feet deep!"

"You are saying we should fight the election as though New Zealand was our opponent?" said Reverend Brown.

"Exactly!" said the Professor. "The faceless men in the shadows who stand for everything wrong."

"It is hard to land a blow on a faceless man in the shadows," observed Reverend Brown.

"And not so easy for a man in the shadows to properly fight back," countered Professor Buchanan. "They will try hard, though. They will try hard."

"A full-blown campaign? Is that what you say?"

"My word!" said the Professor.

"It will cost money," said the Reverend. "The Splendid Islands Party has none."

"How would you spend this money," asked the Professor, "were you to have it?"

"A truck with loud-hailer," tried the Reverend, who was new to this. "Posters. Stickers to put on the windows of cars."

"An official launch of the Splendid Islands Party," added the Professor, warming to the task. "A mailbox campaign. An open letter from you to the voters."

"A good deal of money," corrected the Reverend. "Possibly a great deal."

"How much?" said Professor Buchanan.

"Hmm!" said Reverend Brown, stroking his chin. "At least five hundred pounds."

"My dear fellow, you will spend that on advertising alone."

"A thousand then," said the Reverend, who had no idea.

"I do not believe the money will be a problem," said the Professor. "There is a coalition in America, a coalition from which sufficient funds could be raised."

"What sort of coalition?" asked the Reverend.

"I would call it a nature wildlife coalition, a charity of sorts."

"How much could they provide?"

The Professor watched a bird swoop to the beach below. "More than you could spend, my friend."

"And what of New Zealand? What will these faceless men do in return?"

"What will they do? They will peer into their vast resources, and they will throw at you everything they can."

CHAPTER 35
A ROSE BY ANY OTHER NAME

It takes time for the cogs of government to mesh into place, Professor Buchanan had counseled. But when the great machine began to move, it would be difficult to stop.

The *Jalisco Belle* loitered—that was the word for it, thought Captain Emmet Fullmore—loitered at the wharf at Welcome Harbour for almost three weeks while the negotiations swirled. Tight-faced soldiers. Grim police. Naked wives and daughters. The clergyman, who was somehow involved. The Chairman of the shipping company. The local paper. The Resident Commissioner, whatever he might do. There was no end of intrigue. Emmet Fullmore sighed. He wanted no more than to be back at sea.

'DOCK WELCOME HARBOUR IMMEDIATE STOP LOAD FASTEST AGAINST COMPANY PO STOP NIL REPUDIATION STOP PREPARE SEAL LOG STOP TRIM FOR SPEED STOP ADVISE WHEN LOADEN STOP'. Those had been his instructions, followed by stalemate and silence. Now, finally, he had received a new message from the radio shack behind the bridge. 'RESUME LOADING STOP ESTIMATE PERCENT SALEABLE STOP ADVISE WHEN LOADEN STOP'. Eleven words, without apology or explanation. Still, he would need no asking a second time. He was keen to set sail from the stench of land, even in a place as beautiful as the Splendid Isles.

He gave the orders and watched as longshoremen loaded the sling with crates of produce, which were swung aboard, lowered into the holds, inspected and stowed. The job continued into the night, the longshoremen at one moment caught in the ship's floodlights, the next, receding into the gloom. Eventually, the hatches were sealed, the numbers recorded in the log.

'LOADEN COMPLETE STOP PERCENT SALEABLE 40 STOP TIDE 1600 ZULU STOP STANDBY STOP'. The *Jalisco Belle* was fully loaded. Sixty percent of the produce was rotten. This was a wild guess, of course, which also tried to predict how much more of the cargo would become unsalable during the two-week voyage to Auckland. Most of the fruit was already gone, the first officer explained to Captain Fullmore on the bridge. Spoiled, no doubt, while it sat on the wharf. The vegetables were holding up, but who knew whether a coconut was rotten or not?

'Tide 1600 Zulu' was a hint. It meant the ship could sail with the tide at four o'clock in the evening Greenwich Mean Time; 6 am in Welcome Harbour. 'Standby' meant 'we await your further instruction, but we'll chew our heads off with boredom until you give us the orders to go'.

Captain Fullmore retired to his cabin and was engaged in a game of chess, which he was losing against himself, when there was a knock at the door.

"Pardon, sir." It was the Second Engineer. "Meshing problem with the open worm on the donkey. Request permission to shut her down and idle the main." The donkey was the small, auxiliary engine used to supply power to the *Jalisco Belle* when she was in port. There was something wrong with the gears. The engineer wanted to fire up the main engine for wharf-side power instead.

"Approved!" said Captain Fullmore. He moved a pawn and did not look up.

"Sir," said the Second Engineer, "Wiper Badgley has requested permission to go ashore." A wiper was the most junior member of the engineering team. His job was to clean the engine spaces and wipe down the machinery.

"Now?" said the Captain, glancing at his watch.

"Sir, he wants to report something to the police."

"Nothing to do with us, I hope?"

"No, sir. Something to do with his last shore leave."

"Why wait all this time?"

"Said he'd been thinking about it," replied the Second Engineer.

"Very well," said Captain Fullmore, replacing the pawn and moving a knight.

A few minutes later, the deck plates shuddered as the seventeen-hundred-and-fifty-horsepower main diesel came to life. It was as though the *Jalisco Belle* could hardly wait to get back to sea.

*****

At Trader Mike's sat Randolph Herd and Ned Tanner. A waiter hurried to their outdoor table with a pitcher of their usual cocktail.

"Notice anything?" said Tanner.

"No," said the Resident Commissioner, helping himself to a glass of breakfast.

"The *Jalisco Belle* is gone," said Tanner. "Sailed this morning at first light."

"One less arrow in our back, if you ask me," said Herd, cranking around to squint at the empty wharf.

"I'll drink to that," said Tanner, and drained his breakfast in a single gulp. "Interesting late shift last night," he said, refilling his glass.

"'Interesting?'" said Herd. "I think I'm over 'interesting'."

"Sailor from the *Jalisco Belle*. Covered in grease from head to foot. Fascinating tale about a game of darts."

"All right," said Herd, sitting up, as though he was now in his office instead of the bar.

"Lodged a complaint against Arthur Thomas Bedall, farmer of hereabouts. Tom Bedall," reminded Tanner. "The village idiot."

"Oh, yes. I have him now," said Herd, as though he were a marksman and Tom Bedall a deer in his sights.

"The negotiator," said Tanner, referring to Bedall's role in the toe to toe with Sir Brendan Court, and its much disputed eleven percent outcome. "Also grew the Independence Rose which started all this."

"It's early in the day," said Herd with a sigh. "I need the story in just one piece."

"Tom Bedall rolled Seymour Badgley, a junior sailor on the *Jalisco Belle*, after a game of darts in which both men were drunk. Badgley's story, anyway."

"And stole what?" said the Resident Commissioner.

"You'll love this! A couple of quid, the man's wallet and..."

"Yes?" said Herd.

"The parent of the Independence Rose!"

"That is interesting," said Herd.

"You remember the dossier I sent to New Zealand after the flap?"

"How could I forget?" said Herd.

"Including the theft report, lodged earlier by the QR?"

"Very well," conceded the Resident Commissioner. "I do

forget."

"The QR reported a red rosebush was stolen from the grounds of Government House. We suspect, but cannot prove, the thieving Dan Tehiri and Tom Bedall were responsible, which means the Independence Rose came from two parents, both stolen. 'Independence Bastard Rose' they should have called it."

Both men laughed.

"So!" said the Police Chief. "The question is, what should I do?"

"You've just done it," replied the Resident Commissioner.

"I have?" said Tanner.

"And you must do nothing further," said Herd, "until I hear from my Lord and Master, the Honorable Attorney-General of the wise and just people of New Zealand and, for the time being at least, these Splendid Islands."

"I'll drink to that," said the Police Chief, raising his glass. "To the wise and just people of New Zealand, and the miracle they may continue to govern us." He paused, in search of the right word. "Forever."

CHAPTER 36
TALKING NUMBERS

"Mr. Prime Minister," said Brigadier Gilbert, "it might be of interest to take you through some numbers which I asked my people in Welcome Harbour to collect for your private use." It was typical of the former war hero to lead from the front. Gilbert reached for his notepad, flipped to a dog-eared page, and began to read. "This Reverend is overwhelmingly the popular leader, ninety percent approve of him."

"The man hasn't done anything yet," complained Holyoake. "Wait until he makes an unpopular decision. Then we'll see what his numbers look like."

"On the other hand," the spymaster continued, "there's our whistleblower, Rumsey. Seventy percent think he has done a good job leading the farmers' revolt."

"Must be uncomfortable for our Reverend Brown," said Holyoake. "A deputy so close behind." The Prime Minister was a master politician and could spot a weakness at fifty yards.

"More than seventy-five percent of the population favor independence. No surprise there. Here is the surprise: nearly sixty percent approve of the job we have done running their messy island paradise."

"But they favor independence nevertheless," said the

Prime Minister. "Ungrateful sods."

"People love the idea of the Independence Rose," the Brigadier continued. "Important symbol, I would say."

"Anything else?" said Holyoake, whose tolerance for bad news was wearing thin.

"Their negotiators won points over that deal with Pacific Islands Shipping."

"I'm sure they did."

"We found a sleeper issue," said Gilbert, who had decided to save the best for last. "Forgotten in the turmoil, I would say. The people of the Splendid Isles value their New Zealand passports greatly indeed."

"Even though there are only several thousand working here?"

"Nearly ten percent of their population," reminded Brigadier Gilbert. "And they remit most of their salaries back home."

"So, if their New Zealand passports were threatened in any way," mused Holyoake, talking almost to himself, "by, say, the Splendid Isles gaining independence?"

"Precisely, Prime Minister."

"And sixty percent, you say, think we are not such bad fellows, after all? Perhaps it is time," said Holyoake, "for us to go on the attack."

"I was thinking the same," said Gilbert, who saw himself as something of a James Bond, with the frozen heart of a spy and the cold-blooded mind of a master tactician.

*****

Butterfly cakes landed in a semicircle on the plate between the two men as they sipped tea and sat on the QR's uncomfortable chairs.

242

"There are several matters we must discuss," said Sir Jonathan O'Dowd. "Am I to assume I will read an account of what I say in the *Telegraph* in the morning?"

"I breached a confidence. I apologize for it," said Reverend Brown.

"You achieved your goal," said the QR. "I do not fault you for that." He looked up at the churchman and fixed him with an icy gaze. "I would prefer, however, that no more leaks occur. If you have concerns from now on, please bring them directly to me."

Reverend Brown did not respond, and the QR, professional diplomat that he was, allowed the matter to drop. "You need to review the draft constitution. It is due to be passed by the Parliament in Wellington in the next several weeks. I can leave it with you. I also have something delicate to discuss. More tea?"

"Thank you," said Reverend Brown.

"The *Jalisco Belle* is halfway to Auckland, your produce safe and sealed in her hold."

"At least that is behind us now," said Reverend Brown.

"I think not," said the Queen's Representative.

*****

Later, over cigars and sherry, Reverend Brown and Professor Buchanan reviewed the events of the day.

"In your theory, this is an early shot across the bow," said the Reverend. "But it feels like a blow amidships to me."

"It is a clever move," agreed the Professor, "and it gives you a three-way choice. Absorb the blow. Weather the storm."

"I do not like it," said Reverend Brown. "First, the headlines: 'We have won you thirty percent.' And now? What am I to say? 'More than half the produce is rotten; the shipping company will not pay for it'?"

"You need not put it like that," said the Professor.

"The QR is a slippery man for negating his promise." Reverend Brown mimicked the Government's man: "'For everything you have grown. Whether it is rotten or not.' I am keen to hear the second choice?"

"It is a question of how the numbers are conveyed."

"I do not follow your thinking," said the Reverend.

"My dear fellow, the thirty percent stands. Naturally, you will say, it applies only to produce which is fit to sell. There is sense in that. Or, the other way around: 'We have achieved fifteen percent for all your goods, whether spoiled or not.'"

"I see the line," said Reverend Brown, "and I do not like it. The farmers will say we chased our tail while their livelihood rotted on the wharf. And they will be right to say it."

"In that case," said Professor Buchanan, "there is only one possible course. You will have to go back to Government House."

*****

This time, there were no butterfly cakes. No tea. Perhaps cook had the day off. Nor did they sit in the conservatory on hard metal chairs, but in the QR's private office.

"On the matter of the price for our produce on the *Jalisco Belle*," said Reverend Brown without pleasantries, "what you have proposed is unsatisfactory to us and contrary to your promise."

Sir Jonathan O'Dowd did not rise to the insult. Professional diplomats seldom do. They are trained to ignore such attacks as a sign of weakness, which they usually are.

"The offer was made, informally, privately, and in good

faith, I grant you that," allowed the QR. There was no hint of irritation in his voice.

"I expect you to honor it," said Reverend Brown.

"But it was withdrawn. I made that clear."

Before the churchman could reply, Sir Jonathan raised a hand. "We could go on like this for the rest of the day. Do you have a proposal to put to me?"

Reverend Brown and Professor Buchanan had tugged at this question well into the previous night, but could think of nothing they could surrender that New Zealand might want badly enough to buy.

"They have raised the rotten fruit for a reason," counseled the Professor shortly before retiring to bed. "It is a bargaining chip. Therefore they have something to put to you. They will want something that is valuable to them. With luck, it will be something of little value to you."

"I am sorry," said the Reverend. "Do I have a proposal? I am afraid I do not. Perhaps there will be a way to repay this favor when we are a nation and New Zealand our closest, dearest friend."

The QR produced a thin smile. "Affairs between nations are not like that. We need a firmer footing for a deal to be made."

"What do you want, that is in our power to give?" said Reverend Brown.

The Queen's Representative drew closer and opened his hands in mock despair. "I can think of nothing," he said, and then tilted his head as if struck by a thought. "Maybe," he murmured, as though to himself. "No," he answered a question that had not been asked. "No," he repeated more firmly. The debate was lost. "It is a silly idea."

Reverend Brown did not reply. I am a dancer, he thought, and I am being waltzed around the floor. Provided I do not step on his toes, or on my own, we may get to where he wants me to go.

"Maybe not so silly," the QR teased, more loudly this time.

Still the Reverend held his tongue.

"It is a half-developed thought, inspired by the fisherman across the road."

The Reverend turned to look out the window where an islander in an outrigger canoe cast his net over the flat lagoon. "You want to buy our fish?" he said.

"In a manner of speaking. There may be some small value in your fishing rights."

"We could not fish our own lagoon?"

"I talk only of the international rights," said the QR. "Your own rights would be unaffected."

"Who holds those rights today?"

"New Zealand," said the QR, "since you are our protectorate."

"And in return?"

"The new price for your produce would be honored. However much is rotten."

"This will be in writing?" said Reverend Brown.

"Everything will be in writing," the QR confirmed.

*****

"Luckily," said Reverend Brown to Professor Buchanan, "we have averted what I feared would be a disaster."

"How is that?" asked the Professor.

"New Zealand already holds the international fishing rights, so we have given away nothing that is not already gone."

"Splendid news," said Professor Buchanan. But, perhaps unusually, he missed the point.

CHAPTER 37
TALKING TURKEY AGAIN

RW Rumsey was by no means a drinking man, but he sipped a shandy nevertheless. He sat with *Telegraph* editor Aaron Trieger at what was described as a 'discreet table' at Trader Mike's. There were no discreet tables at Trader Mike's, since almost everyone in Welcome Harbour drank at the town's most famous watering hole. Only a non-drinker like RW could imagine that discretion and Trader Mike's went together. But he saw no one he knew, and therefore imagined his meeting would not be noticed. He was headed, however, for darker shoals.

"Again?" said Trieger, whose own 'poison', as he liked to describe it, was 'whisky, straight up'.

"Very well," said RW, "but a little more lemonade this time."

Whether Trieger obeyed could not be known, but the drink that came back from the bar seemed as strong as the last, and RW was already light-headed.

"I thought we should get to know each other," said Trieger. "After all, you will be our Deputy Prime Minister within the month."

"Oh, there is a difficult path before we get to that—" began RW.

But Trieger interrupted before he could finish. "You are a shy man," he said. "Our readers would like to know you a little better."

RW smiled and took a breath. "I was born—"

Again Aaron Trieger interrupted. "I am more interested in your time working for the New Zealand Government."

"There is little to know. I was an audit accountant in the Finance Department."

"There is more to it than that," said Trieger.

"It is water under the bridge," replied RW who, to his surprise, had finished his shandy.

"Another?" urged the newsman.

His third drink seemed even stronger than the last, but Aaron Trieger was a pleasant fellow, and who can resist talking about himself when asked? Nor could RW resist the human temptation to sound a little grander, a little bolder, than he'd actually been. "I uncovered some irregularities in the imprest account for one of our clients," he said. 'Client' was jargon for another agency of Government.

"What sort of irregularities?" Trieger's questions seemed to have a pull to them, but RW, blurred by alcohol, did not notice.

"Deficiencies in the ledger entries," said RW. He relaxed a little more. Aaron Trieger had neither pen nor notebook. It was not so much an interview as a conversation between friends.

"What sort of deficiencies?" urged the newsman.

Whether it was the flattery of being asked to talk about himself, the alcohol, the attentive company, or a desire to uncork what had been inside him so long, RW found himself unblushing, and in expansive mood. "Cash deficiencies," he answered. "Large ones."

"And where had these—" Trieger labored the word,

"—'deficiencies' gone?"

"I never got quite that far," said RW. "Bundled out. Transferred to a branch office of the Ministry of Works in a place called Taupo. Fishing spot. Bit of tourism. An asphalt depot," he said with disgust. "They transferred me to a job auditing road-building materials in the middle of the country."

Trieger did not seem interested, however, in Taupo, fishing, tourism, road building, or asphalt. He bored in: "You said these cash deficiencies were large?"

"In one month—" said RW "—I shouldn't be telling you this. Seven thousand pounds."

"Doesn't sound like a lot to me," said Trieger. "For a government, I mean."

"From an imprest account?" said RW.

"What is an imprest account?"

"Petty cash, Mr. Trieger."

"And no idea where these funds might have gone?"

By this time RW was on his fourth shandy and his guard well down. Besides, how could it hurt after several years? "The spooky boys," he said coyly.

"By which you mean the intelligence service, whatever its proper name?" This was disingenuous indeed. There was not a reporter alive who did not follow the secret world as closely as he could. The two professions so often swam in the same dark pond. "How can you know that?" Trieger asked.

"The account numbers," said RW, finally realizing he had gone too far. "Really," he tried, "this is nothing to do with anything."

But Aaron Trieger was not put off. "And this imprest account was owned by whom?"

It is the art of the journalist that an answer given, leads straight to the next. For RW Rumsey there seemed only one place to go. "The administration office for a New Zealand protectorate," he said.

"Righty-oh!" said Trieger.

RW had the sinking feeling he had gone too far. But he also seemed to have lost his brakes. "Which we're sitting in at the moment." His lips trembled. Then he began to giggle like a child.

It is not often a reporter loses interest in the middle of a story, but Aaron Trieger did so now. He changed tack and called for fresh drinks. "You're right," he said mildly. "All of that is yesterday's news."

"Oh! It never made the news," said RW, now speeding ahead.

But Trieger ignored the comment. "I'd like to share some information with you. We've done a bit of polling at the paper. You will be pleased to hear you are well regarded in these Splendid Isles. Your approval rating is seventy percent."

RW nodded politely. He was starting, quite suddenly, to feel ill.

"Makes you a natural for the Deputy Prime Minister," said Trieger. And then, archly: "Some say more than that."

But RW Rumsey, island accountant and decent man, was beyond conversation at this point. "I have to go," he managed to say. Fortunately, Dan Tehiri's cab was at the door. He was transported home and straight to bed.

*****

The next morning he could remember little of the previous night. They'd talked of his transfer to the Ministry of Works. He remembered that. And seven thousand pounds, which was terribly indiscreet. He had not mentioned the NZSS, he was fairly sure, since that secret was buried deep inside him and would not be loosened by a few drinks. The thought did not occur to him that Aaron Trieger had gone for the center of things, like a dog for a bone. But the affair had never made the news. How, then, had the dog known where to dig?

There was one exchange that lingered in RW's head and would not go away: 'Makes you a natural for the Deputy,' Trieger had said. 'Some say more than that.'

A tiny seed had been planted. Probably it would never grow.

CHAPTER 38
OVERSTAYING WELCOME HARBOUR

There were no sirens or lights, but it was a grim Police Chief who alighted from the squad car, nonetheless. Flanked by two junior officers, he knocked on the door with the urgency somehow learned by all police: a loud knock that was also a threat.

"Good morning, Mrs. Hana. I wonder whether Titus Bernd Buchanan stays at this address?"

Her eyebrows arched in surprise, but she politely ushered the three men inside. "What do you want with Professor Buchanan?" she asked.

"Police business," said Ned Tanner. "We desire to speak to him, if he is in residence."

"Important business indeed, if the Chief of Police comes himself. Wait here while I go and tap on his door."

Professor Buchanan shuffled into the sitting room in slippers and a dressing gown. Silvery stubble lined his face; he had not yet shaved or had a bath. His sparse hair was uncombed. "Gentlemen," he said, producing a smile, "please take a seat."

"We'll remain standing, thank you," said Tanner.

"As you wish," said Professor Buchanan. His smile slowly drained away.

"You entered the Splendid Isles on a tourist visa. That is correct?"

"I would have to look at my passport to check."

The Police Chief waved the offer away. "Eighty-two days you have been our guest."

"That sounds correct," said the Professor. "Is something wrong?"

"I would like you to come to the station. We can discuss it there."

When they left the rectory, the ker-klunk, ker-klunk of a newsman's camera could be heard as Aaron Trieger circled his prey. The photograph showed the Professor held almost off the ground by two young policemen, with Ned Tanner following close behind.

*****

Reverend Brown was part way through a midweek service when he received a discreet note form his housekeeper. It took an hour for the last parishioner to be shooed away. He hurried from the Church to the old Austin, crank-started by Mrs. Hana and idling patiently in the drive. He drove quickly to police headquarters, where he asked to speak with the Chief. He was ushered to a room, bare except for a table and two cheap chairs.

"Reverend," said Chief Tanner, who arrived, beaming, moments later. "I dare say there are some souls here to save."

"There is one who interests me. It is why I have come."

"I am not at liberty to discuss an individual," said the Chief, replacing his smile with a still pleasant frown. "I may not be able to help you at all."

"I am enquiring about Professor Titus Buchanan. You

took him from the rectory today."

"He chose to accompany us," corrected the Chief, retreating to the leaden politeness police often use.

"What is the problem," said Reverend Brown. "Why is a distinguished Professor from America held by you here?"

Ned Tanner was by no means an evil man. Nor brave. He had a sense for self-preservation, however, and it smoothly kicked in. He had been ordered to pick up this Professor by his boss, the Attorney-General of New Zealand. But standing before him was the anxious churchman who might shortly be Prime Minister, and therefore beholden to no one, least of all Ralph Hanan. "Reverend, we should discuss this in my office, if you will come this way."

"As you wish, but I want to understand what has happened and how it can be set right."

"Of course," said Tanner, as he ushered the Reverend to a more comfortable room. "I would say the same myself. It is a question of formalities."

"That does not sound so difficult to fix."

"Professor Buchanan, innocently no doubt, has breached our immigration rules and has been asked to leave."

"He is to be deported from the Splendid Isles?"

"'Deported' is too strong a word. He has agreed to go."

It was not too strong a word for the next morning's *Splendid Islands Telegraph*, however—'FUTURE PM'S HOUSE GUEST DEPORTED'—or for the story that ran beneath a large photograph of an ashen Professor, frog-marched from the rectory in dressing gown and slippers. A second, more distant picture showed the glazed Professor escorted up the stairs of a waiting Electra aircraft at Briggs Field.

'Police last night deported an American college professor for visa violation,' the story read.

THE MAN IN THE SPIDER WEB COAT

Professor Titus Buchanan, a house guest of possibly soon-to-be Prime Minister and local church leader, Reverend Geoffrey Brown, was escorted onto a TEAL flight to Auckland. From there he is expected to be placed on another aircraft which will take him back to America.

Sources said the Professor had engaged in unspecified work activities during his apparent vacation, and had overstayed his sixty-day tourist visa by twenty-two days.

A police spokesman confirmed it was the first time he could recall an individual being asked to leave the Splendid Isles.

Reverend Brown said he was mystified and appalled by what he described as disgraceful overuse of police power.

Keith Holyoake allowed the paper to fall back on his desk. "This story in the *Herald*," he said with satisfaction, "is identical to a story which appeared in the Splendid Isles. I would say, 'score one for the good guys'. Wouldn't you agree?"

The other members of the kitchen cabinet nodded as one.

"Excellent piece of work, Prime Minister. Truly excellent," enthused Harry Lake.

"The credit belongs to Ralph," said the PM.

"Thank you," said the Attorney-General, mocking himself with an exaggerated bow. "I believe we have stripped our troublesome churchman of his principal advisor, which is good for us and bad for him."

"We have strewn a small rock in the Reverend's path to

power," said Spy Chief Gilbert. "Perhaps we could understand more of the Prime Minister's thinking about our plans now for the Splendid Isles?"

"We should not let them go," said Harry Lake. "They are more valuable as a protectorate than as a free nation state."

"I agree with Harry," said Ralph Hanan, emboldened by his recent glory.

"Gentlemen," said the Prime Minister. "We have already rejected this option. Our decision is made. We cannot turn back."

There was a murmur of assent as the kitchen cabinet fell into line.

"It does not mean," said the PM, "that we should not extract our pound of flesh. Your man in the Splendids, O'Dowd," the PM looked at the Attorney-General, "has already made an excellent start."

But it was Harry Lake who replied. "Indeed!" he said.

"Harry," said Holyoake, responding to the cue, "why don't you fill us in?"

"With pleasure, Prime Minister," enthused the Finance Minister. "We have negotiated, through Ralph's man, for New Zealand to have exclusive international fishing rights inside the economic zone of the Splendid Isles. The zone is presently three miles. There are moves, however, for it to be increased to twelve. Iceland has already achieved a twelve-mile limit. Peru, Argentina, Chile and Ecuador have won a two-hundred mile limit, which we believe may soon be the standard."

"One million pounds a year it will mean to us," said the Prime Minister, cutting the discussion short. "Harry and I have been working to identify other benefits, if we are smart enough to handle this independence in the correct way."

"That is right," said Lake, following the Prime Minister

into the water. "We have found millions of pounds that can, and should, be steered to New Zealand, since our wise leadership has made the Splendid Isles what they are today."

"Bill," said Holyoake to Brigadier Gilbert, "you have also been busy."

"There has been discussion with RW Rumsey," said Gilbert, "the Deputy to our Reverend Brown. He is the whistleblower who came within a hair of causing grief for our Secret Service several years ago. It is unfortunate he moved to the Splendid Isles."

"Out with it," said Holyoake.

"It is why he blew the whistle, Prime Minister. He uncovered a financial facility for certain operations, buried at insufficient depth in the Splendids' accounts."

"A slush fund," said Holyoake. "And we allowed him to move there?"

"Prime Minister," said Gilbert, "he had no reason to ask our permission, and, in any event, could not have been stopped. We shall make the best of the hand we have been dealt."

"Anything else?" said Holyoake.

"As expected, he remains bitter about being removed from his post."

"As expected," echoed the Attorney-General.

"He is also largely a non-drinker," said Gilbert. "Indiscreet when occasionally drunk."

"No surprise there," said the Attorney-General.

"So, for both reasons," resumed Gilbert, "it would be unhelpful for us if this bitter, indiscreet accountant toppled the churchman, and took his place."

"That's never going to happen," said Harry Lake.

"With help it might," said Brigadier Gilbert. "From the

Prime Minister and myself."

"That is correct," confirmed Holyoake. "It was considered."

"A seed of ambition has nevertheless been planted in the whistleblower's treacherous mind," Gilbert added.

"Ambition for what?" asked the AG.

"To be prime minister of the Splendid Isles."

"Even though such ambition is unhelpful for us?"

"The ambition is helpful," said Gilbert. "Its fulfillment is not."

"I am lost," confessed Harry Lake.

"Me too," agreed the AG.

"Bill?" said Holyoake.

"It is another rock in the path," said Gilbert. "An ambitious, disloyal, treacherous deputy is a limit on power. We also considered Thomas Bedall, the man they call 'the village idiot'."

"As prime minister?" said the Attorney-General, incensed. "Would it not be dangerous if a fool were in power?"

"There are two views of our village idiot," said Gilbert. "That he was outsmarted by your shipping chairman, or that the reverse is true."

"That's preposterous," spluttered Hanan.

"Gentlemen," said the Prime Minister, "we are here to review options, not assign blame."

"In any event," said the Brigadier, "we have planned for him a valuable role. And we have cast about the island for another, suited for a particular task."

"Wrapping this up," said Holyoake, cutting Gilbert short, "the churchman is to be their Prime Minister. But his people will pay a heavy price. And the Splendids will not be free. They will only seem to be."

CHAPTER 39
A NEWSMAN CALLS

When Aaron Trieger knocked, it was neither urgent nor a threat; though in truth it was more dangerous than the police who had knocked before.

"I have come to see Reverend Brown, if he is at home," said Trieger, with a newly minted smile, a bottle of the finest sherry, unopened, and a bag of homemade scones from the café in Welcome Harbour.

"I shall see if he is available," Mrs. Hana sniffed.

"I have come on a private matter," said Trieger to his host, once he had been shown to the study. He handed over the sherry. "I know it is your favorite. The scones will help us wash it down."

"You have come to tell me I am to be deported as well?" enquired Reverend Brown. The humiliating departure of Professor Buchanan was fresh in his mind. He already missed the advice of the mysterious academic and his 'thesis', as he called it, which had so far proved correct. "Have the police decided to deport us all? They have made a good start, if they intend to go on."

The question was preposterous, since Reverend Brown was born in Welcome Harbour and a lifelong citizen of the Splendid Isles. He could not be deported and knew it. He unsealed the bottle and splashed generous portions of Trieger's fine sherry into two greasy glasses, which had been rinsed but never with soap, since the Reverend believed soap destroyed taste.

"Hardly," said the newsman. "Professor Buchanan is a topic, however, I wish to discuss."

"I shall be keen to hear your take on it," said the Reverend.

"And there are some other matters," said Trieger. He raised his glass. "A toast to our new Prime Minister."

"I shall drink to that when these Splendid Isles have achieved their independence, and I am chosen by the people to lead them."

"I had thought you needed only the vote of the Party which you head?" said Trieger.

"The parliamentary members. But they are elected by the people, so it is the same thing."

"Not quite," said Trieger. "You require five of nine votes. One of them is already in doubt." He sipped his sherry. "Should we have a scone?"

But the Reverend's mind was no longer on food of any kind.

"Your Deputy has become a risk," said Trieger.

"I do not believe it. RW and I are joined at the hip."

"The fate of our nation is up for grabs," warned Trieger. "You would do well to hear me out."

From the door came the delicious smell of a strawberry rhubarb pie, which sat beneath a dusting of cinnamon and nutmeg, and was accompanied by a bowl of freshly whipped cream. The pie was placed between them. Mrs. Hana left without a word.

The newsman's eyes were drawn to the delicious dessert. He helped himself to a generous slice. The bag of scones lay unopened. "Do you know the background of RW Rumsey? That he left New Zealand almost literally in his socks? That he cannot return to this day? That he covets your job more badly than his own?"

"I know none of those things. I shall be fascinated to hear how you come to know of them, and if they are true," said the Reverend.

"Journalists know a great many things," said Aaron Trieger. "We are the fool with the camera and the notebook. We ask our questions. We write our stories. It is amazing the snippets we are told in our busy day. RW Rumsey breached the Official Secrets Act. Exploited a job he should not have had. Dug deeply for information he had no right to know. And," said Trieger, "threatened to reveal information vital to New Zealand's national interest."

"So he was deported to the colonies?"

"By mutual agreement," said the newsman, "through the kindness of the authorities, he was allowed to resettle here." This was a long way from what had really happened, but Aaron Trieger trotted out the story he had been told to tell. "Where he emerged as President of the Farmers' Federation. Now he is a heartbeat from Deputy Prime Minister—and your job."

Reverend Brown sipped his sherry and unwrapped the cellophane from a cigar. He puffed until he was sure it burned with an even glow. "You make it sound as though it were part of some gigantic plan."

"Do you mind?" asked Trieger, reaching into the box of cigars.

"Not at all," said Reverend Brown.

"It is too large a construction," said the newsman, blowing a smoke ring into the room. "I am not saying there is a gigantic plan. We do not know who he works for."

"'We'?'" said the Reverend.

"The New Zealand Government," recovered Trieger, who was a fine spy and a fine reporter. But it was sometimes impossible to avoid error in his complicated world.

"He is an accountant. With a private practice in Welcome Harbour," protested Reverend Brown.

"It is one possibility," allowed the newsman. "He is certainly so, on the outside at least."

"You are describing something evil and disloyal," said the Reverend.

"I would like to turn your attention to another matter," said Trieger.

But the Reverend's mind was only half on the conversation as he processed what the newsman had told him. RW Rumsey was treacherous and could not be trusted? Clumsy with information he should not have had? A threat to national security? Ejected to Welcome Harbour to live harmlessly on a beach far away? But he was not harmless, if he ever had been. As Aaron Trieger pointed out, the island accountant was a heartbeat from power. Most worrying of all was the seed Trieger had planted that RW was a puppet on someone else's string, that RW Rumsey was, in fact, a spy. Reverend Brown had never met a spy, as far as he knew. His instinct was to avoid them as he would a poisonous spider. He wrenched his attention back to the present. "You said you had something to say about Professor Buchanan and the shameful way in which he has been treated?"

"I have something to say about that," said Aaron Trieger. "Perhaps I can solve a piece of the puzzle. He runs a think tank in New England. It is outside Boston."

"I know where it is," snapped the churchman.

"As we reported," said Trieger, ignoring the Reverend's irritation, "the New Zealand Government believes he has been advising you about the future of the Splendid Isles."

"Your report did not say that, but the Professor and I have talked from time to time," conceded the churchman. "He is a clever man."

"His think tank is richly funded. The source of those funds is a deep concern."

Reverend Brown nodded impatiently. He was keen to glean anything more about the mysterious Professor.

"Navy," said Trieger. "He is funded by the US Navy."

"And the concern is what, if that is true?"

"Navy goes to Defense, which goes to certain three-letter agencies, as they are sometimes called."

"Three-letter agencies?"

"CIA is one," said Trieger. It was a small clue. An amateur —a newsman, for example—would have said 'the CIA'. But Reverend Brown did not notice the tiny slip.

"So Professor Buchanan is now a spy?"

Having approached the line, the editor deftly danced away. "There is insufficient information," he said. "It may not be right."

"The police deported him because the Government believes a sixty-one-year-old professor at a liberal arts university is funded by the Navy, which is tenuously linked to the CIA, and he is therefore an American spy?"

"Reverend, I did not say I could solve this puzzle for you. Merely that I could shed light on a few of its pieces."

"I have a question. How can you know any of this?

"A whisper," said Trieger, "from a highly placed source."

"Hmm," said the Reverend."

"There is one other matter I would like to discuss."

"What is that?"

"Tom Bedall," said Trieger.

"He is a spy as well? For the American CIA? Maybe he drives an Aston Martin like James Bond. Hidden in the shed with his tractor—and his goat, if it has not been eaten."

"Tom Bedall desires your job."

"I will think about what you have said about RW Rumsey. I shall reflect upon the rumors you have heard concerning the United States Navy. But at Tom Bedall, I must draw a line. He is a simple fellow who toils in his field and does not think much about anything at all."

"He dreams of power, now you have given him a liking for the taste of it."

RW a spy? Tom Bedall a traitor? Could these claims be true? Was this the nature of power? Surrounded by friends, smiling to your face, waiting to plunge a dagger into your back?

"I would also like to mention a name," said Trieger. "Daniel Tehiri."

Also a spy? A traitor? But he was not of any consequence. Had played no role in the independence movement or the farmers' blockade, and had no crops. "He drives a taxi," said the Reverend.

"He is one of the best known men on the island. Would you agree?"

Best known because of his reputation for slipperiness, thought Reverend Brown. And the bloated boast on the side of his single cab, which was not yet paid for. "Well known. Yes," agreed Reverend Brown. "As are many people in such a small place."

"A possible candidate is what I thought. It is a mere idea. No more than that."

"Our list of candidates was selected weeks ago. I could not change horses now, even if this man were acceptable, which he is not." The Reverend drew deeply on his cigar and blew a plume of smoke into the air. "Mr. Trieger," he said, "we have never been friends. You bring me sherry, scones and free advice. You must forgive my asking why?"

"It is a fair question and I will give you an honest answer. You will be Prime Minister of this country before the month is out. The Splendid Isles has one newspaper, which I am pleased to own. There is, however, no radio of any kind."

"So this is what you want of me?"

"Also television, which is the future."

"You want a license for a radio and television station?"

"I will prove my value. You will decide."

"I would like to return to your advice that I am surrounded by a nest of vipers who would take my job."

"Reverend, that will always be true. You imagine all around you are loyal and have no ambition for themselves?"

"I had not considered it. Maybe I have lived in a paradise for fools."

"That is the only paradise there is," said Trieger, who perhaps for the first time spoke straight from the heart. "The rest of us live in a more treacherous place. Still," he said, rising to leave, "I cannot think of a more beautiful place for where it should be."

CHAPTER 40
THE QUEEN'S MAN

There is a peculiarity to power which is little understood. The closer one gets to it, the faster things move. It is like the universe in reverse. The planets do not spin around the sun: it is the sun itself which spins. Energy is drawn to it like money to an already wealthy man. Ned Tanner felt the growing power of Reverend Geoffrey Brown and treated him differently: as befits a man who may soon be your boss. The much-conflicted Aaron Trieger felt the power as well. He recognized it immediately, since journalists are used to being in the orbit of powerful men, or those who are headed there. The Queen's Representative felt it too, and it pulled him in many directions at the same time. Lend all assistance short of actual help to New Zealand, said his masters in London. Wellington, however, promised their own reward. Finally, there was his love for the Splendid Isles, where he wished to live out his years, and whose soon-to-be Prime Minister sat before him drinking tea.

Reverend Brown felt it, because a difference between powerful men and those who are not is the speed at which things come at you, and the gravity of the decisions that have to be made.

"I am to tell you your constitution was passed by the

Parliament of New Zealand last night," said the QR. They were at Government House, in the conservatory, perched upon the QR's uncomfortable chairs. "There was an important amendment we have not discussed."

"Amendment?"

"The law is operative, and your elections valid, only if there is a vote for change by two thirds of your people."

"What do you mean, 'vote for change'?"

"The ballot paper will have a box that reads, 'I wish to retain New Zealand's traditional guidance.' If more than one third of voters check the box, then I regret to inform you, your election is lost."

"So it is also a referendum on whether the people want independence or not?"

"That is the net of it," agreed the QR. "Surely you cannot object."

Reverend Brown sipped his tea. 'The men in the shadows who stand for everything wrong', Professor Buchanan had said. He pictured the ashen-faced Professor, frog-marched onto the plane. Now there was a second roadblock, unforeseen. It was the fear of change. If one third of the people did not cast a vote, there would be no parliament of any kind. The Splendid Isles would refasten its chains. Far-away Wellington would remain in charge.

Sir Jonathan O'Dowd faced what is sometimes called the diplomat's dilemma. To lead with the more junior issues, leaving those more important for last? Or tackle the big fish now, so the less important could be dealt with in their exhausted wake? "Tom Bedall—" said the QR, making his choice.

'He dreams of power now you have given him a liking for the taste of it,' thought Reverend Brown.

"—is a thief."

"Is he?" The Reverend could think of nothing more useful to say.

"The charge sheet will say it," said the QR. "Your candidate for North Harbour is to be brought before the court and charged with two counts of theft. It is only fair I warn you."

"Theft of what?" said Reverend Brown. He dreaded the answer he feared might come. Surely they had not uncovered the murky theft of the parent to the Independence Rose? Or the drunken sailor's wallet? Was there something else of which he was not aware? He struggled to recall Tom Bedall's shifting version of events.

"A sailor from the *Jalisco Belle* has reported it," said the QR. "The case is clear. Your candidate will be charged and no doubt convicted of common theft."

"It will be one man's word against another. How can the court possibly decide?"

The QR fixed Reverend Brown with a poker face. "He will be convicted," he said. "You can be sure of that."

The polls were just eight days away. The Reverend ran the gritty tableau through his head. Tom Bedall, cuffed, standing in the dock. The somber, booming voice of the judge: 'Guilty as charged. Both counts.' And the headlines that would immediately follow:

GOVT CANDIDATE JAILED

Below it, a photograph of the village idiot between two burly police. The Independence Rose would be revealed as a stolen bastard child, though the Reverend was not the first to think that. "And all of this will happen before the election?"

"Yes," said the QR.

"I do not know what to say."

The QR waited until his words had sunk in. Firstly, eliminate all hope. Then, a tiny chink of light. "There is an alternative which might be more acceptable. It could be concluded that it is one man's word against another."

"I agree wholeheartedly," said Reverend Brown.

"It would be folly to proceed if that were the case." The QR paused, then asked: "More tea?"

"Thank you," said Reverend Brown. His mind raced. It was not on tea.

"Are you aware of how tax receipts from the Splendids are dealt with in Wellington?"

"I am not."

"There is a delay, of course, before they are spent. We call those funds 'the float'. It would be advantageous to the New Zealand budget if the float for this quarter could be retained."

"You want to keep three months' taxes collected from the Splendid Isles?"

"The funds would be available to you as a loan. On terms acceptable to both governments. In the interests of warm and friendly relations. Do you understand?"

"Perfectly!" said Reverend Brown. The offer was clear. Tom Bedall would be charged and convicted of theft. There would be devastating damage to the Splendid Islands Party, not to mention its symbol, the Independence Rose—at the moment when the nation must go to the polls. Or the charges would vanish, as would the Splendids' tax receipts. Lent back to their owner at some unpleasant rate.

"There is another possibility," said the QR. "Do you know Dan Tehiri?"

Yes, thought Reverend Brown, but I would be astonished if you did. When was the last time the Queen's Representative had been seen in a cab, rather than his official Rolls-Royce?

"Probably it would be better if Mr. Bedall was dropped

from the ballot entirely. Tidier, if he returned to growing his crops," said the QR.

"The taxi driver Tehiri would take his place?"

"He is well known," said the QR.

Certainly in high circles and of late, thought Reverend Brown.

"A popular chap," continued the QR. "If Mr. Tehiri were to replace the thief Bedall, if that were to occur, then funds could be lent to your Government on—" The QR paused to choose his words. A diplomatic surgeon, selecting a scalpel for the bloody job at hand. "—on even more sympathetic terms," he said at last, and smiled.

'Even more sympathetic terms.' The phrase echoed in the Reverend's head. Borrow our own money at a crippling rate and retain Tom Bedall? Or replace him with the slithering Dan Tehiri and borrow our own money a little more cheaply? The carrot and the stick, thought Reverend Brown. How often it came to that. The carrot? The Splendid Isles would be free at last. Do what we say and all will be fine. The stick? Refuse and your world will cave in. He was being asked to ditch Tom Bedall. Replace him with the rapacious Dan Tehiri, whose black cab, by all accounts, matched the color of his heart. Tehiri had somehow become New Zealand's man and was to be parachuted into the Splendid Islands Parliament, a sloping figure in a peaked cap whose loyalty lay with the highest bidder, which was usually himself.

"There is one other matter," said the QR. "Perhaps it is time for a stronger drink."

"It is kind of you," said Reverend Brown, "but I think I shall stick with tea."

"This matter concerns yourself. It is raised because I have no choice."

They have nothing on me, thought the Reverend. His

relationship with Piata? Small beer. Widely rumored in any case. It would not be that. Some scandal linked to Professor Buchanan? The future Prime Minister a puppet on somebody else's string? Probably that was it, but 'undue influence' was all that could be said, unless it could be shown the American Professor represented some sinister force. He braced himself for what was to come.

"There is evidence, considerable it appears, you misappropriated—unthinkingly, I am sure of that—certain funds, a small amount, from the Splendid Isles Christian Church."

It took a few moments for the words to register. Like soldiers landing on a hostile beach, they were repelled at every turn. I stole money from my own Church! The gunfire stopped. The words had gotten ashore.

"A sum of ninety-one pounds." The QR was talking, still. "Misused to purchase an airplane ticket for Miss Tanisha Hana, your housekeeper's daughter."

"I know who she is."

"From Auckland to Welcome Harbour. In January this year. I have the date."

"I am also to be charged with theft? Convicted, no doubt. Jailed this week?"

"The penalty would be decided by the Court."

"Unless I am mistaken...."

"Unless what?" said the QR. For a moment he was genuinely lost.

"Unless I am mistaken, there is to be another deal," said Reverend Brown after a long pause.

"Are you sure you would not like a stronger drink?" asked the QR.

"No. Yes. I am sure."

"There is an aspect of your independence not yet

addressed. Splendid Islanders, as you know, travel on passports issued by New Zealand. It is the same with all our protectorates."

"We shall issue our own passports," said Reverend Brown.

"Unfortunately," the QR continued, "that does not much help."

"Why not?"

"They could not rank with a passport issued by us."

"I do not understand."

"They could not carry the automatic right to live and work in New Zealand, which is much valued, I believe, by your people."

"You are withdrawing our right to reside in your country as a price of independence? It is a cruel cost."

"There is another aspect, quite difficult as well. Three thousand of your countrymen live and work in New Zealand today."

"That is probably right," said Reverend Brown. "Do you threaten to throw them out? Deport three thousand to Welcome Harbour?"

"Not at all," said the QR. "A special visa could no doubt be created, enabling them to stay in place."

"So, the problem is not a problem at all?"

"The greater issue," continued the Queen's man, "is the funds they drain from New Zealand to support their families here."

"I do not see the problem," said Reverend Brown.

But the QR sailed on, a mighty ship of state on a mildly choppy sea. "We should like to create, shall we call it, a monetary export tax? It would not be unreasonably high."

"I think I shall have that drink now," said Reverend Brown, who took a moment to think while brandy was found, glasses located, a cap unscrewed. "I accept," he said, sipping his drink, and making the gravest decision in the blink of an eye. If this was a measure of greatness, the Splendid Isles had found its man. "I accept everything except the dumping of Tom Bedall."

Sir Jonathan O'Dowd was speechless. His mind raced. He did not expect the Reverend to crumple like a cheap suit. The QR was a diplomat, however. His face showed nothing but a polite smile. He rephrased the deal so the churchman's agreement could not be in doubt. "You agree New Zealand shall retain the taxation float for the current quarter?"

"Yes."

"We shall lend you the funds at a rate we agree?"

"Yes."

"And a tax on funds sent from New Zealand to here?"

"In return," replied Reverend Brown, "you will issue a visa enabling Splendid Islanders to live and work in New Zealand. Without restraint."

It was the QR's turn to agree.

"And neither Tom Bedall nor I shall be charged with any offense."

CHAPTER 41
A GLIMMER OF DESPAIR

Piata Hana was slender, nude and unashamed. She lay stretched across the bed, her head supported by a crooked arm. Only her eyes moved. They followed Reverend Brown as he paced the room.

"The cost is high," he said.

"You agreed to it. Is power so important you will do anything to get it? Or did you simply buckle to the blackmail?"

"I have not buckled," said the Reverend. "I have bought time."

"As you say, the cost is high."

He stopped pacing and turned to face her. "If I had choked on their poison instead of swallowing it sweetly, they would have moved against us in the morning."

"It was the risk," she agreed.

"Arrested. Dragged to court. Handcuffed to a sorrowful Tom Bedall, no doubt."

"You are right," she said. "There may have been no recovery from that—whatever the truth of the charges against you."

"There is the passport issue. I had not properly considered that. If the people of the Splendid Isles learn it is the end of their ability to work in New Zealand—"

"A lot of us would look at independence in a new light," she said, finishing his thought.

"And there are the Splendid Islanders living in New Zealand today. Would they be forced to go? It seemed to be the threat."

"You may not have thought it out, but someone did." She paused for a moment and then resumed. "Although I find it hard to believe they would follow through."

"The answer would not come until after the elections," said Reverend Brown. "Which we would certainly lose."

"Perhaps it is for the best," she said, as women will sometimes do when their men are in a dark place from which they see no escape.

"I am not looking for consolation," he said fiercely. "I have eight days to change the world, and no idea how to do it."

"Then let us take the issues one by one. Did Professor Buchanan not advise you how to justify Tom Bedall's theft?"

"'It is only fair this future member of Parliament, for whom you must shortly vote—'" The Reverend struggled to recall the Professor's artful defense. "'It is only fair he stole the rose from the Government which has plundered your Splendid Isles.' It sounded reassuring to me then," said Reverend Brown. "Less so now."

"Your own theft?" she said, "though I had not seen it like that."

"The amount was small. Taken without malice or consideration of the implications. For a good cause. But it sounds like 'Guilty with an explanation, your Honor.' I shall have to do better than that."

"Let us move to the referendum, sprung on us at the last moment," said Piata, still lounging across the bed.

"Wellington will argue they have a duty to govern, unless we can show a clear majority of Splendid Islanders prefer self-rule."

"This therefore is a concession which must be made," she said. "What of their other demands? The seizure of our taxes? 'The float', as they called it."

"Do not forget their generous offer to lend us our own money and to charge us interest for doing so," he added. "It is shameful and outrageous. We cannot live with this."

"Then we shall have to find a way around it. What of the visa they propose to create?"

"So we can enjoy the rights we have today? I do not like it, but I did not consider our right to work in New Zealand might be at risk. I believe we must bow to this."

"And their monetary export tax?"

"Never!" said Reverend Brown. "It is ruin for everyone who relies on the funds their loved ones send home. The icing on a bitter cake. Our people pay their taxes in full. They scrimp. They save. Now they are to be double-taxed on money that is taxed enough."

"I am going to fetch your cigars and sherry," said Piata Hana. "They will help you think."

"I suppose there is no pie?" he asked. Inside every man, a little boy.

She smiled and padded into the kitchen, naked and unconcerned as a newborn babe. Inside every woman, a little girl.

He smoked a cigar, consumed several glasses of the newsman Trieger's excellent sherry, and ate two pieces of hot peach pie wrapped in a pastry God must have made in heaven. "Piata," he said, "how much have we spent on the election so far?"

It is a curiosity of gifted cooks they do not often eat their own food. The housekeeper munched a chocolate cookie rather than her own peach pie. "About two hundred and twenty-one pounds," she replied.

"How much then is left in the account?"

Again the housekeeper did not hesitate. "Four thousand six hundred and fifty pounds. It is the donation from this nature wildlife coalition in America, which is all we have bothered to raise."

"I think," said Reverend Brown, who resumed his pacing, "we should spend the rest at once. Don't you?"

"Nearly five thousand pounds in just eight days?"

"It is a significant sum, I agree. But what do we gain if we save the money but lose the election, if independence is crushed, if our dreams for freedom are at an end? What good will the money do us then? We must spend it now. If we are clever enough, New Zealand will have no time to respond." He paused. "I believe I need Oxide at my side."

"Tanisha may be pleased to hear it," said Piata.

But the Reverend's mind was far away. "What time is it in Boston?"

"Five o'clock in the morning is too early to disturb your son."

"Nonsense!" he said. "Get him on the phone at once."

*****

RW Rumsey knocked on the door at nine.

Reverend Brown greeted him in a dressing gown. The churchman looked as though he had been up all night. A cigar hung loosely from one hand. The other held a glass of sherry. "RW. My friend. You and I have a great deal to do, and only eight days in which to do it."

At eleven o'clock the hissing roar of a steam tractor was

heard. "I came as quick as I could," said Tom Bedall, the man most saw as slow and simple. "What is it you want of me?"

By afternoon, the driveway was greasy from a passing squall. Clouds hung from a slate-gray sky. Piata Hana watched as a blue pickup fishtailed along at breakneck speed and slewed to a halt. There was a knock at the door. "Righty-oh!" a voice exclaimed. The newsman's footsteps receded down the hall.

Next arrived the odious Dan Tehiri, who cheated tourists and pretended his black Ford cab was one of many. The car was left idling beneath a tree.

I wonder whether he has put his meter on, thought the housekeeper, who bet he had. Even the sweet can sometimes be cruel.

"Perhaps we could sit in my study," she heard the Reverend say. There were no footfalls other than the Reverend's slippers, so Dan Tehiri must have crept down the hall. The door closed and stayed shut for a very long time. When they re-emerged, the cab driver nodded curtly to Mrs. Hana and left without so much as a word. His face showed nothing. She could not tell if he was happy or sad.

In the early evening, Sir Jonathan O'Dowd arrived in his black Rolls-Royce, which he drove himself and parked with care.

Most surprising was Police Chief Tanner, who parked his squad car by the church, knocked politely, and greeted Mrs. Hana as though she were a favored aunt.

Later there was a phone call from America. "You will never guess," she said. "Professor Buchanan is on the line."

Still later, a further call. "Someone in New York," she said.

It was past midnight before the rectory went to sleep. Seven days until a nation went to the polls.

CHAPTER 42
COUNTING CHICKENS

"They have agreed to everything, Prime Minister. Harry's monetary export tax. The seizure of their tax receipts." The Attorney-General glowed.

"*Retention* of their tax receipts," corrected Finance Minister Harry Lake. "Retention, as security for loaning them funds for further development of their ungrateful nation."

"Retention, of course," agreed Ralph Hanan. "We retain their money and lend it back to them, secured by the money they entrusted to us."

The Prime Minister chose not to enter this jousting between Ministers. "And our only concession is to create a new category of visa?"

"It is a small chore and costs the Treasury little," said Lake.

"We have also agreed," resumed the Attorney-General, "not to proceed with the prosecution of the churchman and the farmer, believed by some—" he glared at Brigadier Bill Gilbert, "—to be a rocket scientist rather than the village idiot he clearly is. The offer not to prosecute was the carrot."

"And the stick?" asked Lake.

Why, it was the threat the churchman and the farmer

would feel the full weight of the law." replied Hanan. "But I am pleased we do not have to test this stick, which might have been—" he searched for the word, "—awkward."

"Why is that?" pounced Gilbert. "I thought the thefts were cut and dried?"

"Do we really need to go there now?" appealed Hanan to the Prime Minister.

"I should like to hear the answer to Bill's question," said Holyoake, who was sometimes in a hurry, and sometimes had all the time in the world.

The Attorney-General sighed while he gathered his thoughts. "The Bedall case," he began, "turns upon the evidence of a junior seaman, who scrapes his living wiping the grease from our island freighter's diesel engine. When he is not doing that, he is either getting drunk in bars throughout the Pacific or, I regret to say, breaking the law."

"Breaking the law?" said Holyoake.

"The fellow has a charge sheet as long as your arm," said the AG. "Since there were no witnesses to the crime in question, the court would have to decide whether it preferred the testimony of the idiot, Bedall, or this barely educated sailor of dark character. Both men were, of course, drunk at the time."

"So, an uncertain outcome," surmised the PM.

"Particularly in the court of public opinion, which in a political matter such as this...." The Attorney-General faded away. Perhaps he was debating what next to say. "Besides," he resumed, "there were certain technical issues surrounding not only the idiot, Bedall, but the churchman as well."

"And what issues are they?" asked the Prime Minister coldly.

"There is a drafting error in the criminal code, which applies only to the Splendid Isles. For reasons not the fault of my Department, there is a defect, which is unfortunate." Hanan had a habit of waffling when embarrassed.

"'Error? Defect?'" pounced Brigadier Gilbert.

"Criminal law in the Splendid Islands," began the AG with exaggerated slowness, as though he were lecturing an unpromising student, "is based on the New Zealand Criminal Code of 1893, drawn itself from English law going back to 1840." He paused and smiled. "Naturally the code in New Zealand has been modernized several times."

"Naturally," repeated Brigadier Gilbert

"I am tempted to say, 'So what?'" said the Prime Minister.

The Attorney-General's smile developed a frost. "There has been no mechanism for modernizing the law in the Splendid Isles until the new constitution takes effect."

"You are telling us the churchman and the farmer would be tried for theft under laws which have not been updated for nearly seventy years?" said the PM. He was far from a stupid man, and arrived at the heart of the problem without effort.

The Attorney-General's eyes narrowed. His frosty smile became a tight, straight line. "It is an error going back to 1905, when the colony was handed to us by the Queen."

"And the consequences?" said the PM, staying firmly on track.

The Attorney-General's face now turned to granite. He was expressionless as a snow-capped peak. "There are provisions for whipping and flogging. Children as young as seven are treated as adults. There are numerous other provisions, which in these modern times may seem harsh."

"And this law has always applied in the Splendids?" said the PM.

"There is little crime there. It has been unnoticed."

"It would not be unnoticed in the full glare of a trial of their future Prime Minister," said Brigadier Gilbert. "Where top lawyers from New Zealand, and possibly England, or America, could be retained."

"It could be noticed," agreed the Attorney-General. He looked as though he were about to endure an unpleasant medical examination.

"We would be a laughing stock," continued Brigadier Gilbert.

"Who knows of this?" interrupted Holyoake.

"Senior members of my Department. The Queen's Representative, Sir Jonathan O'Dowd, who first raised it with us."

"We have pressed our case, with a measure of threats and concessions, for the good of New Zealand," said the Prime Minister. "Now we learn the threats are hollow, because we would look like fools if we went ahead. If the churchman or the farmer learns of this—"

"They will not learn of it, Prime Minister," said Hanan.

"Sir Jonathan O'Dowd knows!" thundered Holyoake.

"I can safely say, Prime Minister," replied the Attorney-General, "the Queen's Representative is loyal to your Government."

The clock ticked. The Finance Minister shuffled papers. The Prime Minister looked at the sweep hand of his completely silent, space-age watch.

Brigadier Gilbert was next to speak. "We have forgotten Tehiri, the cab driver. The threat of his prosecution for stealing the QR's rose is the stick that brought him into our embrace."

"That has been to no avail," said the AG. "It was the only point on which Reverend Brown stood firm. The thief Bedall will not be displaced by the thief Tehiri. We did not force the issue. The churchman had to win something. It was decided, in the heat of battle, to let him have this."

"And what of the whistleblower Rumsey?" said Gilbert.

"The Attorney-General and I discussed whether it was too late to charge him under the Official Secrets Act," intervened the Prime Minister. Ralph Hanan no longer had a name. He had become a job title that could be dispatched at any time, should the PM decide on a 'Cabinet re-shuffle', which was the name given to retribution against high officials.

"I did not hear of this," said Gilbert.

"We decided not to stir things up," explained the PM. Decoded, this meant the Prime Minister did not want to risk reading about it in the *New Zealand Herald*.

"I am pleased to hear it," said Gilbert. "Threatening Rumsey might blunt his ambition for power, which we have tried to fuel. That card—better, the threat of it—is best played if Rumsey himself becomes PM."

"Very well," said Holyoake. "We have had some surprises." He glared at the Attorney-General. "But we are on reasonable track. In seven days the Splendid Isles shall have their independence, and we shall have them by the throat."

CHAPTER 43
PARTY PEOPLE

Oxide Brown emerged from the L188 Electra as jaunty as a cock robin on a summer morning. The Austin idled at the curb. Piata Hana sat behind the wheel. "Good gracious!" she said, as Oxide threw a large portmanteau onto the back seat of the tiny car. "You have brought the kitchen sink."

"Not at all," said Oxide, who looked little the worse for his long flight from America. "I want to know everything that has happened." The car pulled away from the curb and into the traffic.

In the rearview mirror, had they looked back, could be seen a tall African sliding into the rear seat of a black Ford Custom.

"Where to?" said the cab driver from beneath his peaked cap.

"There is a hotel near the wharf," said the African in Oxford English with the slightest trace of a New York twang. He wore an expensive suit and carried a soft leather case that whispered good taste.

"Trader Mike's," said Dan Tehiri. "It is the only hotel on Welcome Island. It should not be hard to find."

Left waiting at the rank were two exhausted men in slacks, oxblood shoes and crumpled but fashionable Polo shirts. They looked American from head to toe.

"I am so looking forward to seeing our little friend, *Chelonia mydas agassizii*," said Harvey, the taller of the two.

"There'll be plenty of time for chasing turtles," said the other man, from beneath a graying crewcut and from behind dark glasses. "First, we have to get to the hotel. Hopefully Wilson Tuttle will be waiting for us when we arrive." Tuttle had 'hitched a ride to Tahiti with the Navy', as he described the arrangement, and had chartered a Beechcraft Travelair 95 for the six-hour last leg of his journey.

By the time the two men reached the hotel, Tuttle and the African had rendezvoused at an outdoor table and were sitting quietly in the sun. "The Macallan. 1940. Double. Ice," the black man ordered. But the waiter looked nonplussed. "Any kind of Scotch," the distinguished foreigner relented, anxious to create no fuss.

"I'll have a bourbon, straight up," added Tuttle. He spotted the two representatives from the National Turtle Research Foundation, who looked as though they had made the almost six-thousand-mile trip from Washington on foot. "Wendell! Harvey! I want you to meet my very good friend, Alex Quaison-Sackey." The men shook hands. "Alex is Chairman of the United Nations committee responsible for decolonization, and soon to be," he put a finger over his mouth to indicate a secret, "President of the United Nations Security Council."

*****

When the old Austin pulled into the driveway, Piata Hana tooted the horn. The front door flew open and Reverend Brown hurried out to greet his son. After Oxide finished hugging his father, he noticed Tanisha standing shyly to one side.

He looks taller, she thought. And a little fatter. But he has kept his boyish face.

What Oxide thought was not immediately known, since his father took him by the hand like a small child and led him inside. On the dining table sat plates of fresh tuna marinated in lime, chicken curry with banana, vanilla and sweet potato pie, and Oxide's favorite, which had not been forgotten, breadfruit baked golden brown. After the main meal, the Reverend ushered his son into the study, where cigars were lit and the last of Aaron Trieger's superior sherry was poured.

Mrs. Hana interrupted with a large bowl of pineapple and guava in coconut cream, and then the men were finally left to themselves.

"I contacted Professor Buchanan as you asked," said Oxide.

"He telephoned," said the Reverend, "as did this diplomat from the United Nations." The churchman looked at his son. "He has agreed to come."

"Such an important man, all the way from New York," said Oxide. "People will be impressed we have landed so big a fish."

"It is a great deal more than a fish we are trying to land, but I am hoping this man might help us do it."

"Father, he is the biggest fish we can imagine. I do not think you understand the honor his presence will bring to us."

"Perhaps you are right," said Reverend Brown, "although I am not sure he will mean so much to the people here in Welcome Harbour."

"What of Professor Buchanan? He is coming as well?"

"He has been helpful as always," said Reverend Brown, "but, because of the manner of his departure, he cannot be here."

Oxide looked surprised at this news, but did not reply.

"He is sending someone nonetheless," resumed the Reverend. "Several others, as a matter of fact."

"You have summoned me from America," Oxide said, "so I assume there is something you want me to do?"

*****

After a long time, Mrs. Hana poked her head into the study. "Three men have come to see you," she said.

"I am most grateful for your generous donation," said the Reverend, once the men were seated and Oxide had reluctantly withdrawn.

"When Professor Buchanan told us of your need," said the man who had been introduced as Harvey Wesner, "we could not refuse."

"You are a nature wildlife coalition? What is that?"

"Well," said Harvey, "as Wendell would say—"

But this was as far as he got before the man who had introduced himself as Wilson Tuttle intervened. "Turtles," he said.

"Turtles?"

"Yep," said Tuttle. "Your Splendid Isles are smack in the migration path for—" He turned to Wendell Steinbeck, who had not yet said a word. "What was the scientific name again?"

"*Chelonia mydas agassizii*," replied Harvey. "The magnificent green sea turtle. It grows to the size of a man."

"And these turtles swim in Welcome Harbour?" said Reverend Brown.

This time Wendell answered. "They can be difficult to spot, even though they are most certainly here. A facility would have to be built," he continued. "There would be special equipment, scientists. It would not intrude."

"This sounds like a discussion for another time," said Reverend Brown. Everything has a price, he thought. They make a donation, and demand some kind of laboratory in return.

"No problem," agreed Wendell. "We are here to witness your historic independence on behalf of wildlife lovers, as representatives of the green sea turtle. Isn't that right, Harvey?"

"Absolutely," agreed Harvey, who smiled around the edges of his dazzling white teeth.

"Mr. Tuttle?" said the Reverend, turning his attention to the leanest of the three. "Professor Buchanan thought you and I might talk."

Wendell rubbed his hands. "Well, Harvey and I will leave you to it."

"Cigar?" said the Reverend, as the others departed.

"Sure," said Tuttle.

"I have a rather unusual problem."

"The Professor told me."

"There may be some small danger involved."

"I am a SEAL," said Tuttle.

"Seals, turtles. Every kind of sea creature seems to have found its way to my door."

"Navy SEAL," clarified Tuttle, lest he be confused with the semi-aquatic marine mammal. "You know what that is?" Navy SEAL stood for 'special operations—SEa, Air and Land'. But Reverend Brown could not, in fact, have heard of SEALs, since they did not officially exist until the following year. A secret cadre of US Navy demolition frogmen was in training in 1961, however. Perhaps the American was a member of this and trying out their future name. It was one of numerous possibilities.

"Some kind of soldier?" guessed Reverend Brown.

"Uh-huh," said Tuttle.

"I would like you to almost start a quite small war." The Reverend could think of no other way to describe what he had in mind. An almost war, which would have to be almost fought. It would take the Splendid Isles almost to the point of catastrophe, if such a thing could be almost achieved. He explained his plan to the Navy SEAL, if that indeed is what he was.

Tuttle listened expressionlessly, and did not ask a single question. "No problem," he said. "You haven't got any bourbon have you? I like to drink when I smoke a cigar."

*****

There were neither migrating turtles as big as a man, nor seals of any kind, when Oxide and Tanisha strode the beach.

"You seem very grown-up," she said. They watched as breakers smashed onto the reef.

"I am twenty-six," said Oxide. "Almost a graduate engineer."

"I did not mean it that way," replied Tanisha. But she was in one conversation and he in another.

"Do you still think he is dangerous?" Oxide asked.

"Who?" asked Tanisha.

"The last time we sat on this beach, you told me my father was a dangerous man."

"Did I?" said Tanisha. She wrinkled her nose. "I had forgotten that. No. He is not dangerous. Not to us."

"Dangerous to some? Is that your view?"

"He is a great man. I did not see it before."

"Not dangerous then?" Oxide pursued.

"All great men are dangerous," she said.

"And Professor Buchanan? What is your opinion now of him?"

"Oxide," she said, "must we speak of this? You have been away so long. I thought we could talk of other things."

But Oxide waited for her answer nevertheless.

"My opinion of him has not changed."

"And our independence movement?"

"It is a living thing. It cannot be stopped."

"And my father, a great man?" he said, circling back.

"He is a great man," she said, taking his hand. "And so are you."

*****

At the rectory, Reverend Brown made a show of hunting for a fine Scotch whisky he did not have. "No Macallan," he said, after pretending to check. "But I do have sherry, if you will have a glass."

"Sherry would be wonderful," replied Alex Quaison-Sackey.

"I am honored you have come to see us."

"Nonsense," said the African diplomat. "I am delighted to visit your nation on the historic eve of its independence. You will be the third country to achieve it this year."

"I am reassured the path is so recently trod," said Reverend Brown. "No wonder the ground is so hard."

"And dangerous," said Quaison-Sackey. "Even though the illustrious Professor Buchanan is trying to make it less so."

"We are fortunate in dealing with New Zealand, which is one of the more benign powers," said the Reverend. "But we are not there yet. We may still fail."

"None of them are as benign as you think," said the diplomat. "Samoa, a neighbor of yours, has struggled for independence since she was seized by New Zealand during World War One. She was on the edge of it thirty years ago. Much as you are this very day."

Samoa, in fact, would finally achieve independence within a few months, on 1 January 1962. Intriguingly, the tiny island kingdom had also escaped Professor Buchanan's predictions, which meant his much-vaunted thesis still had flaws.

"The New Zealand military killed eleven civilians and a member of the Samoan Royal family during a peaceful protest. Pressed hard enough, they could do so again." Alex Quaison-Sackey sipped his sherry and looked closely at Reverend Brown. "There is one other thing I must say to you. If there is bloodshed, I cannot intervene."

CHAPTER 44
LIGHTING THE WAY

Oxide borrowed his father's car, cranked it himself without breaking his wrist, and drove to the library, which was next to the school. A fan swung slowly overhead but did little to break the heat of the day. There was a faint smell of books roasting on the shelf. Mrs. Tahata sat on a stool, date-stamping volumes that had been borrowed and returned. Welcome Harbour's meticulous librarian was notorious for levying ferocious fines for anything even slightly overdue. In her other life she manned the Tasman Empire Airways Limited Office at Briggs Field, where she ruled with a softer hand. Books were her life; issuing air tickets merely a job. After much thought she had agreed also to be a candidate for Parliament in the forthcoming poll.

"Mr. Oxide Brown, I do declare. It is a long time since I have seen you here. How is your father?"

"He is fine," said Oxide. "I have come—"

"And Piata?"

"Mrs. Hana is in excellent health," replied Oxide patiently.

"Tanisha?" asked Mrs. Tahata. "She has become beautiful, do you not agree?" But before Oxide could answer, she cut him off. "I do not have all day to gossip. If you are here for some purpose, let me hear it now."

At last Oxide was allowed to speak. "I have a request which is probably beyond the resources of our humble library," he began.

"I shall be the judge of that," replied Mrs. Tahata, bristling at the innocent slur.

Oxide tried again "I need to know everything there is to know about stage lighting."

"Everything is a lot to know," she replied frostily, "but if you require an introduction to the subject, I shall see if we have anything here." Mrs. Tahata swished past him. Sweet perfume hung in her wake like dust on the corner of a country lane. She climbed a step-ladder and reached for a leather tome on the topmost shelf. "A Method of Lighting the Stage," she announced, "by Stanley McCandless." She looked over the top of her glasses to make sure Oxide was listening. "Published 1932. I think this will do the job."

"Maybe something a bit more modern?" suggested Oxide, who had the disdain of the young for anything old.

"Do you know who Stanley McCandless is?" she asked.

Oxide shook his head.

"He practically invented stage lighting." Mrs. Tahata placed the book on the counter. "This," she said reverently, "is the bible."

*****

At the control tower at Briggs Field lay the pristine office of airport manager, parish president and Gardening Club treasurer Iwi, who had no other name. "Come with me, young man," he said, after Oxide had explained his mission. In an un-padlocked shed, under a dust-sheet, sat a searchlight on a trailer with four narrow tires. "Left behind by the Americans after the war," Iwi explained. "Perhaps it still works." Iwi whipped the cover from a second trailer. He was like a conjurer performing a trick. "This," he said, "is the generator, which I know still works since we use it occasionally, even today." Of equal value to Oxide, however, was the much-thumbed operations manual that hung from a chain.

Oxide thanked Iwi and drove to the Welcome Harbour movie theater, where he met the president of the local dramatic society, Mrs. Tiro Wiriwi, who was also office manager of Pacific Islands Shipping and, after much agonizing, a candidate for a seat in the forthcoming Parliament.

"Our storeroom is at the back," she said, fiddling with a key.

On a wooden floor, in a room that smelled of mothballs, sat mannequin dummies, mirrors surrounded by lights, boxes filled with makeup, racks of suits, papier-mâché swords, a lance made from a curtain rod, and other props from shows long past. Mrs. Wiriwi looked at the collection sadly. "There is not much call for real theater anymore. People prefer movies from Hollywood." She stepped over the theatrical junk into a smaller room off to one side.

"Ah!" said Oxide. "This is exactly what I want."

"I should think so, young man" she said, surveying the scene. "There is an inventory here which we shall check." She cleared her throat, pulled out a pen. "Six by five-hundred-watt ellipsoidals. Twenty-two by four-hundred-watt, six-inch Fresnels. Two by two-hundred-and-fifty-watt baby spots." She seemed prepared to go through a long list.

"Whoa!" said Oxide, raising a hand. "We shall be here all day. I will take the lot."

*****

"It is said that people will commit suicide when they judge their misery to be intolerable, inescapable and interminable," the Reverend murmured. It was the morning before the nation would go to the polls. Reverend Brown and Piata Hana lay entwined in bed. The sun shot a beam of yellow light into the room.

"Wherever did you hear that?" said the housekeeper, nestled in his arms.

"I wonder if it is what I am doing to the Splendid Isles," said Reverend Brown.

"Marching us to suicide? That cannot be so. You are giving our people the right to decide."

"Is our situation so intolerable?" he said. "Interminable?"

"We have endured it for sixty years," replied the housekeeper.

"Is that a point for or against?" The Reverend pounced. "The larger question is whether it is inescapable."

"It will be escaped tomorrow," she said. "You cannot doubt it."

"Oh, we may escape to independence, if my plan succeeds."

"You mean if it almost succeeds," corrected Piata, playfully, referring to the Reverend's instructions to the mysterious Wilson Tuttle to almost start a war.

But he ignored his lover's joke. "Of what use will the escape be if we are crippled by it? Impoverished. Shackled to the country that supposedly sets us free?"

"You are in strange mood," replied Piata, "for a man who will be Prime Minister tomorrow night."

"I have promised no bloodshed, as the Professor's thesis requires. But we are at the brink of it nonetheless," he lamented. "I do not know how things will turn out."

She leant over and touched a finger to his lips, a mother hushing a small child. *"Que será, será,"* she said, "Whatever will be, will be." It was the popular Doris Day song from the Alfred Hitchcock thriller, *The Man Who Knew Too Much.*

"I wonder if that is me," said the Reverend. "The man who knew too much—and destroyed a nation because of his own vanity."

*****

If there was to be a war, Wilson Tuttle was certainly dressed for it. He wore khaki pants, a T-shirt the color of dirty water, and canvas jungle boots. He had a web belt with a hunting knife. A borrowed .303 Enfield rifle hung from his shoulder. A metal box labeled 'DANGER EXPLOSIVES' sat beside him on the rectory porch. He was ushered into the kitchen. It seemed the right room for a man of war. Eat, drink and be merry, for tomorrow we die. He sipped coffee and waited for the others to arrive.

RW and Tom Bedall came together. 'Before I die, I would like to be involved in something important,' RW had said long ago. 'Even if I were to die because of it.' But he did not look much like a warrior. He wore his once-white shirt, though the armbands had been removed and the sleeves rolled up. The chain of his fob watch disappeared into the pocket of his trousers, which were cinched at the ankles. For protection, thought Reverend Brown—but protection from what?

Tom Bedall wore threadbare pants and workman's boots.

The Reverend hurried the two men inside, lest they be seen on the porch. He felt like a cartoon John Wayne about to deliver a speech at the Alamo. Piata Hana looked on. "The most important thing—" he began boldly, "—is to be safe," he finished lamely.

"No problem," said Tuttle.

If the Navy SEAL was part of the nature wildlife coalition, he reminded Reverend Brown of neither turtles nor seals. 'Red of tooth and claw' came closer to the mark. The Reverend watched as the three-man militia exited the rectory and vanished into the trees. Tuttle led with long, sure strides. Tom Bedall and RW skipped along in his khaki wake.

The kitchen had also gone to war. It shimmered with heat like a shore battery guarding the mouth to a palm-fringed bay. Bags of flour and sugar lay strewn about. The oven door opened and shut like the breech of a gun that fired apple pie and strawberry tart.

"My god!" said Oxide, surveying the scene. "You're baking enough to feed an army." It was perhaps not far short of the truth. Kitchens throughout Welcome Harbour were hard at work. "Father," he said, turning to the troubled Reverend, "you are looking at not merely an electrical engineer, but a son who is now expert in stage lighting."

"I am pleased to hear it," said Reverend Brown. "Tell me what you have done."

"Set up a General Electric World War Two searchlight which can throw eight hundred million candlepower of light up to twenty-five miles. Naturally, this is too much for our needs. I have found a way to turn it down."

"A wise decision," said the Reverend, "since our goal is to light the path to independence, not bleach it to the bones."

""I have also applied the McCandless Method, which is to use three spots upon the stage." The famous technique enabled an actor—a politician perhaps—to be shaped by light so they became the total focus of the spectator's eye.

"McCandless?" said the Reverend, unfamiliar with the name.

"Oh, Father!" said Oxide, feigning despair. "Everyone has

heard of him." And then, more seriously: "But I am a bit player behind the scenes. Is there no more important role for me than this?"

"Son," replied the Reverend, "you are producing, I would say literally producing, the self-government of a tiny nation, which, like your borrowed lights, has been in darkness far too long. This will be a moment in history, my boy, as you once said to me. One day, when I am gone, you will lead these Splendid Isles to greater things."

"There will be many competitors for that job," said Oxide.

"But you," said the churchman, "will be positioned to win."

Piata Hana opened the oven door and removed a tray. It exuded the most delicious smell. Through the kitchen window could be seen whole families as they made their way behind the flame tree and along the path past the rectory. They carried baskets, rugs, folding chairs.

And so the afternoon wore on. The numbers grew until a river of people flowed uphill. Cars and bikes clotted the road. In Welcome Harbour, canoes rubbed against their ropes and heaved as one on the gentle swell.

*****

Police Chief Tanner arrived at five. A walkie-talkie chattered by his side. "We are estimating the crowd at three thousand," he said. "I am talking of those already here."

"As many as that?" said Reverend Brown.

"More," said Tanner. "At least a hundred canoes are on their way."

"The outer islands are coming too?" Reverend Brown was astonished by this, since Aowai, which meant 'world of water' and was furthest, was three days' sailing, and the passage rough. None of the islands were less than a day away. Yet from the rectory and beyond the reef, outriggers seemed to march across the sky.

"We have closed the road by Tom Bedall's shack," said the Police Chief. "There are so many cars, it is impassable."

The road—if the muddy track could be called a road—was one of only two ways to the high pasture that housed the Gardening Club and the 'meeting of all our people', as the posters had proclaimed. The other path flowed past the rectory. The crowd thickened. Police materialized and directed traffic.

"We are estimating seven thousand more," said Tanner.

"I am sorry?" said the Reverend. His attention had turned to other things.

"It is the largest crowd I have ever seen. I have not enough men to police it," warned Tanner, "if it gets out of hand."

But the Reverend would have none of that. "The police presence," he said, "must be light."

"Very well," said Chief Tanner. "You are our Prime Minister."

"With the will of the people, that may be so."

"Reverend Brown," said the Police Chief, "they are already here."

*****

At Briggs International Airport, as it was grandly known, a Hercules C130 landed and taxied to a discreet corner of the tiny field. On the tail could be seen the star, red slashing line and circle of the US Navy. Stairs were lowered. An elderly man clambered out. He walked stiffly to a waiting black Ford Custom with whitewall tires.

CHAPTER 45
AN OLD FRIEND

The calculation that landed Professor Buchanan on the steps of the rectory had three parts. Officials would be distracted on a day such as this. A new administration would soon be in place. And third, his deportation and return would not become an issue if he maintained a low profile and was little seen. The Professor's thesis demanded neither his long journey nor his presence in Welcome Harbour; only the fact of independence, or the failure of it, was now required. The risk were therefore no more than indulgent whim. At a human level, however, the old Professor simply found he had to come. As proof of his first calculation, no one had been on duty at the airport, except a single guard, and Dan Tehiri's taxi was waved straight through.

It was also true that though all around was mayhem, Reverend Brown found himself in the eye of the storm. The planned events would unfold or not; and the laws of show business demanded his latest possible arrival at the rally, still hours away. So there was nothing whatever at the moment to do. He and Professor Buchanan sparked with energy but were slowly becalmed. They puffed cigars and gulped sherry while excited people streamed past the rectory, the harbor bloated with vessels, and the police rushed from place to place.

"It is a brilliant plan," said the Professor through a haze of smoke. "None can say whether it will work, but it is brilliant, nevertheless."

"Its illumination is one thing," said the Reverend. "Whether it will work is another, outside my control." He had spent the day like this, whipsawing between depression and glee.

But the Professor would not be further drawn. "Do you know much about electrical circuits?" he asked.

"No."

"Nor I, it must be confessed, until of late. You understand the basic principle?"

"Electricity is contained by wires, which transport it from one place to another?" tried the Reverend.

"Circuits are about the management of power," said the Professor. "It has occurred to me this is the next step in my thesis, which is not yet considered."

"I do not think human behavior has much to do with electric circuits," said Reverend Brown.

"They direct where the power is to go," said the Professor. "How it is to be applied, and in what measure. Is this not what you are doing? Coursing power through circuits designed by you?"

"Perhaps what you say is true," said Reverend Brown, sparring with the Professor out of politeness. His mind was elsewhere.

"Your Splendid Islands Party is a source of power, which is itself the redirected energy of the Farmers' Federation and the Gardening Club. You have also harnessed the power of RW Rumsey, and the Bedall fellow who stole the rose."

"I have harnessed their power, I am encouraged to think, but perhaps they have harnessed it for themselves."

"Reverend Brown!" said Professor Buchanan, delight in his voice. "This is the proof of your closeness to power. Your first fear you might lose it."

"I do not yet have it to lose. My fear is certainly not of that."

But Professor Buchanan chose to ignore the reply. "You have also harnessed the power of the police, and possibly your governor."

"Queen's Representative," corrected Reverend Brown patiently. "America has governors. We have a Queen's Representative."

But again, Professor Buchanan could not be diverted. "You lunge for power because you know it is needed to shape a nation."

The Reverend, however, did not respond. His cigar had gone out. He searched for a match.

"Power is neither created nor destroyed," said the Professor. "It is merely converted from one place to another. This concept is most important—" He stopped mid-sentence, interrupted by the opening of the study door and the arrival of Police Chief Ned Tanner. The two men looked at each other, the deporter and the recently deported.

A walkie-talkie crackled at the policeman's side. "Professor," he said, an English gentleman greeting a colleague on a morning stroll.

"Captain!" said Professor Buchanan, guessing at Tanner's rank, and puffing more energetically on his glowing cigar.

The Police Chief turned his attention to Reverend Brown, who watched the exchange in silence. "There are reports of explosions and gunfire on the mountain, a mile or so from the Gardening Club."

"That is indeed alarming," said the Reverend. His reply, however, seemed unalarmed. Meant for the record? History, perhaps? "Have you sent men to investigate?"

"I am afraid we lack the training for such a task." The conversation seemed stilted, rehearsed.

"New Zealand soldiers are still camped on the beach?"

The Police Chief nodded.

"I recommend you contact their Major for assistance while we face this grave threat." The disturbance had now become a 'grave threat', though neither man had the slightest information about its source or purpose. That at least was their official stance.

"Excellent advice," said Tanner. He looked like he might rub his hands with glee. "Our priority must be to secure the crowd." With that he turned, said: "Good evening, Professor," and left the room.

*****

It is a phenomenon that men covet what they train to do. It is the reason firefighters sometimes moonlight as arsonists; politicians make laws when there are plenty enough; emergency workers respond to crises when they are off duty, unequipped, and of little use.

The sixty-two soldiers of Six Para had bivouacked in paradise these past few months. The food was local and excellent: fresh reef fish hauled from the sea, fruit and vegetables plucked from nearby fields, cases of beer, chilled on ice; their camp just a stone's throw from the turquoise lagoon. In the ranking of military assignments, it was possibly the sweetest of all. Yet, in their hearts, they yearned for what military men describe as 'action', so the mood of the camp quickened when Ned Tanner's squad car screeched to a halt. Its blue light strobed like a lighthouse on a storm-lashed coast.

Within a few minutes, soldiers emerged with their boots

on, helmets buckled, rifles held across their chests. They ran to their trucks, vaulted aboard and waited for the signal to move out.

*****

In the high pasture above Welcome Harbour, the crowd had swollen to more than eight thousand, according to the official estimate, possibly the most mysterious black art, as anyone who has tried to count more than twenty people will quickly attest. Tents had been erected. Inside were tables that groaned with food. Battalions of coffee urns stood silent guard. Squadrons of ice cream sticks doubled as spoons. Air wings of insects circled supply dumps of sugar. Armies of youngsters swished coconut fronds to keep them at bay. Oxide's volunteers adjusted speakers, tested microphones "one-two-three", and checked the generator, which purred with pleasure like a well fed cat.

And still they arrived, until the whole pasture was dotted with chairs. Men and women stood in clumps, sipping coffee from wax paper cups. Children played fighter jet with their arms outstretched. Teenage boys and girls stood in small, separate tribes. They made eyes at each other, too shy to cross from one tribe to the other.

In the distance was heard the odd rifle shot. Every so often, a much deeper boom.

The Major considered his most sensible course. He had no orders from his chain of command, which was days away and out of touch. The decision to act was his alone. Had an armed militia stormed ashore? Camped in the hills? Planned some kind of bloody assault? The truck passed a dog asleep by a tree. A cat snoozed on a nearby porch. Should he commit to a jungle march? Engage this militia in lethal battle?

In the back of the trucks, soldiers rubbed camouflage paint onto their cheeks, loaded their rifles, and retightened the laces on their combat boots.

Or should he go straight to the rally and secure the crowd, which the police had urged? The choice came down to military action against an unknown force, or protective duty to guard the crowd. Whether he yearned for the first could not be known and, in the absence of orders, could not be done.

The trucks headed to the lookout above Welcome Harbour. The soldiers sprang to the ground. They double-timed along the mountain path to the high-pasture home of the Splendid Isles Gardening Club, which had become some kind of independence cathedral for the huge, still-gathering crowd.

They stormed past the clubhouse in wedge-shaped squads. Their boots thudded on the hard, trampled ground. Commands were shouted to 'secure the space'. Sixty-two soldiers took up their posts. "Order arms," barked a Sergeant. A blur of movement, and then each trooper stood at rest, each rifle against a soldier's leg, each barrel pointed upwards towards the sky.

CHAPTER 46
THE ALMOST WAR

Dual Fresnel spotlights were fastened to the roof of the slowly collapsing Gardening Club. Their oval beams found Reverend Brown and followed him as he made his way to the rough wooden stage. He was bathed in the glow of the World War Two searchlight set up on a ridge a mile away. "My friends," he said. His voice seemed to drift in the cool mountain air. He was like a god, lit by a hot, distant sun. "Tomorrow, if you so vote, we shall be a country. Tonight we will understand what that will mean."

He stopped mid-speech, descended from the stage, and walked wordlessly to the nearest paratrooper who stood, rifle at his side, staring straight ahead. The Reverend's microphone cord snaked on the ground. "Tell me," he made a show of examining the stripes on the soldier's arm, "tell me, Sergeant, is it?"

But the Sergeant was a Lance Corporal, as evidenced by the single chevron on his sleeve. He did not reply. He had no orders to do so. Nor any idea what he should say.

"Very well," said Reverend Brown. "Sergeant will have to do. You have a rifle at your side. Why is that?"

Once again, the unhappy soldier did not respond.

The Reverend moved to the next in line. "And you!

Corporal is it? I see you also have a gun. Pray tell me, who are you hoping to shoot?"

This went on for some little while, until he arrived at the much older officer he guessed was the boss. This paratrooper wore a sidearm, did not carry a rifle at all, and had an epaulette boasting a small, single crown. "You are in charge?" He thrust the microphone into the man's face. A spotlight followed, close behind.

"I am the Commanding Officer," responded the Major in his strongest voice.

"Why are you here?"

The crowd was silent, but the Major did not reply.

"You do not know why you are here?" asked Reverend Brown in his most reasonable voice.

"Orders!" tried the Major.

"You have been sun-baking on our beach, swimming in our sea, grilling our fish these last months because of orders?"

"I am not at liberty to say," said the Major. He was trapped between the microphone, the spotlight, and the churchman. The crowd, police would later report, had grown to almost ten thousand, far larger than the small farming town where the Major was raised.

"So you have been on our beach with your hundred armed men all these months, but you cannot say why? Is that it?"

It is known people will sometimes make disastrous mistakes in the public glare. Political veterans, captains of industry, ruined by a question they should ignore but which is answered once a microphone is thrust into their face. The Major, wanting not to look a fool, made the mistake now. "We are here to protect you," he said.

"By sleeping on our beach? By sending your trucks for

beer at Trader Mike's?" The Reverend waged his own almost war. There were no bullets or shells. It was cruel and bloody, nevertheless.

"No!" said the Major miserably.

"I see," said Reverend Brown, turning to face the crowd. "We did not send for them, but they are here to protect us, these heavily armed soldiers." He turned back to the Major. "And tonight?" he said. "Why are you here on the very eve of the day when we will throw off the shackles with which your master has bound us?"

"What was the question again?" said the Major, overrun and dying in his trench.

"He does not know why he is here!" said the Reverend, spraying words into the dying man. "But I shall tell you. It is to show muscle! To intimidate! To remind us who is in charge as we go to the polls."

"There has been a disturbance," tried the Major.

"Really?" said the Reverend. "Are we out of apple pie?" There was loud laughter from the crowd. "What is this disturbance? I do not see it."

"Gunshots," said the Major, and fell silent again.

"Oh, those!" said the Reverend, and darted back to the stage, the spotlight on him every step of the way. "Major!" he called. A small spot lit the officer. Dark shadows appeared beneath his eyes. He looked like the Devil—a stagecraft trick of Oxide's lights. The Reverend cupped his hands for theatrical effect. "Major! Can you hear me?"

"Yes, sir," came the reedy reply. The Major's authority ebbed away.

"Yes, sir," repeated Reverend Brown. The crowd laughed again. "They have come to protect us from gunshots which were fired by some enemy force. Is that right, Major? Pirates have come to cut our throats?" Reverend Brown pressed his own assault. "I am going to produce these murderous privateers for us all to see."

Nothing happened for a few moments, and then could be seen the paunchy figure of RW Rumsey and the simple farmer, Tom Bedall, bathed in light as they emerged from the trees. They sprinted to the stage. Their ancient Enfield rifles hung almost to the ground.

"Here they are!" said the Reverend. "It is the President of our Farmers' Federation together with the gentle, future member for North Harbour. "RW," he said, holding the microphone to Rumsey's face. "Have you come to invade us?"

RW, still breathless, managed a laugh. "Not at all," he said. "Tom and I have been out this afternoon dispersing mynah birds which were attacking his mangoes." Mynahs were an introduced species, common to the Splendid Isles, and a pest.

"It is why you have guns?" said Reverend Brown.

"Time got away on us," added Tom Bedall. "We came straight here."

"There you are, Major!" said the Reverend. "The gunshots are explained. We are perfectly safe." What the Reverend had not mentioned were the explosions, forgotten also by the crowd. Move on quickly, the Professor had advised, so the churchman dared not linger too long.

Another spotlight swung through the trees and came to rest on the Major's face.

"Well?" pressed Reverend Brown. His voice boomed from the darkened stage.

The crowd munched pie. Drank coffee. Enjoyed the show.

"Atten-shun!" said the Major, loud and crisp. "Fall in!" The crowd watched as the paratroopers formed a humiliated line in front of their boss. "By the left. Quick march." Within moments they disappeared into the gloom. Their boots thumped along the track. They retreated to their trucks, whose engines idled, far below.

Reverend Brown watched from the stage. "In a few hours —" He paused with a flourish to look at his watch. "In a few hours, you will be asked to vote on the most historic moment in the history of these Splendid Isles."

There was polite clapping. Children made airplanes with their arms.

"But I want you to know what kind of Government you are voting for. I want you to understand the truth of the colonial power that has ruled us until now, and which, by your actions, if you so deem it, tomorrow we shall leave behind. Tom," he indicated Tom Bedall, "RW," he turned to RW Rumsey, "and I have been threatened with jail if we do not bow to the demands of Wellington."

A few people looked up, set their pie or coffee to one side. What did he say? Did they hear 'jail'?

"I am to be jailed for stealing ninety pounds from my own church."

The crowd fell silent. Something important was being said.

"I took the money." He paused. "Guilty as charged."

There was deep silence now, of the kind pervading a funeral home where the battle is lost; or the intensive care ward of a hospital, where it might still go either way. The children sensed something momentous was happening. They shuffled to the foot of the stage and sat cross-legged on the grass, as if a show were about to begin. Whether it was scripted, and if so by who, would be hotly debated for decades to come.

The spotlight tightened on Reverend Brown. "Do you want to know how the money was used, these funds stolen from the church, which represents all of our people?"

"It was spent on me," said a soft female voice from the back of the crowd. The voice was amplified by a microphone that smoothly appeared. Within seconds a spot found her as well. Tanisha Hana was lit up for all to see.

"Don't be shy," said Reverend Brown.

"It paid for my trip to New Zealand," Tanisha said a little more confidently. "Where I confirmed the Reverend's fear."

"And what fear was that, my dear?" he asked in honeyed voice.

"That we were being bled white by the greedy shipping company." She was fully confident now. Defiant. "Who sold our produce in Wellington for twenty times more than they paid our brave farmers." 'Our brave farmers.' The words echoed across the field. Farmers were not merely hard-working or loyal. They were now pronounced 'brave' by a pretty girl. In the crowd, men stood a little more tall.

The churchman turned to RW Rumsey, who hovered by him on the stage. "Who is the owner of this greedy shipping company?" he asked quietly.

"The New Zealand Government," boomed RW.

"There you have it," said Reverend Brown. "I am to be jailed for spending our own money to confirm what we all suspected. These masters in Wellington rob us blind. 'Stealing' is the word for it. 'Stealing' our crops, so they might profit, while we starve."

The crowd was silent. For the first time, the food tents stood empty.

"Now I am going to tell you of RW's terrible crime. He is a spy. A traitor to us all." It is a trick of showmen to sometimes let silence do the work. The accusation hung in the air, a weight suspended from a fraying thread. The simple accountant a traitor? The President of the Farmers'

Federation a turncoat? "Shall I tell you what he did?" The churchman's voice roared, teased the crowd.

People rose to their feet, as though a saint or a prophet were in their midst. "Yes!" they cried.

"RW discovered seven thousand pounds stolen from these Splendid Isles by the New Zealand Secret Service. When was this money taken?" asked the Reverend, turning to face his deputy. They were bathed together in magnificent light.

"Why, the money was taken every month," said RW, face upturned, perfectly framed in the spotlight's glare. Were it not for the once-white shirt and cinched pants, he could have been an adoring cherub from a Rubens painting.

"They took this huge sum—our money—every month?"

"Every month," RW confirmed.

"So they could spy on us?"

"It is so," said RW.

At the front of the crowd, Aaron Trieger stopped scribbling notes, looked uneasily behind him.

"I take it you are not a spy," said Reverend Brown.

"No!" RW shook his head.

"You have a .303 rifle which struck fear into the hearts of a hundred soldiers." Laughter came from the crowd. The mood had changed. "Do you have a Walther PPK in a holster beneath your shirt?" The legendary gun of the famous James Bond.

RW patted his shirt to show it could not be true.

"An Aston Martin in your garage?" 007's famous car.

There was loud laughter now. The cow was milked. The next heifer entered the stall. "Tom," he said, turning his attention to Bedall.

"I didn't do it," said Tom, playing the role he had been told to play. The village idiot, but a little less so.

"Now, Tom," admonished the Reverend. His finger wagged. "I haven't asked you yet. Is it correct you stole the parent of the Independence Rose from an innocent sailor on the *Jalisco Belle*?"

"No sir!" said Tom. "I won it fair and square. He welched on a bet and gave me the rose."

"So!" pounced the churchman. "It is your word against his." But before Tom could reply, the churchman continued, "I wonder if Police Chief Tanner could join Tom and me."

There was a murmur in the crowd. What surprise lay in store? A spotlight found Tanner, pushed him along.

"Citizens of the Splendid Isles," said Reverend Brown, as though the polls were already decided, "I give you Ned Tanner." In the reins of the right rider, even police could be led to water and made to drink. "Chief Tanner," said Reverend Brown with scrupulous formality, "can you tell us if this un-named sailor from the *Jalisco Belle* has a police record?"

"Yes, sir," said Tanner, "both in New Zealand and here."

"Very well," said the Reverend.

"Also in Tahiti, Samoa and Niue," added the Chief. "We have not yet heard from the authorities in Port Moresby, but they are often slow." Port Moresby was the capital of New Guinea, the largest and most lawless of all the islands in the South Pacific.

"So he has 'form', as you chaps in the police would say?"

"Oh yes!" confirmed Tanner. "A long record. Assault, dishonesty, drunken behavior." The policeman seemed ready to go on, but Reverend Brown had raised a hand.

"Did you say 'dishonesty', Chief Tanner?" Before Tanner could respond, the Reverend opened his arms, a symbolic hug which embraced the entire, teeming crowd. "Who do you prefer?" he said. The churchman took Bedall's hand and held it aloft. "Who do you prefer?" he repeated. "The word of an honest, simple farmer," he paused again, "or a drunken criminal working as a sailor in the pay of the greedy shipping company?"

There was silence as the crowd digested this. They were fed the story a bite at a time.

"Which is owned in turn by who?" The Reverend pressed. But there was no need to answer. The case was made.

There was disturbance as a man in a peaked cap elbowed his way onto the stage. "I, too, was threatened with jail," said Dan Tehiri into an out-thrust mike. If not popular, he was at least well known. Who among them, at one time or another, had not ridden in the Tehiri cab, been forced to pay his savage fare?

"You are also a thief?" asked the Reverend. There was silence at this, since many in the crowd believed him to be so.

"They said I stole the other parent of the Independence Rose. From the QR's mansion."

"'They?' said Reverend Brown. "Who has accused you of this?"

"The New Zealand Government," replied Tehiri.

"So!" said Reverend Brown, allowing the word to float in the air.

"Not so," called a well-modulated voice from deep in the crowd. Well-modulated and with a microphone already to hand. A spotlight located the patrician figure of Queen's Representative, Sir Jonathan O'Dowd. "My cook gave Mr. Tehiri the rose."

"So Tehiri Transportation Services is not a thief?" said the Reverend.

"Not of my rose," called Sir Jonathan. "Beyond that I cannot say."

There was broad laughter at this, an inside joke understood by all.

But Reverend Brown was not yet finished with the island cabbie. "Dan, if I may call you that. You said 'threatened with jail'?"

"That is correct."

"Under what law was this threat made?" But Tehiri looked lost and did not reply.

It took a few moments for people to realize it was the QR speaking again, still 'miked up', as they say in the trade. "The Criminal Code of 1893," he called.

"Did you say 1893?" said Reverend Brown. "There is no more modern law than that?"

"It is the 1893 law which is to be applied."

"And what are the penalties under this law?"

"Death by hanging. Flogging with a cat-o'-nine-tails. Whipping with a rod."

The Reverend interrupted before Sir Jonathan could go on. "And this ancient law applies to our masters in New Zealand as well?

"Certainly not," replied the QR. "Their criminal code has been revised many times."

"But not ours?"

"It is an oversight," said Sir Jonathan.

The Reverend seized the word. "An 'oversight' we are to be hung, flogged, whipped?" The spotlight swung away from Sir Jonathan O'Dowd. The Queen's man had played his role. Dan Tehiri, unnoticed, vanished into the dark. His moment of fame had also passed.

The churchman stood on the edge of the stage while the searchlight bounced slowly across the crowd. A mirror was set up behind him. Ten thousand people, mesmerized, watched themselves.

"An oversight we are to be hung, flogged, whipped!" the Reverend roared. The searchlight found a family group. "Perhaps *they* are to be flogged?" A young couple, hand in hand. "Or these innocent lovers?" This time a child with a wide-eyed gaze.

"Enough!" said the Reverend with a snap to his voice. "Shall I tell you the price they want us to pay? The price for the loyal RW, the simple Tom Bedall, the innocent Dan Tehiri, and myself, to stay out of their jail?" Behind him, the mirror was taken away. "New Zealand wants to confiscate the taxes they have collected from us—our taxes." He built his anger, brick by brick. "But that is not the worst of it. They offer to lend us our own money. Charge us to borrow it. Money you and I have slaved to earn." He turned to RW, who appeared at his side. "You are an accountant, RW. What else do they plan to steal, these people who accuse us of stealing from them?"

"They threaten to impose a monetary export tax," said RW mildly. When one is angry the other is calm. "All funds remitted from New Zealand are to be double-taxed." The crowd gasped; many families gratefully received funds from their loved ones abroad.

"Taxed twice you mean, since their wages have already been taxed before they are received!"

"That is correct." RW whispered, but was heard by all.

"Did you say 'taxed twice'?" said the Reverend, re-hitting the nail.

"Yes!" said RW, more loudly this time.

"And this applies to the citizens of which nation?" 'Nation'! 'Citizen'! Like the farmers before him, the glowering churchman sowed his seed.

"The Splendid Islands," said Rumsey. "Only our people

are to be taxed this way."

"Unless you and I will go to jail?" This was their most dangerous ground, since voters could decide they preferred jail for a few to a new tax for all. Years later, pundits would conclude this was the Reverend's finest hour. There are hills to die on. For Reverend Geoffrey Brown, portly churchman of the Splendid Isles, this was his. On one slope, disgrace, ruin and jail. On the other, salvation as leader of the world's newest sovereign state.

At this moment, the spotlight found a tall African man, slim as an athlete, beautifully groomed. He strode to the stage in a magnificent coat, a collarless smock with an intricate pattern slashed in gold, black and red. It was a kente coat, its weave inspired by a jungle spider spinning its web. Some called him the man in the spider web coat, though none to his face. Reverend Brown reached down and helped this man onto the stage. They embraced like lifelong friends, though the friendship was only a few days old.

"If we are to be a nation tomorrow—" said the churchman. His voice quivered for the first time. "If we are to be a nation tomorrow," he repeated, "it is this man before you tonight, who is the true father of these our Splendid Isles." Reverend Brown stepped back. Only the black man was center stage. Lit by Oxide's McCandless Method, he appeared a giant. If silence could be purchased, it was over-subscribed.

"My name is Alex Quaison-Sackey," the giant said simply. "I am chairman of the Non-Self-Governing Territories Committee at the United Nations." The crowd hushed. "I have flown from New York in America, to be with you tonight."

Ten thousand pairs of eyes filled with tears. This powerful man had flown halfway around the world, from a city with buildings that reached the sky. If there was a god tonight, it must surely be he.

"You stand on the eve of the most important day of your lives, and the lives of your young ones yet to be born," He was speaking again, but it took a moment to register, so humbled were they by his glorious presence. They did not know what a non-self-governing territories committee was, nor what it did. But they'd heard 'chairman', 'United Nations', and 'New York', and were enthralled as children on Christmas morning.

"Tomorrow you must make the most important decision of your lives, and for many generations still to come." Alex Quaison-Sackey was a diplomat, who mixed with kings, presidents, potentates. He held the crowd gently in his hand, as if it were a half-drowned kitten that trembled in fear. He did not roar or scream, beseech, harangue, plead or demand. He spoke softly; a father, perhaps, to an innocent child. "The decision is a difficult one. Each of your four leaders is threatened with jail."

The taxi driver, Dan Tehiri, is now a leader? thought Reverend Brown. It was a small error. Perhaps the only one. The crowd did not notice, or did not care, so fabled had the night become.

The diplomat continued, "If you do not demand your freedom, you shall not have it. You shall not deserve it. You must stand with your leaders, including this great man." Quaison-Sackey looked directly at Reverend Brown, smiled, extended a hand. Then he removed his spider-web kente coat and held it up in front of the crowd. "This coat is a symbol of democracy in Ghana, far from here." The coat shimmered in his hands. "We fought the British for our freedom. We lost, but we never gave up. We did not achieve independence until fifty years after our struggle began. By your vote tomorrow, you shall achieve freedom in less than one.

"This sacred coat," he continued, "belongs on another man tonight." He leaned forward and placed the coat around the Reverend's shoulders. "He is a great man, you know. A humble churchman, leading you to the nation you must become."

Reverend Brown stood motionless in the exquisite jacket. For a moment, silence prevailed, and then, like a force of nature, ten thousand people roared as one.

Doris Day's "Que *Será Será*" boomed from loudspeakers, "Whatever will be, will be." It was a strange choice, but somehow it struck the mood. Destiny was only hours away. Children and parents snaked down the trail in a conga line.

Nothing else to be said or done. Save for Aaron Trieger, who drove to his newsroom and placed a call.

CHAPTER 47
SELLER'S REMORSE

Leaden clouds sailed the sky, driven by a high wind which swept sodden leaves into the air and dumped them in pools of water pockmarked by rain. Election Day brought the first winter storm of the season, which had come unseasonably soon.

Wilson Tuttle and Alex Quaison-Sackey huddled by the boarding steps while their chartered Beechcraft Travelair was readied for flight. A few minutes later, the twin-engine plane taxied onto the only runway at Briggs Field, accelerated to a high-pitched scream, circled once and disappeared.

At the rectory, Professor Buchanan and Reverend Brown sat unshaved in dressing gowns.

Aaron Trieger telephoned to report drenched voters outside polling booths since before first light. An early turnout meant eager to vote—but to vote for what? A brand new nation or an unchanged world? Trieger had covered many an election overseas and knew how risky prediction could be. He had assembled a team of part-time reporters, 'stringers', as they are known. They would monitor the voting on Welcome Island. The other places were said to be more certain, since the 'outlanders', as they were sometimes called, would hopefully vote as a single block. Then again, worried Reverend Brown, they might not.

When an informal count was available, well before the official result, Aaron Trieger would be first to know. The churchman, he promised, would be second, though who else was on his list was not discussed. Trieger was also a worried man. RW Rumsey had gone too far. Seven thousand pounds a month to spy on the Splendids. The question was: What else did the whistleblower know? Could the trail lead to Trieger himself? The end of everything he'd worked to build? A deeper question gnawed away. The slush fund had not been spent on him. So, where on earth did the money go?

Dan Tehiri was in buoyant mood. 'Each of your four leaders is threatened with jail,' the UN chairman had told the crowd. "Each of your four leaders.' He savored the words. 'Four leaders.' 'Four.' Reverend Geoffrey Brown; Rumsey; the village idiot, Tom Bedall; and of course Tehiri, too. New Zealand had thought the island cab driver was their man, but at the last minute he had ever so wisely changed his mind. Any fool could see the Reverend would win. A new Prime Minister in his debt. A new Prime Minister now aligned. There were plans for Tehiri Transportation Services. Dan Tehiri's dream soared, even as the rain plunged to the ground.

At the Governor's mansion, the QR ate butterfly cakes and stared sadly into his tea. He had crossed a line marked 'No Return.' The parent of the Independence Rose not stolen after all? He was either a liar or a half-cocked fool. In either case, a dead man once his masters in Wellington heard the tale. Unless, of course, the Reverend won.

At Trader Mike's sat Ned Tanner and Randolph Herd. The Resident Commissioner's breakfast lay undisturbed. "It is very fine for you," he said. "You have played the ball. I have not even been asked to try-out for the team."

Tanner was in expansive mood, since he judged his own position was now secure. Police Chief? Certainly! Commissioner of the Civil Service? Possibly. Cabinet Minister? Not unless he were some day elected to Parliament. Still, it could not be ruled out. If Randolph Herd fell away, there was no knowing where Ned Tanner might go.

Herd, meanwhile, was in his cups. He had no particular alliance with his masters in New Zealand. Nor was he in the orbit of the Reverend's political party, which within hours might be in power. Nor on more than nodding terms with the future Prime Minister. Tossed out to grass, with so much more to give.

"Ned," he said. "We have always been friends."

"Agreed," said Tanner, who could afford to be kind.

"If the Reverend becomes the new Prime Minister—"

"Yes."

"If you have a position of some influence with him—"

"OK."

"If the occasion arises before it is too late—"

"Uh-huh."

"Would you put your oar in the water for me?"

"That's a lot of ifs," said Tanner. "I will do what I can."

Herd looked uncomfortably at his colleague, whose assurance did not sound like an assurance at all.

RW Rumsey sat, while the rain drummed the roof above his head. I was not much in the spotlight, he thought. Even though I am to become the second most powerful man in the land. Our leader is thirsty for the public gaze, while I am expected to bask in the shade. Like the rain above, Aaron Trieger's words drummed in his head. "Makes you a natural for Deputy," the newsman had said. "Some say more than that."

Tom Bedall huddled in his shack and ate goat stew. He had been adopted by a cat, which guarded the door. If Tom Bedall was a leader, he was the loneliest of all. 'I want you to play the village idiot, but less so.' The words repeated in his mind. I am the village idiot, he thought. It is what they think I am.

At the rectory sat Reverend Brown, staring out the window at the slate-gray day. "I confess to no sense whether victory lies within my reach." He stirred his tea.

"My dear fellow," replied Professor Buchanan, "you have done everything it is possible to do. You must wait now to see if the power will come to you."

"I have made many mistakes," said the churchman. "Last night worst of all."

"Nonsense," said the Professor. "Oxide has told me the evening went well."

"Sugar!" said the Reverend, dipping a spoon into his cup. "I fed them sugar. Oceans of sugar."

"They did well on it, by Oxide's account."

"Their sweet humor last night is not what concerns me," said the Reverend. "It is whether, in the light of day, it has turned to something more bitter."

"Tell me of these errors," said the Professor.

"Firstly—" said Reverend Brown, but he was interrupted by a plate of cassava, coconut cream, sugar, eggs, cheese and honeyed ham, which had been baked into a breakfast so divine, everything else was set aside.

"Ah, Mrs. Hana," said the Professor, eyeing the housekeeper with his usual zeal. "We have been saved by your perfect meal."

"More tea?" she said, splashing fresh brew into their cups.

"You were saying?" said the Professor.

The Reverend replied, "I have put upon one side of the scales jail for a few, and on the other, new and vicious taxes for all. We cannot know which way the scales will tip."

"I agree," said the Professor. "It was your bravest move, and I counseled against it. You have threatened an election, to be decided within hours, against a risk that is many months away, and which you might also be able to fight. It makes you a great man, or a lesser one. I cannot say. Still, your astonishing support from the United Nations might tilt the balance in your favor."

"Not support from the United Nations," corrected the Reverend. "From one man who tiptoed in and who has now most certainly tiptoed out. Nor was it 'astonishing', since you yourself arranged his trip."

"Who brought him here is not the issue. And whether Quaison-Sackey has gone already does not matter. He called you a great man. Whether official or not is beside the point."

"Also," said Reverend Brown, "I have sown a seed with the treacherous Tehiri. He was grouped by your UN diplomat as one of us. Rumsey, Bedall, myself and the cab driver, who is loyal to no one but himself. It was unwitting and no one's fault, but he is more closely identified with me because of it."

"That is not today's issue," said Professor Buchanan. "As a powerful man, you must learn the art of dealing with each problem in its own time."

But Reverend Brown was unappeased. "I was cruel to the Major who came to protect us."

"All great men are cruel," said the Professor. "The 'almost war', as you described it, was your most brilliant stroke. Like your secret destruction of the Independence Rose, you did not shrink when destiny called."

"Ned Tanner?" said the Reverend. "The Queen's Representative? They played their roles, as I asked of them.

Now I have debts to repay." He was like an ancient knight looking for chinks in his armor. But it was already too late. The fight was over. Only the verdict remained unknown.

"My dear fellow," said Professor Buchanan. "As Prime Minister, you will be in the debt of many people, because such a journey cannot be achieved as a solitary man. When the great Sir Edmund Hillary conquered Mt. Everest, do you think he climbed alone? They have played their role, these men you describe—the governor, the police chief, the cab driver, the diplomat from the UN. But they did not do so from any special love of you. Each will expect a reward."

"Trapped in a web of IOU," said Reverend Brown. "What kind of funny power is that?"

"These debts are yours to pay or not. Some men you will honor. Others you will not. It is the hope of favors that drives them to you."

"Including RW Rumsey and Tom Bedall?"

"Including them," the Professor agreed.

"My son, Oxide? Does the hope of favors drive him as well?"

"Ah," said the Professor. "We should leave these things for another time. But you are right. The destiny of these Splendid Isles is upon the scales. We shall see if it is the greatest or the worst day of your life. We shall learn soon enough what is brought to you."

CHAPTER 48
CHECK!

"So," said Prime Minister Holyoake," let me summarize what I have been told." He looked at Brigadier Bill Gilbert with fraying good humor.

"I can hardly wait for this," whispered Attorney-General Ralph Hanan. Gallows humor, because Hanan was in the crosshairs as well.

"Our man Tehiri, this cab driver, recruited by you—" the PM's humor snapped, as he looked soberly at his country's head spy, "—has been recruited back into the arms of this cursed churchman, who has become our most deadly threat."

"Unhappily," said Gilbert, "that is so." He bowed his head like a choir boy at vespers.

"More than a deadly threat, Prime Minister," interjected Harry Lake. "They shall achieve statehood within hours if our fears are correct."

"Their Police Chief—" resumed the PM, as if he had not been interrupted.

"Ned Tanner," prompted Hanan, the island policeman's ultimate boss.

"Tanner," said the Prime Minister, looking directly at the Attorney-General, "has also abandoned whatever loyalty he had to New Zealand—and to you."

"It is the only way the sailor's criminal record could be revealed," added Gilbert. "So you are right, Prime Minister. Their Police Chief has also betrayed us."

"Our attempt," resumed the PM, "to—I do not know the correct word. Is it 'sway'? 'control?' Or something worse?"

"'Sway' will suffice," said Gilbert, who seemed to know what was coming.

"Very well," said the Prime Minister in a leaden voice. "Our attempt to sway this man, Rumsey, is also in shreds."

"Again," said Gilbert, "it is my sad duty to agree with your view."

"And," resumed Holyoake, "the Queen's Representative, before whom we dangled a juicy new job—"

"Yes, Prime Minister. The offer was clear," said Hanan.

"Clear, maybe, but not juicy enough," replied the PM, "since he has disowned his own police report that his rose was stolen from his Government mansion."

"Once again, correct," said Gilbert.

The Prime Minister's eyes shifted to the hapless Ralph Hanan. "He worked for you, since the Splendid Isles are part of your remit."

"Officially," protested the Attorney-General, "he reported to the Governor-General, Viscount Cobham." This was a particularly narrow view of the QR's official loyalties, but the kitchen cabinet let it pass.

"Viscount Cobham has been uninvolved in any of this," said the Prime Minister. "Too busy opening school fêtes, making speeches and drinking other people's champagne. Is there anything else to add to this fiasco?"

Emboldened, Harry Lake stirred the pot. "The humiliation, perhaps, of Six Para? Our nation's finest, ordered back to their barracks, as though they were children sent to bed."

"I'd forgotten that," said Holyoake. "At your feet again, Ralph."

"Their Commanding Officer did not report to me," protested the Attorney-General. "It was his decision to protect the locals from two farmers out shooting birds."

"Rumsey and the so-called village idiot are much more than farmers," corrected Brigadier Gilbert. "And the bird-shooting incident does not ring true."

"OK," said Holyoake. "I will bite."

"We are expected to believe," the spy resumed, "two leaders of the independence movement went shooting mynah birds at this critical time."

"Put like that," said the Prime Minister.

"There were also reports of explosions which were never explained."

There was silence for a moment while the kitchen cabinet considered this.

"Nor," said the spy, "do I buy Ralph's view that this Bedall is a fool. He outsmarted Sir Brendan Court. That is my view."

The Attorney-General opened his mouth to protest again, but Holyoake smartly waved him down.

"The military were enticed to respond. I believe that is clear," said Gilbert. "It was part of a wicked plan so they could be humiliated in front of the crowd. Left them with an awful choice. Heavy-handed jackboots, overshadowing the peaceful wishes of a peaceful rally, or shameful retreat in shameful disgrace. There are several other matters I wish to raise. May I go on?"

"Do not play the fool," said Holyoake. "One is enough." If there had been any doubt they were taking heavy fire, there was none now.

"The entire independence campaign was funded by

foreign nationals."

"That is disturbing news," said Holyoake.

"A check for ten thousand American dollars—nearly five thousand of our pounds—was deposited into the Splendid Islands Party bank account some weeks ago."

"By whom?" said Holyoake.

"The Nature Wildlife Coalition."

"Never heard of it," the Prime Minister shot back.

"So far as we are able to tell, it is controlled by a group in Washington DC. The National Turtle Research Foundation." The Brigadier paused. "There is worse to come. This turtle foundation, masquerading as a wildlife coalition, is actually funded by the American Navy."

"Which I suppose also funds the think tank of our mysterious Professor," guessed the Prime Minister.

Brigadier Gilbert nodded. "Who has a Yankee White security clearance, which means—well—we do not know what it means."

"We deported this Professor," said Hanan. "And good riddance to him."

"There is intelligence," said the Brigadier slowly, "Professor Buchanan has returned to the Splendid Isles."

"What!" spluttered the Attorney-General. "He must be seized."

"The report is unconfirmed, but others of interest are also there. The Chairman of this turtle group, one Wendell Steinbeck, and its Secretary, Harvey Wesner. Also, Alex Quaison-Sackey," added Gilbert.

"The head of the UN Committee?" Holyoake spluttered. "From New York?"

"There is one other thing," said Gilbert. "A chartered Beechcraft departed Welcome Harbour at dawn today. The

UN diplomat, we believe, was on board. He left the island with another man."

"Who?" said Holyoake.

"I regret to inform you we do not know."

And so the 'great machine', as Professor Buchanan described it, had not yet learned of Wilson Tuttle.

"Is that all?" said Holyoake.

"HUMINT in Welcome Harbour reports that Harry's planned tax levy was revealed to the rally last night." 'HUMINT' meant human intelligence or, even more simply, a human being.

"Brigadier Gilbert," said the Prime Minister, "you are closest to this. How long do we have before the outcome of their elections is known?

"Three hours," replied Gilbert. "Four at the most."

"I am concerned by all of this," said the Prime Minister. "The United Nations and the US Navy have developed interest in what should be a local matter."

"And Britain," reminded Lake, adding fuel to the fire. "That business with the note from the Queen's Private Secretary."

"And Britain," agreed Holyoake. "We also have a sinister political movement, about to seize control of a lawful New Zealand territory, which has been run by us justly and with great compassion. This movement is controlled by men who lie, steal, and," he paused for effect, "breach our state secrets whenever it suits them."

"Yes! Yes! And yes!" said Ralph Hanan.

"Finally," said the Prime Minister, "we have sixty crack troops on a beach a few minutes away." Holyoake turned to Brigadier Gilbert once again. "These men would be armed with what?"

"Light weapons. Rifles. Several machine guns."

"Sufficient," Holyoake asked, "to impose our will?"

"To suppress a nation of forty thousand would require eight hundred," said Gilbert. "One to fifty is the rule of thumb."

"So the position is hopeless. We could not win?"

"On the contrary," replied Gilbert, "I do not believe we would have to suppress forty thousand, or any number remotely like it. There is no great animosity to New Zealand in the Splendid Isles. Most would simply go along."

"So it could be done!" said the PM.

"At a pinch," agreed Gilbert, "it could be done."

"Without violence or loss of life?"

"Maybe," said Gilbert. "We could not be sure."

The Prime Minister now swung his guns on to Ralph Hanan. "Let us assume the elections are over, our churchman has won."

"Very well," said Hanan.

"Is there a basis in law to set them aside?"

The Attorney-General, who had last worked as a lawyer fifteen years ago, considered the question. "We might argue," he began, "that their elections are tainted by funds from a foreign group. Also a murky Professor, deported once and since illegally returned, exerted influence behind the scenes." Hanan paused again. "And therefore, an injunction might be granted by the Court."

"So," said Holyoake, "it could be done."

"It would require a finer legal brain than mine, but yes, Prime Minister, it could be done."

"So there is military action," said the PM, "and legal action, either of which would kill their elections at the moment of birth. Against this, however, is the slight possibility of a bloodbath; and international acceptance for our actions may not be so easy to secure. It is finely balanced. Everything is upon the scales." The Prime Minister leaned forward and spoke again. "You are all dismissed," he said. "This decision is mine to make."

CHAPTER 49
CHECK AND MATE!

Balanced thus, the day dragged on. Six Para, fresh from their humiliation, were ordered to occupy a triangular patch of wet grass at the turnoff between the airport and Welcome Harbour. They lolled there, sullenly smoking cigarettes and doing the things soldiers do when they are becalmed between one order and the next. They were to be 'battle ready', so they wore their helmets, which dripped with rain. A line was run from the airport and connected to a field phone by the Major's side.

In an unprepossessing brick house at 41 Pipitea Street, Wellington, with an oil company on one side and a brewery a few yards down the road, sat New Zealand Prime Minister Keith Holyoake. A nearby construction site threw off a fine mist of powdered concrete. A jackhammer was also loudly at work. The PM stirred his tea, ate cookies filled with what might have been strawberry jam, and pondered whether to sue or attack the Splendid Isles.

*****

Three thousand four hundred and thirty-two miles northeast of Wellington, in a whitewashed rectory, next to a flame tree, and connected by a short path to the Splendid

Isles Christian Church, sat the Reverend Geoffrey Brown. Showered and dressed, he slumped at his desk, drinking sherry and smoking a stale cigar. Professor Titus Buchanan did the same. Neither man spoke. Everything to be done, already done. Everything to be said, already said.

"Father," said Oxide Brown, "when do you think we shall know the vote?"

"When it is counted," said the Professor patiently.

The sky cleared. The rain eased. The clouds slowly rowed away.

Tanisha Hana, in a cotton skirt and gingham top, knocked politely at the door. "There you are!" she said to Oxide. "Reverend," she said firmly, "I have come to take your son for a walk."

"It might be better if I waited here for the phone to ring," protested Oxide. But like all men, he was putty in the hands of a pretty girl, though Tanisha had always seemed more like a sister to him.

"I want to know what you are thinking," she said, when they reached the beach.

"My father has decided we will lose," said Oxide "As the hours pass he grows more sure of it."

"And you?" she asked, taking his hand.

"I shall return to America and find a job."

Tanisha considered this. Her nose wrinkled in disapproval. "And if your father wins?"

"I have not really thought of that."

"Liar!" she said.

"I might stay in Welcome Harbour," he conceded.

She cupped his face in her hands, looked into his eyes. "I would like you to stay," she said. She kissed his cheek, placed her hands flat upon his chest. "I would like you to stay," she repeated, and kissed him on the mouth.

There was no plan to it, not on Oxide's part, but he found his hands had moved behind her back, snared her in a tight embrace. "Tanisha," he whispered.

"Sh-sh!" she said, leading him to the shade of a nearby palm and pulling him down to the warm, damp sand. "I think it is time we made a pact."

"A pact?"

"That I love you and you love me."

His lungs filled with her scent. Her hair caressed his face. Then she slowly unbuttoned his shirt, and Oxide forgot all about America, the elections, his father, Professor Buchanan, and the lizard that watched unblinking from the water's edge.

Afterwards, when they had dressed, he realized it was not a lizard at all. It had a lizard's neck, but behind that was a large turtle shell. They watched as the huge reptile, the size almost of a man, used its flippers to bury an egg in the golden sand. As Harvey Wesner would have said: "*Chelonia mydas agassizii,* our little friend."

*****

The shrill sound of the telephone came from the hall. Piata Hana raced from the kitchen and got to it before Reverend Brown or Professor Buchanan.

"Of course he is here," they heard her say. "Reverend!" she called.

"Uh-huh!" said the churchman into the phone. He replaced the handset, walked back to the study, and poured measures of sherry into glasses. Then he relit the remains of his dying cigar and sighed loudly. "Mrs. Hana," he called. "Please join Professor Buchanan and me in the study at once."

The housekeeper strode anxiously into the room. She wore an apron. There was a splotch of flour on one cheek. She walked to the Reverend and clutched his hand. If Professor Buchanan noticed, he did not say. Such was the tension on that day.

Reverend Brown, however, seemed in no hurry at all. "Was it the Romans," he asked, "who said, 'Eat, drink, be merry?'"

Professor Buchanan leapt to his feet. "'For tomorrow we die!'" he cried in sudden despair.

"Not at all!" said Reverend Brown.

A smile spread across the Professor's face. "We have won?"

"A landslide," said Reverend Brown, hugging his housekeeper in a most un-housekeeperly way. "We have secured more than ninety percent of the vote."

"That is marvelous news," said Professor Buchanan, raising his glass. "I give you a toast to the first Prime Minister of these Splendid Isles."

The toast could not be sealed, however, not in any event by the clinking of glasses. Mrs. Hana pulled the Prime Minister's head down and kissed him fully on the lips.

"It is a small secret," the Reverend confessed.

"Not to me," said Professor Buchanan, marshaling a frown. "Or to anyone else in Welcome Harbour. It is the largest open secret in the whole of the South Pacific, I would say." But the Professor was smiling now, and Mrs. Hana kissed the new Prime Minister again.

Before the Reverend could reply, the telephone rang again.

*****

It is said the test of a politician is to do what you do not want to do, and pretend to enjoy it; the test of a great one, to do what you do not want to do, and to love the doing of it. If politics is the art of the possible, then a great politician loves only what is possible to do. By this measure, Keith Holyoake was a great politician. Moments after taking a call from Brigadier Gilbert, he picked up the phone and asked to be connected to Major General Sir Stephen Weir, Chief of the New Zealand Army. He, in turn, phoned the country's Land Component Commander, before a call was finally placed to a field phone, which buzzed on a triangular patch of grass between the airport and Welcome Harbour. The Six Para Major answered, listened, stood, saluted, and ordered his men to quickly fall in.

*****

The Reverend took the phone from his housekeeper's hand.

"Prime Minister Brown?" asked a distant voice.

"Well," said the churchman, "I am not yet used to being called that."

The man at the other end chuckled. "I am calling to congratulate you."

"Thank you." Perhaps this is what it is like, thought Reverend Brown. Strangers I have never met offering congratulations to a man they do not know.

The man continued. "On behalf of the people of New Zealand, I want to welcome the Splendid Isles to the fellowship of nations, of which you are now, I believe, our fifth smallest member." It was true only the Vatican, Monaco, San Marino and Liechtenstein were tinier than the five specks of land which comprised the world's newest sovereign state.

The Reverend's brain whirred. 'On behalf of the people of

New Zealand?' But he dared not guess. "I am sorry," he said. "Things are in chaos here, as you can imagine."

"We have not been introduced," said the voice on the end of the line. "Keith Holyoake. I am calling you from my home in Wellington."

"Prime Minister!" said Reverend Brown at once.

"Call me Keith," said the PM, "and I in turn would like permission to call you Geoffrey. You should come for dinner. Once things in the Splendids have settled down."

"I would like it very much—Keith," said the Reverend.

"Excellent," said Holyoake and hung up.

"You will never guess who that was." But before the Reverend could say any more, the phone rang again. Like the ripples from a stone thrown into a pond, the news had spread quickly. There were calls from RW Rumsey, the QR, Police Chief Tanner, Sir Brendan Court, who cooed sweetly, Aaron Trieger, who requested an interview for the next day's paper, the Attorney-General Ralph Hanan, whose voice dripped with pleasure, and many others, including the Chairman of the Turtle Research Foundation and an awkward call from Sir Randolph Herd, the Resident Commissioner.

*****

At Briggs International, as the tiny airport was grandly named, a pair of trucks lumbered onto the runway. They drove to a plane with the markings of the US Navy on its tail. Sixty-two men poured up into the aircraft's stifling insides.

"Howdy!" said the loadmaster. Welcome aboard."

The soldiers unhooked their packs, sat on uncomfortable canvas seats, lit cigarettes and did their best to settle in.

After a few minutes the loadmaster reappeared. "Change of schedule," he brightly announced. "Quick ride up to

Barbers Point, and then we're ready to take you home."
Barbers Point Naval Air Station was a few miles outside
Honolulu, and nearly two thousand miles in the wrong
direction.

But their 'ride', as the loadmaster described the flight,
was a generous gift from the US Navy. So the frustrated
Major had no choice. "No problem." He managed to smile
through gritted teeth.

A black Ford Custom pulled up by the plane. Two middle-
aged men climbed stiffly aboard. "Wendell Steinbeck," said
the older of the two, "and this here is Harvey. Sorry we're
taking you a little out of your way."

"Jesus!" complained a Private to the Sergeant beside him.
"Wellington via Hawaii is like going to England via the South
Pole. They're not even soldiers, just bloody civilians."

"The only thing I know for sure," replied the Sergeant
through the side of his mouth, "is they have more pull than
you and me."

*****

Reverend Brown had just completed his dozenth call.
"Prime Minister," said Mrs. Hana. She tried out the title for
the first time. "A special treat. Off with you. Down to the
pier."

I might be the Prime Minister, a ruler of men, thought
Reverend Brown, but I do not yet seem to have escaped the
power of a woman. In this, his position was the same as his
son. Once the new Prime Minister left, Professor Buchanan
made a long-distance call.

*****

The foul weather that day was the distant breath of the
season's first storm. Dark clouds scudded across the sky, and

the wind amplified the children's waves. Two boys rode one ashore. There was a faint smell of cooking in the charged air.

Across the road from the pier, a trim, small figure in an apron emerged from the rectory, ran across the road to the pier towards a short, pot-bellied man in suit pants and an unbuttoned white shirt.

"Prime Minister," she called, once she judged he was in range. "Telephone. From America."

The pot-bellied man hurried across the road in the excited wake of his housekeeper, and on into the house.

There was a brief pause before the operator came on the line. "Is that Prime Minister Geoffrey Brown?"

"Yes, of course," said the Reverend, whose new title still seemed strange.

"This is the White House operator. Please hold for the President of the United States." There was a hollow sound, as if the call were coming from the bottom of the ocean, which thanks to the undersea cable, indeed it did. Then Reverend Brown heard a warm Boston accent, a silken voice.

"Prime Minister," said the President. "My congratulations to you on this wonderful day."

"Thank you," said Reverend Brown, who could think of nothing more momentous to say.

"I have watched your progress to nationhood, and it is a tribute to all the peoples of your island, and to the folks down there in New Zealand, that so peaceful a change has been achieved. You must come up to the White House sometime. Jackie— Mrs. Kennedy—and I would love to meet you."

*****

And so it finally came to pass, the world's fifth tiniest nation was born at last. Reverend Brown pondered the job before him, but brightened as a familiar tantalizing smell drifted towards him. "The Pacific's greatest statesman deserves a reward," said his housekeeper, her face in a grin.

"For goodness' sake," said the new Prime Minister with a gentle sigh.

Piata Hana had baked a pie.

END

ACKNOWLEDGMENTS

Special thanks to Sir Geoffrey Henry, the two-time former Prime Minister of the Cook Islands in the central Pacific. Sir Geoffrey gave me a valued insight into the affairs of a tiny nation adrift in an ocean of global politics. Sadly, he died before the book achieved its final form.

Thanks also to Henry Puna, who was kind enough to have dinner with me on the eve of his ascent to the Prime Ministership of the Cooks in late 2010. It was fascinating to chat with a man just a few hours from taking the reins of a nation. He was re-elected in July, 2014, so he must have done a few things right.

I am also bound to acknowledge the contributions of Jean Mason and Sally Voss from the Cook Islands Library and Museum. They helped me source a huge range of books and research papers on subjects ranging from globalization and governance in the South Pacific through to strategic cooperation and competition. I also learned a great deal about fish and the vagaries of the fruit export market.

At a more tangential level, I want to acknowledge Leonard Casley, the self-styled Prince of Hutt River Province. The seeds for *The Man In The Spider Web Coat* were truly sown many years ago, after the wily Prince Leonard claimed to have seceded his wind-swept wheat farm from Australia. I wrote a feature article for Penthouse Magazine (Australia) in the early 1980s, in which I wryly described Hutt River

Province as the second biggest country in Australia. Prince Leonard was a charming host and I shall never forget his wife, Princess Shirley, chasing the cat around the kitchen with a broom while Prince Leonard and I discussed grave matters of state.

I also want to thank Air Vice Marshal William Henman of the Royal Australian Air Force whose insight into global strategic politics helped to re-shape some of the story, though he knew it not.

Others with valuable input included Eilish Hegarty, Jim Farquhar, Min Somers and Tom & Mary Barbour.

Special thanks to Michael Burnet, whose astonishing ability to detect inaccuracy improved the book immensely. Any remaining errors are mine alone.

Also to my wife, Bernadette, whose support and encouragement made the book possible.

Finally I must salute the pioneering work of retired Professor Gene Sharp from the University of Massachusetts, who has been dubbed by one wag as the "Machiavelli of Non Violence". Professor Sharp's seminal works on non-violent revolution are said to have inspired the governments of Lithuania, Latvia and Estonia during their separation from the Soviet Union in 1991. Other accounts say his theories have also been applied by leaders of the Arab Spring, the series of uprisings which threatened—for a while at least—to rejuvenate the Middle East.

ABOUT THE AUTHOR

PHILIP R. ACKMAN

Philip R. Ackman is a journalist and businessman who has worked for a wide variety of newspapers and magazines in Australia, New Zealand and South Africa, as well as reporting from the Middle East and the central Pacific. For several years he produced a current affairs radio program for the wife of Australia's then Federal Leader of the Opposition, before producing a weekly Ackman Report networked into 17 radio stations along Australia's east coast. He also wrote a column for a national computer magazine, and against all the odds, was named Australia's Funniest IT Writer in the late 1990s.

He has held a variety of mostly disastrous operational and executive roles for global vendors in the IT market. He has run a distributor in Australia, a consultancy developing strategy for IT vendors and a start-up in America, which got killed in the global financial crisis. He washed up on the beach in Switzerland and then Asia, where he got to thinking (See Preface) about the (give or take) 200 world leaders who rule the other seven billion of us. What was required, he wondered, to land such a job, where victory meant enormous power and possibly great wealth, but defeat meant consignment to obscurity, or, in many countries, loss of life or liberty.

The satire, *The Man In The Spider Web Coat*, gradually took shape, mostly on the beaches of Asia and far northern Australia, where Ackman now lives with his wife, a dog rescued from death row and a cat plucked from a drain.

IF YOU ENJOYED THIS BOOK

Please write a review.

This is important to the author and helps to get the word out to others

Visit

PENMORE PRESS

www.penmorepress.com

All Penmore Press books are available directly through our website, amazon.com, Barnes and Noble and Nook, Sony Reader, Apple iTunes, Kobo books and via leading bookshops across the United States, Canada, the UK, Australia and Europe.

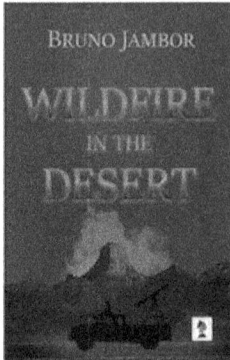

WILDFIRE IN THE DESERT

BY

BRUNO JAMBOR

Action Adventure, Crime, Mystery,
Southwest History

Highly entertaining, well researched
and original:

A Navy veteran returns home to his ancestral land to escape the pace of modern life. His nephew begs him to hide the drugs he is transporting to escape his pursuers.

An astronomer trying to find a replacement for his estranged wife finds solace in his work with the stars.

Police and the drug cartel try to recover the missing shipment, regardless of consequences, ready to sacrifice any opponent.

The antagonists crisscross the desert of Southern Arizona in a chess game where the loser will be eliminated.

Unexpected help comes from a famous missionary who blazed new paths through the same desert three centuries ago.

The climactic resolution will captivate readers of this thriller with deep spiritual undertones.

PENMORE PRESS
www.penmorepress.com

A Gathering of Vultures

Donald Michael Platt

Murder, mutilation, and carrion... in paradise?

"There shall the vultures also be gathered, every one with her mate." -ISAIAH 34:15

Professional ballroom dancers Terri and Rick Hamilton aspire to be world champions. Unfortunately, Terri's recurring back and health problems place that goal well out of reach. They travel to Terri's birthplace, Florianópolis, on the scenic island of Santa Catarina off the coast of Brazil to vacation and visit their best friends and mentors.

Along the picturesque beaches, dead penguins and eviscerated bodies wash up on the shores of paradise, and Antarctic blasts play counterpoint to the tropical storms that rock the island. The scenic wonder is home not only to urubús, a unique sub-species of the black vulture, but also to a clique of mysterious women who offer Terri perfect health and the promise of fame—at a terrible price.

Praise for "A Gathering of Vultures

PENMORE PRESS
www.penmorepress.com

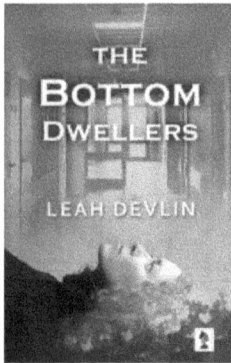

THE BOTTOM DWELLERS

BY

LEAH DEVLIN

Bioengineer and Party Girl...

Lindsey Nolan has it all: inventions paying large dividends, a dream job in the scientific village of Woods Hole, Massachusetts, and a stable of eager playmates. But when Lindsey wakes up in rehab with no memory of how she got there, her world is turned upside down. Her roommate, an HIV-positive teenage prostitute named Maggie, is the most volatile patient on the ward. The facility is plagued by disturbing thefts. And another theft unfolds when her competitor, an engineer named Karen Battersby, discovers and steals Lindsey's astonishing new invention from her Woods Hole lab. Lindsey and Maggie must face the consequences of past transgressions if they hope to deal with present perils and ascend from the desolate world of the Bottom Dwellers.

PENMORE PRESS
www.penmorepress.com

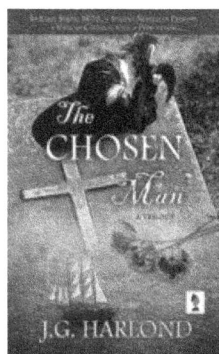

The Chosen Man

by

J. G Harlond

From the bulb of a rare flower bloom ambition and scandal

Rome, 1635: As Flanders braces for another long year of war, a Spanish count presents the Vatican with a means of disrupting the Dutch rebels' booming economy. His plan is brilliant. They just need the right man to implement it.

They choose Ludovico da Portovenere, a charismatic spice and silk merchant. Intrigued by the Vatican's proposal—and hungry for profit—Ludo sets off for Amsterdam to sow greed and venture capitalism for a disastrous harvest, hampered by a timid English priest sent from Rome, accompanied by a quick-witted young admirer he will use as a spy, and bothered by the memory of the beautiful young lady he refused to take with him.

Set in a world of international politics and domestic intrigue, *The Chosen Man* spins an engrossing tale about the Dutch financial scandal known as tulip mania—and how decisions made in high places can have terrible repercussions on innocent lives.

PENMORE PRESS
www.penmorepress.com

Penmore Press
Challenging, Intriguing, Adventurous, Historical and Imaginative

www.penmorepress.com

www.ingramcontent.com/pod-product-compliance
Lightning Source LLC
Chambersburg PA
CBHW051710020426
42333CB00014B/924

9 781942 756484